HUNKY DORY
(WHO KNEW?)

Laurence Myers

**The best I can remember from
twenty years at the heart of
'60s and '70s rock and pop**

B&B
Books

First published in 2019 by B&B Books

Copyright © Laurence Myers 2019

ISBN 978-1-912892-29-7

Also available as an ebook
ISBN 978-1-912892-28-0

Jacket photography: Getty Images
Front cover images of Mick Jagger and Marianne Faithfull
copyright Gered Mankowitz

Typeset by Tom Cabot/ketchup
Cover design by Simon Levy
Project management by whitefox
Printed and bound by Clays

Hunky-dory

[Huhng-kee-daw-ree]

adj. informal

Fine: going well

Oxford English Dictionary

For

(in order of appearance)

Marsha,

James, Peter, Beth

CONTENTS

Introduction

1.

2.

3. The History...

4. The Early Stages...

5. How...
& On...

6. ...

9. ...
of the...

10. The...

11. ...

12. ...

13. The...

CONTENTS

Introduction 7

1. The Forties – The War Years 11

2. The Fifties – The Finsbury Park Years 17

3. Manners Maketh a Man But a Dark Suit Does
   Not Maketh an Accountant 27

4. The Early Sixties – Qualified, But for What? 29

5. How Goodman Met Myers and Goodman Myers
   & Co., Chartered Accountants, Was Born 31

6. Mickie Most – My Parachute into the Heart of
   the London Music Scene 35

7. Don Arden 46

8. Midem – The Music Industry Annual Get-Together 50

9. Allen Klein – The Man Who Changed the Business
   of the Business 54

10. The Greek Tycoon 71

11. Pirate Radio and The Star-Club 87

12. Tetragrammaton Records and Tiny Tim 92

13. The Later Sixties – Showbiz, Here I Am! 98

14. The Society of Distinguished Songwriters – The SODS . . 103

15. Tony Macaulay 107

16. Music Publishers, Freddy Bienstock and Elvis 114

17. The Rolling Stones 121

18. Rupert Loewenstein Comes on the Scene and The
Stones Break with Klein 140

19. The Jeff Beck Band and Rod Stewart 147

20. The Beatles and Apple Corp 151

21. Mike Leander – the Man Who Encouraged Me
to Change my Business Life 160

22. Gem Productions – Mike Leander, Tony Macaulay 169

23. David Bowie 171

24. The Plan to Launch Bowie 182

25. Stevie Wonder – An Interlude in the Bowie Story 199

26. Postscript on David Bowie and Tony Defries 232

27. GTO including David Joseph and The New Seekers . . . 235

28. Arcade Records 255

29. Mike Leander – Rock and Roll Pt. 2 269

30. GTO Records – Dick Leahy, Donna Summer,
Billy Ocean, Heatwave 280

31. Gem Records – My Swan Song in the Record Business . . 290

Acknowledgements 303

Index 305

INTRODUCTION

Once upon a time, a long time ago, a young ex-student of the London School of Economics sat at my desk in my Regent Street office. He was a nice young man, skinny with long hair and a distinctively large mouth. He was a singer with a band; I was his accountant and he was interested in pensions.

'After all, Laurence, I'm not going to be singing rock'n'roll when I'm sixty,' he said in his south London accent.

'No, you're not,' I agreed. How we laughed at the thought ... Nearly sixty years on, my client – Mr Jagger – is not only still singing rock'n'roll, he is still fronting the greatest rock'n'roll band in the world – and he certainly does not live off a pension.

Six years after that meeting, another skinny young man with long hair, also a singer, sat opposite me at a different desk. I was no longer an accountant. I was managing artists. I thought that he was extremely talented but one thing slightly troubled me. Although his wife was by his side, he was clearly flirting with androgyny. It was the received wisdom of the times that it was mostly teenage girls who bought records, so their pin-ups should be handsome in an alpha-male way. After I agreed to take him on, I asked the young David Bowie his views on this.

'Don't you worry about that, Laurence,' he said, 'I know what I'm doing.' And he did ...

A music-business journalist once asked me: 'What was it like to be at the heart of the British music industry in the fantastic sixties and seventies?' I truthfully answered, 'Who knew?' At the time, although the people I was dealing with on a day-to-day basis were exciting and interesting, I had no idea that – years later – many of them would be of historic interest and that much of the music I was then involved with would still be relevant more than fifty years later.

They say that, in life, timing is everything and 1964 was the perfect time for me to get involved with the music business. The rock/pop business had burst into the public psyche with a four-to-the-floor drumbeat thumping out the rhythm of a youth revolution. In America young men were burning their draft cards as a protest against the ongoing war in Vietnam. Youth in the UK were rebelling against the general mess that they were going to inherit from the post-war generation – the established class system that pigeon-holed the populace according to their accents and anything else that would upset their parents – especially their taste in music.

Unlike today, when a kid can make a record in his bedroom, records had to be made in expensive recording studios. Record sales, along with the rest of the economy, were booming. The major record companies had a total lock on the recording industry and took advantage of the artists who were providing the music that reflected the desires of the youth of the day – which were, largely, sex and dancing. The contraceptive pill had been introduced in 1961, encouraging the sixties to swing.

'Let's spend the night together,' suggested the Rolling Stones, and many did.

There was a real need for young business brains that would protect the artist against the rapacious practices of the record companies. Whom, you may ask, was amongst the first to fill this need? Twenty-eight-year-old me! How, you may ask, did I begin? Well, here's how – although if, like me, you sometimes skip the early years chapters in biographies, go straight to chapter six. I won't be offended.

1. THE FORTIES – THE WAR YEARS

I was born in London in 1936 within the sound of the Bow bells. This means that technically I am a cockney, but I spurned my birthright as soon as I could toddle, already hating the idea of having to learn to walk with shoulders rolling, thumbs in my braces, doing 'The Lambeth Walk' and shouting 'Oi!' Besides, I didn't think that when I grew up I'd want to wear suits that were covered in pearl buttons. Little did I know that through the eras of teddy boys, flower power, glam rock, new romantic and punk, I'd flirt with far worse.

I was three years old when what my generation call 'The War' broke out. It was *The* War because, like the misnamed 'The War to End All Wars' twenty-odd years before it, there was only one war that made the papers. I recently read that currently there are people trying to kill each other in something like three hundred 'conflicts' – as little wars are called – around the world. There is also, of course, the global war against terrorism. Will we ever learn? It seems, sadly, not.

War can be fun … if you are a child and protected from its true tragedy by your parents. For my contemporaries and me it

was an ever-changing adventure. Too many changes of schools
to take education seriously, and no expectancy to do well. Lots of
disruptions from air-raid warnings, fire drills, gas mask practice
and, of course, many bomb sites to play on. All wonderful stuff
but, to this day, if I ever hear a siren that has been programmed
to sound like a wartime air-raid warning, my stomach turns.

Like most kids during the war years, I went to a variety of
schools. Between 1940 and 1945 I attended a convent in Hitchin,
Hertfordshire, a boarding school in High Wycombe, a school in
Soho for refugee kids from Malta and a school for future gang-
sters in East Ham. There were other schools that I was sent to
for just a few days, as I was shunted around the country so that
Hitler could not find out where I was.

My father's parents came from Russia and my mother's
parents came from Poland and they were both very influenced
by the *Fiddler On The Roof* experiences of their recent heritage,
when Jews were thrown out of countries just for being Jews. This
was a generation that generally instilled in their children a need
to have their own businesses because:

A)   You could not get rich working for someone else. Being
rich was perceived as the best insulation from anti-Semitism.

B)   It was feared that anti-Semitism would inhibit the
advancement of Jews working in the general marketplace.

This was not as paranoid as you might think. In the 1930s,
National Socialism was politically and physically active against
the Jews in Germany, and Mosley's fascists were gaining trac-
tion in the UK. The 'ruling classes' may not have been overtly
anti-Semitic, but the cooks in the stately homes of England had
no need to learn how to make chicken soup or kosher salt beef

for expected Jewish guests, unless the guest was a Rothschild, which supports A) above.

In 1939 when the war started, my parents were operating a small hairdressing salon on the Barking Road, East Ham. During the war my mother Alice, a wonderful woman whom I adored and respected, battled on to operate the salon during my father Gerry's absence in the army. Our home was above the shop – a proud Jewish tradition that meant she could work all hours to make ends meet: an even prouder Jewish tradition.

I loved my father but found it hard to respect him. He was something of a Willy Loman figure, the titular character of Miller's *Death of a Salesman*, who relied on being liked to get him through life, happily allowing my mother to be the strength of the family. He was adorable and one of the funniest men I have ever known. He used to send me letters from 'your Daddy at the Front'. The 'Front' being the beach-front, Cleethorpes, the seaside town where he was safely stationed away from the London Blitz being endured by his wife and child.

According to my father, on one occasion when his platoon was strung out along the coastal terrain during one of the many invasion scares, he dropped his rifle, which fired a round. Anxious not to frighten his fellow soldiers, he shouted out: 'Don't worry, it's me, Gerry!' By the time the message was passed along to the ninth lookout, it had Chinese-whispered into a panicky: 'It's Gerry,' which was of course one of the slangy names for Germans. The alarm was raised, barracks were mobilised, Winston Churchill probably scrambled into his siren suit, and my father was lucky to only be punished with guard duty for a month.

Towards the end of the war, having feigned madness to avoid being posted abroad to Singapore where bullets were being exchanged in anger, he was committed to an army mental hospital in Bristol. Here there were three categories of inmates: the poor unfortunate, genuinely ill; the malingerers like Dad trying to get out of the army; and the army spies planted to try to distinguish one from the other.

Family legend has it that he conducted an orchestra that had no instruments and that he fired the second violin for playing the wrong note. There's a bad-taste sitcom in that story somewhere. In later years I asked my father how he, as a Jew, could not possibly wish to fight fascism, something that I was secretly ashamed of. He told me that the anti-Semitism in the British army was so strong that, in action, more Jews were shot in the back than the front. I am sure that this was not true, but I am equally sure that many Jews got a hard time from some other servicemen.

Whilst my father was fighting for democracy in the Palais de Dance in Cleethorpes, back in war-torn, dangerous London my mother and I lived between the shop in East Ham and the central London home of my maternal grandparents Peter and Annie Levenberg. My grandparents lived in a large flat in Bedford Square in the now trendy area of Bloomsbury. One of my earliest memories is clinging to my mother in a taxi as we drove there from East Ham through the blazing London docks during the Blitz. Grandpa Peter was a master tailor in the Mile End Road. I used to love going to his workshop where he and my uncle David would sit cross-legged on a counter, making bespoke suits built to outlast the Taj Mahal. There were huge heated pressing irons hissing on a gas range, the workshop smelled of tailor's soap, and I was allowed to sit cross-legged with my grandpa, pulling out basting stitches with an ivory pick.

When I was aged six or seven, my mother would often put me alone on the 106 bus at East Ham for my grandmother to meet me an hour later at the Tottenham Court Road stop, where the conductor to whom I had been entrusted would help me off. No thought of danger from strangers … different days.

Tottenham Court Road tube station was the nearest designated bomb shelter to Bedford Square. The trains stopped running, the electric rails were switched off and we slept on the station floor for many a night during air raids. I still have to resist getting undressed on platform three when I go down there to catch a tube train home from Soho.

I have a vivid memory of VE Day when the war was finally over. I was nine and my cousin Alan – who was five years older than me and was my boyhood hero – took me to join the celebrations on the streets of the West End. There was much spontaneous singing and dancing and I particularly remember a sailor. I assume he was a sailor because he was completely naked other than wearing a sailor's hat, his modesty barely covered by a skimpy Union Jack flag, as he pulled us into a circle of revellers for a knees-up.

Once the war ended, my grandparents' flat in Bedford Square was very much the focus of family life. We were a close-knit bunch. Grandpa Peter's brother Nussan had married my grandma Annie's sister Brandel. In the next generation, my father's brother Hymie had married my mother's sister Betty. Don't spend too much time trying to work that out, just be assured that there was no incest involved down the line. I was very close to my cousins Alan and Marlene Myers on my mother's side and Roy and Patsy Bloom on my father's side and we were socially pretty much self-contained. I had other cousins who were born after the war but we never had the opportunity to be that close. I was never that involved with my grandparents on my father's side, maybe because my father was not close to them himself.

On Thursday evenings my parents and my aunts and uncles, together with their children, all met at the Levenbergs' flat at Bedford Court Mansions. I have wonderful memories of the warmth and closeness of those family gatherings. Parents, uncles, aunts and cousins, eating, laughing, shouting and more eating. Grandma was a great cook.

When my cousin Alan was sixteen, his best pal was Marty Feldman, who used to come to my grandparents' flat and practise his clarinet – my first introduction to show business. Alan also introduced me to jazz and American big band music at a very young age, for which I thank his memory.

My father had worked as a hairdresser before the war and when he was discharged from the army in 1945, he got a job at a Mayfair salon. He was, by his own admission, a lousy hairdresser and claimed that his inept use of scissors inadvertently produced asymmetrical haircuts long before they became fashionable in the swinging sixties.

In spite of – or maybe as a result of – my patchwork education, aged eleven I passed my scholarship exams and spent a term at East Ham grammar school, before the family moved to Finsbury Park, where I attended Holloway County grammar school.

2. THE FIFTIES – THE FINSBURY PARK YEARS

My mother had been in a terrible traffic accident during the war and it was painful for her to stand, so being a hairdresser was not a great idea. My father was still a hopeless hairdresser and it was decided they should both change careers. In 1947, when we moved to Finsbury Park, my father bought a small tobacconist and confectionery shop.

Dad had an envious eye on his brother-in-law Len, who had three confectionery and tobacconist shops in north London. A multi-retailer! My parents had no capital and Len altruistically financed my father's acquisition of the Astoria Candy Stores, a small outlet opposite the Astoria cinema on Seven Sisters Road.

The Astoria was a showpiece cinema built in the thirties and was decorated spectacularly in the style of an Andalusian palace. There were silhouettes of Andalusian architecture around the auditorium and a large mosaic fountain in the foyer. When the house lights went down, the roof was a beautiful dark sky twinkling with stars. It was truly magnificent. I had a free pass to

The Astoria – if you kicked the third emergency exit door on the Seven Sisters Road side in the right place, it would open and allow you to pass freely into the splendid auditorium. In later years The Astoria would become The Rainbow rock venue and I would promote shows there. The first thing I did when I took over was to secure the third exit door on the Seven Sisters Road side. It is now a church and you can get in for free. Where's the fun in that?

Finsbury Park now has the wonderful Park Theatre, opened in 2013, a two-minute walk from where I once lived. Many years later I produced plays there. You can take a boy out of Finsbury Park, but you can't take Finsbury Park out of a boy.

My dad had a board outside our sweet shop that advertised the current weekly variety bill at the nearby Finsbury Park Empire. For this we were given two tickets for each of their weekly shows and I saw most of the acts that played there. There was always a mixed bill of supporting 'specialty acts', known in the trade as 'spesh acts': jugglers, acrobats, magicians, cycling acts, dog acts, knife throwers … Variety in the true sense of the word. Table tennis was very popular at the time and Viktor Barna, the Hungarian world champion, used to tour the halls giving exhibition matches. Artists such as the Beverley Sisters were advertised as 'Decca Recording Stars' in recognition of having received the great accolade of a record deal, and comedians famous through radio often topped the bill.

The site of the Finsbury Park Empire is now a mosque where Abu Hamza, the infamous cleric with the hook for a hand, once preached his particular brand of brotherly love. On the spot where the cleric more recently spewed venom, Arthur

Askey, Jimmy James, Jimmy Wheeler, Max Wall and a host of
other legendary comedians spewed jokes. These artistes toured
the UK and usually played any particular theatre once a year
so never had to change their act, and we would have hated it if
they did. The comedians' routines, polished and refined by years
of practice, were eagerly anticipated and if one was missed we
fretted. Their acts were so good that over sixty years later I can
still recite chunks out of most of them, and to my wife's dismay
I frequently do. Their example taught me to insist that the acts
that I managed always featured their hits in live performance, no
matter how bored they were with performing them. 'Give your
audience what they want.'

My favourite singer was Josef Locke: a large, usually drunk,
Irish tenor with the voice of an angel. His big song was 'The
Soldier's Dream'. There was a line in the song where he put his
hand to his ear and shouted: 'Hear the guns' and we, the cogno-
scenti in the audience, shouted it out with him. I have tortured
my children and, indeed, selected friends to this day by insisting
on playing the song from my iTunes collection and expecting
them to holler 'Hear the guns' at the appropriate moment.

Josef Locke did not believe in paying tax. In order to keep
ahead of the Inland Revenue he would perform his sell-out
concerts billed as Mr X. In 1991, Ned Beatty played him in a
film called *Hear My Song*. Any of my kids who didn't go to see
that film would have been cut out of my will. If you don't buy the
DVD, you'll be cut out as well.

Comedian Max Wall was a particular favourite. He announced
himself with: 'The name's Wall, Max Wall, my uncle was the Great
Wall of China.' He used to come on stage clown-like as Professor

Wallofski, sporting a long and wild wig, wearing black tights and slap shoes. His absolute showstopper was the Max Wall walk. It is impossible to describe his act and I urge you to look him up on YouTube. His career was ruined in 1955 when, as a married man, he was caught in bed with Miss Great Britain, twenty-six years his junior – something that today would guarantee him a book deal, a spread in *Hello!* and a spot in *Celebrity Something-or-Other*.

In 1974 when he was quite old, I filmed his classic Professor Wallofski act at the Richmond Theatre before an invited audience, which included Richard Attenborough and many other celebrities, all devoted fans of Max. Max was a bankrupt and I paid him in cash, which he said 'saved his life'. He was also working by that time as a serious actor. I went to see him in John Osborne's *The Entertainer*. He was magnificent and a reviewer said, 'Max Wall makes Olivier look like an amateur.' Max died in 1990, but there is still a Max Wall Society and I have given them permission to distribute *Max Wall Funny Man*, the film I lovingly made, to its members.

From the age of eleven I received a steady education at Holloway grammar school, a ten-minute bus ride from home. My popularity there, I'm sure, had little to do with my parents owning a sweet shop and sweets being rationed until 1953!

After an undistinguished school career, I left at sixteen with a modest six O-levels. I had no idea what I wanted to do, other than becoming a Latin American percussionist. My preferred dream would have been to be a drummer but I could only afford to buy a set of bongos, hence the Latin American bias. Telling my mother that I wanted to be a drummer of any sort would have been an intriguing way to commit suicide, so I did not even suggest it. I had to choose from the post-war Jewish Mother's List: doctor, lawyer, architect, dentist, accountant. This was very brave on my parents' part as none of these professions provided a living prior to qualification and it was going to be a struggle for them to support me. I went down the list, rejecting the suggested professions for no sensible reasons. My mother threatened me with a career in hairdressing if I did not say yes to something, so I agreed to accountancy.

I became an articled clerk to a small firm of chartered accountants in Holborn. The firm consisted of two brothers, and I was their first and only employee. They did not even have a secretary and did all of their own typing. They were very nice men, but the practice was tiny and I received no real training. At a time when a sixteen-year-old school leaver was earning about five pounds a week, my pay was a Dickensian fifteen shillings, seventy-five pence in today's currency. Hard to believe now, this covered my daily fares of one shilling (five pence), and lunch money of two shillings (ten pence). It *was* a long time ago.

I earned the occasional few shillings as a newspaper reporter. Well, more of a tiny cub reporter. The *Daily Express* used to pay for contributions and if I saw a road accident I would call them from the nearest phone box, exaggerate the severity of the incident and get sent a five-shilling postal order. I used to walk about hoping to see a car crash, preferably fatal. Well, I was young and very broke.

As my parents could not afford to subsidise me, I earned my spending money working on Sundays in the street market on Club Row Waste, an extension of the famous Petticoat Lane market in London's East End. Sunday was a big, busy day in the Astoria Candy Stores so after the market I helped out in the shop. I was no martyr, my parents worked hard and so did I. In the market I rented a stall from which I sold mainly old confectionery provided by my father's connections. This was before the concept of sell-by dates, which is just as well, because most of my stock would have had Roman numerals. True to the Finsbury Park ethos of dealing in hooky gear, a man only known to me as Cecil delivered my more current stock to our shop in the middle of the night. I never questioned the source of the remarkably cheap and invoice-free goods.

In the summer I sold cold drinks from a large, galvanised tin bath on which I balanced a huge block of ice. The ice, which was extremely heavy, was schlepped by my only employee, Reg, aka Chicken. It was a ten-minute walk with the ice water melting on his back, from an ice factory in not so nearby Wentworth Street. Chicken was an illiterate meat-market porter, who could be the subject of his own book as well as many a police charge sheet. I went to his wedding to a hooker who was pregnant with twins. Chicken proudly claimed that 'one's mine an' one's me mate's.'

Market grafting is only romantic to those who have never done it out of necessity. For me it involved borrowing a vehicle that may or may not start; loading up at six o'clock on Sunday morning come rain, shine or flu; and struggling to make about five pounds, and there's not much romance in that. It was, however, a most valuable part of my education, and the fiver a week that I earned kept me in spending money. I could also afford my first set of wheels, but only two of them, on a Lambretta motor scooter. It cost about eighty pounds; more money than I had ever possessed, so I bought it on hire purchase.

After a couple of years I became a multiple retailer, having rented a second stall on Club Row, an adjacent market, the stall manned for me by my pal Colin Levine. The doubling of my business outlet enabled me to double my wheels from two to four and I bought an Italian-made Isetta bubble car. Messerschmitt also made a bubble car but in those days Jewish people did not buy German cars or any cars that were green. The German antipathy was because of the recent war and green was considered to be unlucky.

Market grafters are a fascinating bunch of characters. Some, anecdotally, did so well that when they drove home to their mansions in the country, they swapped their beat-up old vans for their Rolls-Royces. On one occasion, the rarely seen but legendary Red-Faced Sam came to the market to work the 'run-out', a fraudulent auction resulting in some poor punter going home with a box full of swag (worthless junk) for which they had handed over their Christmas Club savings. I saw him avoid repaying a very large and very angry husband of a woman he had conned, who caught him as he was packing up. Sam explained, as well as he could with a docker's hand around his windpipe, that he would love to give a refund but he had 'closed the books for the purchase tax' and would get into trouble with the authorities if he gave the money back today. The docker, suckered by Sam's patter, and clearly ready to join up against the authorities, apologised profusely and agreed to return next week for the promised 'no-questions-asked full refund'. Needless to say, Sam had no plan to return to the market for some years.

Most market grafters had a philosophy that was 'As long as they don't cut my tongue out, I'll earn a living selling *some-*

thing.' I had a huge, warm duffel coat, which I wore for the cold winter mornings. It was really scruffy but even after I was married I kept it in my cupboard for some years until I felt confident that I could earn a living as an accountant. Some market grafters went to jail, some prospered, and one became Alan Sugar.

In 1948, when I was twelve, my brother Roger was born. At that time it was not unusual to have a large gap between children. The threat of war delayed families having children, and they were inclined to wait a few years after the war before starting again. Roger was a gorgeous baby and I loved him to bits. I still do. We were obliged to share a bedroom until I was about eighteen, but I never for one moment resented him. When I was sixteen I ventured up west to the Queensway ice skating rink, sometimes taking the cute four-year-old Roger with me as a pulling prop. It worked, and there I met fourteen-year-old Marsha Bloom, who would be my intermittent girlfriend for some ten years and, ultimately, my wife.

Marsha lived just off the Edgware Road. I called it Paddington but she called it Marylebone. The argument persists to this day but it was undeniably classier than Finsbury Park, and her family was so posh they had fruit on the table when nobody was ill. We were married in 1962 and – more than half a century later – she is still the love of my life.

My father's shop did well with the sweets and cigarettes because of the queue that formed outside of the cinema opposite. In the fifties there was no competition from television and everybody went to the cinema at least once a week. The Astoria was full every evening no matter what was showing, and the lines would form early. Sweets were on ration and had to be weighed up for sale out of seven-pound jars. Rationing required cutting out coupons for each sale, and from the age of eleven I had to work in the shop every evening to deal with the cinema pre-opening rush. I'm sure that I can still pick out a handful of sweets to weigh a quarter of a pound with great accuracy.

On the actual day that sweet rationing ended in 1953, we sold every single sweet in the shop. The shelves were absolutely bare and for some weeks to follow we opened for just an hour a day to sell the little stock my father had managed to find. Unlike now, where concessions are the major money-earner for cinemas, the venue itself did not need the revenue from selling any drinks or snacks. With rationing ended and TV inexorably taking cinema audiences, so the owners looking for more income introduced kiosks selling packaged sweets.

The disappearance of the cinema audience market caused the inevitable demise of the Astoria Candy Stores and in 1954 my father was about to go broke. It was not only our business that was threatened; it was also our home as we lived above the shop. My father was incapable of dealing with this, so aged eighteen, I had to. I went to Uncle Len, my father's brother-in-law, and begged him to help out financially, which he generously did. I went to see the bank manager and persuaded him not to foreclose. This episode took away what little confidence my father had and, at eighteen, I effectively became head of the family. We put a little hairdressing salon on the ground floor behind the shop and, enduring the physical pain from her bad leg, my mother went back to work as a hairdresser. For a while, my father still ran the sweet shop at the front. To accommodate the salon, we lost our bathroom and our only bath was moved to the middle of the kitchen. They say that you should never be ashamed of your own home, but I was acutely embarrassed at the thought of my friends seeing this.

After a couple of years we sold the shop, and my parents opened a proper salon in a parade of shops in nearby Manor House, where we rented a flat in the block above. Still living above the shop, but least I now had my own bedroom, and the bath was in the bathroom. My father – who had been such a lousy hairdresser before the war – now worked alongside my mother and eventually got back a little of his confidence and self-respect.

3. MANNERS MAKETH A MAN BUT A DARK SUIT DOES NOT MAKETH AN ACCOUNTANT

I am still entitled to use the initials FCA – Fellow of the Institute of Chartered Accountants – after my name, although I cannot remember the last time I did so. Each year when it is time to pay the annual subscription, I wonder why I am spending the few hundred pounds that it costs to continue membership. Then I think about how hard it was for me to get the qualification, and pay up.

I found studying for my exams really hard. We were prepared for exams by correspondence courses, which required great self-discipline, which I had heard about but did not have. I was supposed to study for an average of three hours an evening. I would tell my parents that I was going to the public library to study but then spend the time at friends' houses, listening to music or going to a film. At weekends, when not helping in the shop, I spent my evenings at clubs like The Poubelle, Cy Laurie's, the El Toro, the Whisky A Go-Go and the Cage D'or, perfecting my jive and bongo playing. Few of these clubs had licences to sell alcohol, it cost little to get in, and they were mostly rather grotty but I went to them because I loved to dance.

There is an unfair generalisation that accountants are boring. People can be boring no matter what their job is. I have known some famous actors who are really boring off-stage. However, I found that there was no quicker way of stopping the irritatingly chatty person sitting next to me on a plane than answering the inevitable 'and what is it that you do?' with: 'I'm an accountant.' If this did not work, I used to add, 'with the Inland Revenue' ... at which point they would move seats.

My lack of fascination with the structure of consolidated balance sheets meant that I struggled with my accountancy exams. There were intermediate and final exams that had to be passed, with six papers in each of the different subjects. If you failed in one, you had to take all six again. I twice failed one paper in each of the exams, resulting in my taking two years longer than necessary to qualify. For me, the problem of those years was that my life was on hold until I qualified, and there was no certainty that I would do so. I eventually earned my qualification at the end of 1960, and the day that my results came through was the most emotional day of my life. I started my proper grown-up life by becoming engaged to Marsha Bloom, the gorgeous girl that I had first met at the ice rink some ten years before.

4. THE EARLY SIXTIES – QUALIFIED, BUT FOR WHAT?

Whilst I was engaged to Marsha, Cyril Myers, a distant cousin, approached me with an opportunity to operate bingo one evening a week at the Rio cinema on Canvey Island. Showbiz called!

Cyril was an extremely nice guy about the same age as me. With a loan of four hundred pounds from Marsha's stepfather, the lovely Billy Levene, we ventured east to Canvey Island. It's a small mass in the Thames Estuary joined, I do not recall how, to the mainland. Canvey Island in the winter was decidedly lacking in sun-seekers and indeed sun. In the sixties, it was a drab wilderness of caravan parks and miserable stony beaches. The Rio cinema, a local fleapit, was generally patronised by holidaymakers and did not operate in the winter. Bingo was just becoming a big business, so where could we go wrong? Read on and find out.

We had an ambitious marketing campaign consisting of a couple of tiny ads in the local paper and a hand-made sign outside of the cinema. On our first night Cyril and I waited for the rush. Twenty-seven people – mostly Essex ladies with a definite resemblance to Les Dawson in drag – rushed to join the club and we were in business … sort of. I was the bingo caller, an experience which soon eradicated the tiny voice inside me that thought I could entertain in public. I had learned the bingo lingo: 'two fat ladies, eighty-eight', etc, and also decided that the way to build the audience was to tell a few jokes. I can tell you now that Jewish humour does not travel to Canvey Island. Our highest crowd was about sixty and we never made enough to pay the rent.

The law at the time was that you had to be a member of a club for twenty-four hours before you could actually play. This was to avoid the ladies going wild and squandering their sixpences without time to reflect on their folly. We were so short on punt-ers that I let a middle-aged lady in without her having waited the statutory twenty-four hours. She was strangely pedantic. 'So, you are letting me in without my having to wait for the statutory twenty-four hours?' This should have rung a warning bell, but we were so short of members, I just patted her bum in a 'cheeky-chappy' way and waved her through.

The Essex constabulary force had a female sergeant of middle-age who looks like Dot from *EastEnders*. I was charged with offences against the Gaming Act and I had visions of headlines in the popular press along the lines of 'Chartered accountant in bingo scandal' ruining my future chances of a knighthood. In the event, my cousin Cyril, being a gentleman, took the main rap and I was fined five pounds for contravening the Gaming Act. Cyril was fined fifty pounds and that was the end of our bingo empire. Had I not been busted, I am convinced that we could have doubled our miserable attendance to about a miserable hundred and I could today still be calling, 'Number one, Kelly's eye,' to an adoring crowd of elderly ladies in Canvey.

5. HOW GOODMAN MET MYERS AND GOODMAN MYERS & CO., CHARTERED ACCOUNTANTS, WAS BORN

Having had a very poor training at the firm to which I was articled, coupled with my great disinterest in accountancy, I was untrained and fearful of holding down a job. I decided that the best option was to be my own boss so that only me could fire me.

In 1962, Alan Carter, a long-time friend from the ice rink days, had also recently qualified as an accountant, and he introduced me to fellow graduate Ellis Goodman. Ellis had been to public school and wore dark suits, which in my book meant he was a proper accountant. The idea was that the three of us would start up a new accountancy firm. In the event, Alan dropped out and Ellis and I decided to go into business together. Goodman Myers and Co., Chartered Accountants, was thus born.

In April 1962 Marsha and I were married. Marsha's father, Jack Bloom, had divorced her mother many years earlier. He was

a very successful antique-silver dealer and made our wedding
party a modest bash for three hundred guests at The Dorchester
hotel in Park Lane. Most of our friends at the wedding we have
kept to this day, and at our thirtieth anniversary I counted eighty
people who had been at our big day three decades earlier. We
are soon to celebrate our fifty-seventh wedding anniversary and
inevitably there will be fewer of the original guests there. Jack
and Marsha's other family helped us to buy our first home, a tiny
house in Abercorn Place, St John's Wood. Jack was a wonderful
and generous man and his support had a very positive effect on
my life. He encouraged me to dare and, most importantly, he was
someone I felt provided me with a safety net should I ever falter.

Goodman Myers & Co. initially consisted of Ellis, a secretary
and myself. Ellis's father – a delightful man called Manny Goodman – was coming to the end of his career as a provider of posters
for the film business and we based ourselves at his tiny office in
Blenheim Street, just off Bond Street. The offices were on the third
floor, and to get to it you had to walk up rickety stairs past a tailor's
workshop and Bev's Blenheim Club, a tiny drinking establishment on the second floor. As well as buying a dark suit, I invested
in a bowler hat and umbrella in the hope that I would pass as a
city gentleman. We had very few clients but Ellis had managed
to find some sub-contracting work from a large accountancy firm
that he knew. Ellis's clients included Petula Clark, which – with
my latent show-business aspirations – made me most jealous.

Soon we developed some clients of our own and were able to
take on our first employee, a delightfully eccentric young Indian
clerk called Mitra. Mitra came from quite a wealthy family in
Delhi and was to go back and face an arranged marriage as soon

as he qualified as an accountant. He therefore took a delight in failing his exams, thus ensuring an income from India and a continued pursuit of cricket and English girls. I once found him in the office, eyes closed, doing up and undoing a bra on a modelling bust that he had brought to the office. An explanation? 'Tonight, Mr Myers, I am taking a girl to the cinema and am therefore practising the removal of her brassiere in the dark.'

Mitra had a vivid imagination. He was always late and always had improbable excuses. His best, in his delightful Indian accent, being: 'I was thinking that I had the diabetes. The doctor told me to provide him with a urine sample, which I expressed into the small bottle that he provided. I left this in the toilet of the house I am sharing with some English girls. Later on, unbeknown to me, one of the girls had left her own urine sample in a bottle in the same lavatory and by some mistake I was taking her bottle instead of mine to the doctor. This morning the doctor asked me to urgently attend his premises where he told me, "Mitra, you do not have the diabetes but you are pregnant." That is why I am late.'

On another occasion I was sitting with one of our few clients, reviewing some accounts that Mitra had prepared. Having a small query, I called for Mitra to come into my office. This he did, immediately dropping to his knees, hands held protectively over his head, imploring, 'Please don't beat me, Mr Myers. Please don't beat me.' I have many Mitra stories but they really don't work without his fabulous accent. He eventually left us, before I did him actual bodily harm, and I often wonder if he ever returned to India to face his arranged bride.

Ellis ran the practice. There was no fight over this as he was much better at running a business than me, and I knew it.

In later years, had he run all of my businesses, he would have prevented me making many of the big mistakes that I made left to my own devices. Ellis went on to be an extremely successful businessman. He now lives in the USA, but we are still close friends and Marsha and I have enormous affection for him and for Gillian, his wife.

6. MICKIE MOST – MY PARACHUTE INTO THE HEART OF THE LONDON MUSIC SCENE

It was my relationship with legendary record producer Mickie Most that got me into the music business. In 1964 my accountancy partner, Ellis Goodman, had a chance meeting on an airplane with a man who wanted to back Mickie Most in opening a record company to be called Warrior Records. The man was looking for an accountant to represent the company and Goodman Myers & Co. was duly appointed.

We were by no means a successful firm yet and we welcomed a new client. Aware of my personal passion for music – I had actually bought 'The House of the Rising Sun', the hit that Mickie produced for The Animals – Ellis agreed that I should take over the account.

As they say, the devil is in the details, and the Warrior Records deal was far from done. It quickly became apparent that Mickie and the potential investor had different views on how the venture should be run and Mickie decided not to go ahead with the deal. A court case ensued, and the investor understandably thought that we would support him, but I really thought that Mickie – who had no business experience at that time – had been badly misled by his would-be investor, and Ellis and I decided to support him. It would be hard to resist accusations that ethically we had done the wrong thing. It is said that there are three phases in a businessman's life. 'Dishons' is the time when you do things that you would rather not, in order to get on; 'Hons' is when you want to be regarded as an honourable, 'his word is his bond' type; and 'Honours' is when you want to be recognised with some glory – be it a knighthood or being enrolled in the Rock'n'Roll Hall of Fame. Backing Mickie Most against the man who brought him to us was definitely in the first category, but without Mickie I would not have had the entrée to the music business that has given me a career.

Born Michael Peter Hayes to a military family in Aldershot, Mickie Most had left school at fifteen. As a wannabe pop star, he worked as a singing waiter at the influential 2i's coffee bar in London's Soho, where, incidentally, Peter Grant – the future Led Zeppelin manager – was working as a bouncer. Mickie, with Alex Murray as his partner, had an undistinguished career as a part of the pop duo The Most Brothers. In 1959 he followed his wife Christina back to her native South Africa and had some local success as Mickie Most and the Playboys. He came back to London in 1962, where he briefly tried his luck again as a singer, before deciding that there was a better future for him as a record producer.

The producer's function was to choose a song, outline the arrangement of the music, and then supervise all aspects of the recording in the studio. A great producer is like a master chef. He just knows how to mix the ingredients, and what needs adding to season the dish. Most importantly he knows when to stop adding more. In 1964 the producer was, in most cases, pivotal to the making of a hit record. With the right song, a skilled producer in a well-equipped studio could make a great record out of the most limited of singing talents. Tamla Motown famously made great tracks of great songs and then decided which artist got to sing on the track. Phil Spector with his wall of sound – arguably the most influential record producer of his era – could have had his hits with almost any artist he chose to work with. Of course, there were exceptions to this very general rule. The Beatles had unlimited talent but even so, it was George Martin, their producer, who fashioned them into a hit factory.

Mickie's first successes as a producer came in 1964, with The Animals. 'Baby Let Me Take You Home' was released in April, followed by 'The House of the Rising Sun' in October. It was just after this release that Mickie came into my life.

It was a great time to be involved in the music business, which was going through a worldwide revolution starting out in England, and I was lucky enough to be involved at the heart of it. Popular music had changed in the fifties. And not just the music, but also the way the public heard it and bought it. The forties were the golden age of radio and being a radio star was an accolade second only to being a film star. The public bought records that caught the magic of an artist who had established themselves via film, radio or personal appearances. Frank Sinatra's bobbysoxers, the first of the hysterical girl fans, were created by his personal appearances and radio shows with the Tommy

Dorsey Band. Teenagers did not exist as a defined cultural group until the mid-fifties, when both in America and in the UK a very few radio programmes started catering to the younger audience. This was no doubt due to the fact that sponsors were recognising that teenagers had spending power and spots on their faces that needed clearing up. When teen-oriented programmes were on air, kids would be glued to the radio. Suddenly a recording by a relatively unknown artist could be a hit. Records by Frankie Laine, Johnny Ray, Eddie Fisher, Al Martino and their contemporaries were instant hits with kids, mainly young girls. The first chart published in the UK was in 1952 and the first No. 1 was Al Martino's 'Here In My Heart', a big romantic ballad.

Young boys were to find their own idols when rock'n'roll came in a few years later, pioneered by Bill Haley's 'Rock Around The Clock' in 1954 and exploded when Elvis released 'Heartbreak Hotel' in 1956. The British soon created idols of their own with Cliff Richard, Marty Wilde, Billy Fury and many others, nearly all pale imitations of the American pioneers. Radio exposure now made the record king. A star could be created by radio play alone, without the artist needing to rely on personal appearances or film.

A record producer was to a record what a director was to a film. In the world of early sixties' pop music, the independent producer picked the song, usually written by someone other than the artist, supervised the musical arrangements and the sound created in the studio. A good producer listened to a song that would be presented to him with just a piano or guitar accompaniment and had a vision of what it would sound like with a change of tempo or a specific arrangement. Most importantly the producer crafted a record that *the teen public would want*.

Previously, the best recording studios were owned by major record companies. The growth of the independent producer encouraged a proliferation of independent studios. The creative power of the major companies was being eroded, although they still controlled manufacturing and distribution as well as the all-important financial power to pay for recordings and marketing. Staff A&R men – their initials showing they were responsible for Artists & Repertoire – were employed full time by the major record companies. They were usually under-salaried and undervalued.

I knew Norrie Paramor, who was a staff producer at EMI records. He produced, amongst many other artists, Cliff Richard, Frank Ifield, Helen Shapiro and Ruby Murray; all top stars of their time. He had produced more No. 1 singers than any other producer of the day working in England. He once told me that, having heard that American producers got a royalty on sales, he approached Joseph Lockwood – the feared and respected head of EMI Records – and timidly suggested that, like his American counterparts, maybe he himself could get some small royalty on sales of the records that he had produced. He had heard that the going rate for top US producers was 2 per cent of the retail-selling price of a record so, not wishing to push it, he suggested getting a half per cent. Lockwood said that he would consider it. Norrie was later summoned back to the great man's office.

According to Norrie, Lockwood said, 'Paramor, we have run the figures. Do you realise how much money we would have paid you at a royalty of half a per cent?'

'No,' replied the frightened Norrie.

'Well,' thundered Joseph, 'it comes to over two hundred thousand pounds!'

Norrie told me that he was so appalled at the thought that he, a mere employee, could earn that sort of money, he had apologised profusely for his temerity and settled for a raise of a thousand pounds a year and a new Ford Cortina. Even George Martin is on record saying that he was on a salary of two thousand pounds a year from EMI when he started producing The Beatles – making millions for the company.

I could see that all of this was going to change and I was determined to be one of the people who helped make it happen.

Mickie was also producing Herman's Hermits, who were signed to EMI, and The Nashville Teens, who were with Decca. Although he had had some success, his deals were poor and he was not in a position to pay us any fees for the work we would have to do as his accountants. I was reluctant to let him go as a client, as I really believed in his talent, and I had a passion for the music that he was making. I suggested that instead of fees, we would take a 10 per cent stake in all of the companies, and Mickie happily agreed. We set up three companies: Rak Records, Rak Music Publishing and Rak Management. Peter Grant, his old friend from the 2i's, had worked for a variety of people as a road manager and tour manger, but he was currently unemployed and Mickie asked him to head-up Rak Management. Peter was a huge figure of a man who, long before he became the legendary manager of Led Zeppelin, tried his hand as a film extra and professional wrestler.

Mickie's younger brother Dave would take care of the publishing interest, having had no previous experience – but there was no school for music-business executives and the independent side of the business was so new that anybody could get a shot at getting involved. Mike Jeffery, who managed The Animals and later on Jimi Hendrix, was running a coffee bar and some music venues when he signed The Animals for management. The only company that had activity from day one was Rak Records, because Mickie was already recording artists. I was now unquestionably involved in the music business and was really enjoying my life.

State-of-the-art recording studios of today can record voices and instruments on a virtually unlimited number of different tracks and have the ability to infinitely vary the sound on each of those tracks in hundreds of ways and even auto-correct a singer's out-of-tune note. This technology was not available to Mickie, who used to record at the Kingsway Recording Studios in Holborn. Kingsway had a very basic four-track desk and this meant that there were only four separate mics available during recordings. In simple terms, he only had the ability to add a little echo and reverb. Sessions were booked in three-hour blocks and Mickie could make a hit single *and* a B-side in this limited time. 'The House of the Rising Sun', which sold millions, probably cost under two thousand pounds to record and mix. Today, many artists spend hundreds of hours and hundreds of thousands of pounds to make a record. Eventually Mickie opened his own recording studio in St John's Wood, and it is still run by his widow Chris today.

Mickie and Chris became close friends with me and my wife Marsha. We went on holiday together and frequented the trendy restaurants of the day. The most 'hip' was the trattoria Terrazza, where it was essential to be seated in the back room along with the likes of Michael and Shakira Caine, Roger and Luisa Moore and many stars of stage, screen and rehab clinics. The funny thing is that the back room was a late addition to the already fashionable restaurant, and Mario, the owner, once confided in me that he thought that nobody would want to sit in the space that was windowless and nothing particularly special. Alvaro, the manager, who later went on to open his own eponymous restaurant, worked the magic to make it desirable. Whenever anyone phoned for a reservation, he would say, 'Of course, but I regret I do not have a table in the back room.' In no time at all, being seen in the front room was unthinkable. This was a reminder of how easily we the public can be manipulated to be 'where it's at'.

Our most frequented clubs were Tramps, which is still going, and the Ad Lib, and it was a great thrill to hear the DJ play a record that Mickie had produced. There were lots of clubs where musicians hung out, like the Bag O' Nails and The Cromwellian, where you would often see a Beatle drinking with a Rolling Stone.

The legendary Marquee Club in Oxford Street, which moved to Wardour Street in 1964, was the venue to see great bands. the Stones, The Yardbirds, Jimi Hendrix, The Who, Led Zeppelin and other big bands of the sixties and seventies all played there and it was a hangout for A&R men who were looking for new talent.

One of my earliest memories of being with Mickie was on a flight to New York with Andrew Oldham. Mickie and Andrew commandeered a spare wheelchair and blanket before boarding the flight. Andrew sat on the chair, tucked his knees under his legs and covered them with the blanket. In those days, airplanes were always boarded by a flight of stairs and Andrew allowed himself to be carried up the stairs by two struggling stewards. Once on the plane, he jumped up, thanked the stewards for their help and walked jauntily down the aisle towards our seats. I was convinced that we would be thrown off the plane. We were not, but for me, it got worse. We were sitting in first class, and in those days you could smoke at the front of each cabin. Andrew produced a joint which he lit and shared with Mickie. There were not many passengers in our cabin and most had chosen to sit at the rear. I looked nervously towards to the passengers at the back, hoping that the plane's air-conditioning did not allow the smoke to drift backwards. There was only one other passenger in our row: an attractive young woman of about twenty. Mickie offered her a toke which she declined with a smile. I declined too – not out of morality, but out of fear. Before they finished the joint, he once again offered it to the young lady, who said 'I'd better not, my father's the chief pilot.' Uncharacteristically, I took advantage of the free bar to recover my nerves.

Early in 1965, Mickie, Chris, Marsha and I went to a party at composer Lionel Bart's house in Seymour Walk, off the Fulham Road. The house was wonderfully over the top, as you would expect from the outrageously profligate Lionel. There were bowls of joints everywhere and the finest of wines were served in abundance. We once met Lionel in Positano, where he had taken a suite and several rooms at The Splendido for the entire summer. The hotel was, and still is, one of the most expensive hotels in Italy, but Lionel had reserved one room for himself, one for his boyfriend and the other rooms for friends passing through.

Lionel was delightfully crazy. On one of the several occasions that his mate Liza Minnelli got married, he hired a private jet and took his entire crowd to the wedding in New York. UK taxation was high in the sixties and none of Lionel's wild extravagancies were tax-deductible. Even for the man who had written many hit songs including 'Living Doll' for Cliff Richard and *Oliver!* – the greatest ever British musical – he was spending way too much money.

Lionel was a lovely man and in the early seventies I would try to extract him from his self-created financial quagmire. He had already sold all of his future royalties, including his interest in *Oliver!* and he was being pursued by the tax man and many creditors. American Express ('Membership is a privilege') were particularly intransigent and, after exploring all other possibilities, I told him that he had no choice other than to declare himself bankrupt. Apart from the financial implications, this was a terrible blow to his ego and it was one of the most difficult conversations I've ever had.

Years later he came to our home for dinner so drunk and/or stoned that he bent his fork leaning on it as he fell asleep at the table. When he left he said that he wanted to go to a club to 'find some pretty company' and asked me if I would kindly arrange a car to take him. Of course, I said yes and, concerned that Lionel would not find his way home, told the driver to 'keep the car at Mr Bart's disposal for as long as he needs and charge the cost to my account.' Lionel kept the car throughout the night, the following day and the following night. It was impossible to be angry with Lionel. Marsha and I were both really fond of him and we were delighted when Cameron Mackintosh – a mensch if ever there were one – as a condition of producing a highly successful revival of *Oliver!* at The London Palladium, negotiated that, during his lifetime, Lionel would have his income back from the production.

We were at the first-night party and Lionel came over to me and said that he couldn't remember if he should love or hate me. They say if you can remember the sixties you weren't there. I assured him that he had no reason to hate me. Even though *Oliver!* was once again hailed as a huge hit for Lionel, he was not working productively and once again I tried to help him. Every composer wanted to collaborate with him, but he did not want to actually work. Don Black, the Tony and Olivier award-winning lyricist, told me that whenever they met for a work session Lionel suggested that they first had a cup of tea. He would then reminisce about the old days until the planned time was up. Don reckons that Lionel was afraid that his talent had deserted him and was frightened to put his head back above the parapet.

7. DON ARDEN

My first major music-business meeting involving Mickie Most was in 1964, with the legendary Don Arden, father of the now famous Sharon Osbourne. Don, who in his early days had been a singer/impersonator working the variety circuit, was by then a very successful promoter. He brought over Chuck Berry, Gene Vincent and other big US acts to the UK, and had recently promoted a UK tour by The Animals. Some months later, he had still not paid them the six thousand pounds that they had earned. The Animals' manager, Mike Jeffery, was in America at the time and asked Mickie if he could persuade Arden to pay up.

I wanted to show Mickie the great value of my accountancy acumen and suggested a meeting with Arden. Mickie explained to me that in the course of a dispute with the Bee Gees' manager Robert Stigwood, Don had dangled Mr Stigwood out of a window by his ankles. In Mickie's opinion the only thing that Don understood was violence, and this was something never covered in the exams to be a chartered accountant. Mickie had a plan B. He asked the mountainous Peter Grant, who had worked for Don as a tour manager, to come to the meeting. Being very confident the law was on our side in this issue, I was against bringing along a 'heavy', but as it was very early days in my relationship with Mickie, I went along with it.

I put my accountant's dark suit on for the meeting. Don had a posh office in Mayfair and as we waited, I heard Don screaming down the phone in his American gangster accent, threatening to have someone's legs broken. I thought that the accent was rather poor but smiled weakly as we were shown into his office. Don knew why we were there and without the usual formalities a screaming match kicked off between Don on one side and Mickie and Peter on the other. Even in my dark suit I was totally ignored but eventually plucked up the courage to nervously intervene. After all these years, the details of the meeting have stayed in my mind.

Me: 'Excuse me, Mr Arden.'

Don: 'Who are you?'

Me: 'I am Laurence Myers and I formally represent The Animals in this matter.' (Thus far, I was quite impressed with myself.)

Don: 'Oh, yeah?'

Me: 'Would you like to see my authority?'

Don: (To Mickie) 'Who is this schmuck?'

Mickie: 'He's their accountant.'

Don: (Looked at me as if I were an accountant.) 'So, Accountant, what do you want?'

Me: 'You owe my clients money arising from their last tour.'

Don: 'Do I now?'

Me: (Smugly I gave Don a pristine copy of the accounting I had prepared.) 'Yes, you do, Mr Arden. Six thousand three hundred and seventy pounds.'

Don: 'So?'

Me: 'So you have to pay them.' (I looked at Mickie, sure that he
was impressed.)

Don: (Without a glance, he tossed my beautifully presented
accounts into his bin. There was a pause.) 'Fuck off.'

This was not in my script. Pulling myself up in my chair and
pausing for dramatic effect, I said, 'Mr Arden, if you do not pay,
I ... [another pause for dramatic effect] am going to issue a writ
on behalf of my clients.' I gave a self-satisfied 'get out of that'
nod and sat back in my chair.

Don replied, raising his eyebrows, 'Are you now?' He picked
up his bin, walked over to a window – no doubt the same one
as Mr Stigwood had been dangled from – and threw out the
basket. 'Listen, you little pisher,' Don growled. 'Get out of my
fucking office or you're next out of that window.'

I paused, before offering a weak, 'You'll be hearing from
our solicitors' and hurried out of the office. Mickie followed
me, laughing. Peter Grant stayed behind to execute plan B –
smashing up the office – but, to my knowledge, Don never paid
The Animals.

Later on, Don and I became friendly to the point that one
day he felt impelled to call me to warn that he was very sorry, he
liked me very much but he was going to have to give my brother-in-law Larry Levene 'a good smacking'. Larry had financed
the making of a record by an artist who had been through Don's
hands. The disgruntled artist had called the B-side 'Take the
Money and Run', and had credited the writer as being D. Arden.
Don, who was surprisingly sensitive for a man who hung rivals

out of windows, perceived this as a slight, hence his wish to reward Larry with a smacking. Larry had the good sense to call Don and resolve the issue without being smacked.

8. MIDEM – THE MUSIC INDUSTRY ANNUAL GET-TOGETHER

Midem, standing for *Marché International du Disques et de l'Edition Musicale*, is a music business market/trade show that takes place in Cannes, France. It has been going for fifty years and I went to the very first one and didn't miss a year until the eighties. We had a home in Cannes and by the seventies the Midem party that Marsha and I hosted was a very much sought-after invitation.

Before the demise of the independent music publisher, owners of music copyrights met at Midem to buy and sell territorial rights. There are two copyrights in a record. One is in the written words and music of the song and is owned by the music publisher, and a separate copyright is in the recording, owned by whoever paid for the session. If you own the music copyright in the song of, say, 'White Christmas' (you should be so lucky) you'd never have to work again. Every time the song was used on a record, or played in public by anybody, you would be paid a royalty. If you owned the Bing Crosby recording of 'White

Christmas', you would earn only from the sales of that record, from the public performance or use of that particular record, maybe in a film or in a commercial.

Midem used to be full of people who had owned a record master or a publishing copyright, licensing their product on a territory-by-territory basis. Now Midem is attended by tens of thousands of people and takes over the whole of Cannes. The focus is the Palais des Festivals where participants take small booths as offices. The first Midem in 1967 was attended by about five hundred people. The English representatives were Mitch Murray and Peter Callander, very successful songwriters in their own right. They had invited Mickie Most – being an important producer and user of songs – as an honoured guest. Marsha and I together with Chris Most went along for the ride. The rooms at the Martinez hotel had been turned into offices and small independent music publishers from all over the world scurried from room to room, buying and selling copyrights. This was before the Common Market and it was possible to own the rights to a song in any European country. Now it is mainly populated by the large companies who use the date to arrange their own international conferences, and there are more lawyers than what we used to call 'record men'.

The gathering was closed by a gala concert featuring Nina Simone, Sonny and Cher and a young singer called Oliver, one of the early one-hit wonders. Oliver's hit was 'Good Morning Starshine' from the musical *Hair*. The record was produced by the proudly gay Bob Crewe. Oliver had a wonderful voice but was not very charismatic. He was, however, very pretty. I'm just saying …

Miss Simone took the opportunity to rant to her audience about how the industry, i.e. most of the people in the room that night, had cheated artists in general, black artists in particular, and very specifically, herself. She was not entirely wrong in her assertions and it must have been an irresistible opportunity for her to vent her spleen, but it sort of killed her performance.

After the concert there was a big party and everybody including Sonny and Cher were on the dance floor. As was the style at the time, everybody danced with everybody else and I had my few minutes of bliss dancing with Cher. I think it is what inspired her to write 'Little Man'.

In 1973 Stig Anderson, a Swedish publisher, was working Midem, trying to place his recording of the Swedish entrant to the upcoming Eurovision Song Contest. It was a time when Scandinavian countries usually scored '*nil points*' in the contest and he only managed to get deals in a few territories because some small record companies were prepared to take on this certain loser as a favour to Stig, who was a well-liked and much respected individual. Also 'Waterloo' sounded like a terrible title for a pop song. Cut to 1976, three years later, and all of the territorial deals for Abba were up. I was chatting with Bob Summer – the worldwide head of RCA Records – when he excused himself: 'Sorry, Laurence, I have to run over to the Carlton hotel. It's nearly three o'clock. Stig now wants to make a worldwide deal and has told the head of every major record company that he will be available at three. I have to go and line up with the others outside his suite.' I guess that Bob was not early enough in the queue because Stig signed Abba to Polydor.

At one Midem, Marsha and I found ourselves playing late-night poker with a bunch of guys including Mike Stoller who – with lyricist partner Jerry Leiber – were arguably the most successful writers of the era. They wrote many of Elvis's early rock'n'roll hits including 'Jailhouse Rock', 'Hound Dog' and 'King Creole' as well as brilliant songs like 'Is that All There Is' for Peggy Lee. They also co-wrote 'Pearl's A Singer', one of my favourite songs of all time, for Elkie Brooks.

Mike and I became business friends and I often met with him and Jerry when I was in LA. We usually met at Nate'n Al's, a very famous deli in Beverley Hills. There, nobody had a prestigious table and the waiters were famously indifferent to celebrities who ate there. Mike always teased Jerry for parking in the public car park thus saving a few dollars, but they were as close as brothers, and for a songwriter groupie like me spending time with them was a joy. At one point, Mike's wife Corky, herself an accomplished musician, wanted to write a musical about lyricist Al Dubin. He and his composing partner Harry Warren wrote many of the songs for the hit musicals of the forties, including the outstanding *42nd Street*. Al Dubin was an alcoholic and he died, unrecognised, in a gutter when he was fifty-four, broke and forgotten. I thought that it was a brilliant project and offered to get involved but, for a number of reasons, it never made it to the stage.

For me the most amazing thing about our friendship was going to Mike's home where he and Jerry would pitch their latest compositions to see if they would be of interest to any of the artists that I was involved with in the UK. *Jerry Leiber* with *Mike Stoller* at the piano, singing and playing their songs, hoping they would please *me*. It was like me auditioning Shakespeare for a new play.

9. ALLEN KLEIN – THE MAN WHO CHANGED THE BUSINESS OF THE BUSINESS

Allen Klein, who was to be a huge influence in my business life, also first became involved in the music business as an accountant. He was studying for his qualification while working for Fenton & Co., a New York firm that specialised in the entertainment business. He was not a disciplined employee and was soon fired for always being late. He did not bother to qualify but started his own small accountancy firm with a friend who had the necessary licence for the firm to able to practise.

Allen earned a meagre living from accountancy for clients recommended by Don Kirshner, a close friend who was working for a small publishing firm in the Brill Building. This was the fabulous art deco office block on the corner of Broadway and 49th Street in Manhattan. The Brill Building was crammed full of music publishers and songwriters in small offices and studios; a one-stop-shop for anyone looking for a hit song. Don became one of the most successful music publishers of his era. He

discovered and nurtured Gerry Goffin and Carole King, Barry
Mann and Cynthia Weil, Neil Sedaka, Neil Diamond and Phil
Spector. In the sixties, he was given the task of finding songs
for *The Monkees* and called upon his old Brill Building writers
to provide some hits. He was in no small way responsible for
the incredible success of that show. Later on he did the same
thing for *The Archies*, an animated TV series. It was for good
reason that Don was known as the 'the man with the golden
ear'. Don features heavily in *Beautiful*, the wonderful musical
about Carole King. I enjoyed it hugely, although it was strange
seeing somebody I knew being portrayed on stage. I remember
being halfway through a New York call from him when he said,
'Hang on, Laurence,' the line going dead for a minute, 'I'm going
through a tunnel.' This was 1964 and he was calling me *from his
car*, a truly astonishing thing more than fifty years ago.

Both Allen and I used similar methods to audit record
companies on behalf of our clients. I would start with the vinyl
pressing orders. Having verified the number of records actually
manufactured, I then established the difference between that
number and the number on which they had actually paid royalties to the client, which was always considerably less. The record
company would ascribe the difference to promotional copies,
reserves for returns, discounts to retailers and other semi-fic-
tional explanations, but in truth some of the major record
companies institutionally cheated.

Allen also invariably found unpaid monies for his artists. His
pitch to attract prospective clients never changed (except for
the figures). He would say, 'I can get you a hundred thousand
dollars.' Even if he didn't get that amount he always got them

something substantial for which they were quite rightly grateful. Later, he refined this approach and the promised amount became considerably bigger.

This is how Allen got to Mickie and came into my life. Sam Cooke – whom Allen would later manage – was signed to RCA records. When The Beatles were at their most successful, Allen asked Joe D'Imperio, his contact at RCA, what he would pay The Beatles if they switched to his label from EMI. 'A million dollars advance and a royalty of 10 per cent' was the answer. Allen then contrived a meeting with Brian Epstein, The Beatles' long-time manager, and said: 'I can get you two million dollars' (he thought it was more impressive and figured that RCA would go for it if pressed) 'and a royalty of 10 per cent'. Brian had signed The Beatles and all of his other acts to EMI and, thanking Allen for the offer, said that he would stay loyal to EMI. They were paying The Beatles one old penny per single sold – about one-sixth of the payment Allen was offering, but Brian was not interested.

Allen's thinking was simple, but genius. If you asked a record company what they would pay an artist who was now successful on a rival company's label, the answer would of course be a huge amount. It was like betting on a horse when the race was finished. If you asked them what they paid their own newly signed and unproven artist, the answer would be very different.

I did not know Brian Epstein well but at a meeting we had some years later when I was trying to get his artists to record my writer's songs, he confided in me that Allen was not someone that he would want to do business with. Brian was the most charming man but did not pursue my offer to provide him with songs from my songwriters, so maybe he didn't want to do business with me either.

In September 1964, Mike Jeffery, the manager of The Animals, was in New York meeting with top agent Jerry Brandt about possible work for the group. Jerry was a business friend of Allen, and introduced him to Mike. Through Mike, Allen learned that Mickie Most produced The Animals and that Mickie was a hot producer. The Dave Clark Five were going to appear in *Get Yourself a Girl* with Nancy Sinatra. Featuring in a Hollywood movie was something that no other contemporary British act had ever achieved, and this impressed Mike no end. Allen – with no basis of truth whatsoever – told Mike that he could get The Animals into an MGM movie and that they would be paid ten thousand dollars for the day's work. Mike was definitely impressed and in return agreed to introduce Allen to Mickie.

Allen Klein arrived in London and asked Mickie and me to meet him at the Grosvenor House, a swanky hotel on Park Lane. His reason for asking us to go to where he was staying was that he had sent his clothes to the laundry. It sounded a bit strange, but so what. At the appointed time, the door to Allen's impressive suite was opened by his wife Betty: a petite, pretty brunette. She ushered us into the suite's parlour, where Allen sat wearing a bathrobe and holding a pipe. Allen was in his early thirties, and even with the pipe looked younger than I had expected for a guy who was powerful enough to get pop artists into movies. The pipe was not alight, and when we became closer he confessed that it was just a prop. Allen thought it made him look wise and he could suck on it if he needed a moment to think before answering.

He did not get up but said, 'Hi. Would you like some tea?'

We said, 'Yes, please', and exchanged pleasantries until room service delivered the refreshments. Allen gave the waiter a stack of silver coins from a row of such stacks that he had lined up on a table beside his chair. It was an obviously over-generous tip and I think that we were supposed to be impressed, but we were not. Betty left the room after serving the tea and Allen said, 'Mickie, I can get you a million dollars.' Now we were impressed.

What followed was, for me, a master class in the intricacies of the record industry. Allen knew the cost of every aspect of the manufacture and distribution of records. In 1964 the retail price of a single was six shillings and four pence, about thirty pence in today's money. The cost of manufacture was maybe five old pennies. Even taking into account the retailer's margin, royalties for music copyright and the cost of physical distribution, the record company's profit margin was about fifteen old pennies; they could easily afford to pay artists *and* producers much more than the few pennies they did. As mentioned above, *The Beatles* were being paid *one* old penny per record, and even this was subject to arcane deductions. Allen made us realise what huge potential power a successful artist had.

Mickie's deals for The Animals and Herman's Hermits were with EMI. Allen offered to renegotiate the deals so that Mickie would be guaranteed that million dollars for future productions. During the conversation it became clear that Allen had decided that I was the key to Mickie agreeing to take him on and he gradually switched his sales pitch from Mickie to me. We said little as he talked in thousands and millions and I told him that we would think about his million-dollar proposition. We thanked him for the tea and left.

Once outside the door, we practically fell about laughing at the thought of Mickie getting a million dollars, a sum equal to approximately ten million dollars today. Mickie was doing well, with an income measured in the tens of thousands, not millions. He lived in a small suburban house in Wembley, probably worth about four thousand pounds. I was drawing twenty-five pounds a week from my practice and gave Marsha eight pounds a week for housekeeping. The average wage was less than one thousand pounds a year and you could buy a nice family house in Chelsea or Hampstead for less than fifteen thousand pounds, so a million pounds was a *lot* of money to both of us.

In the 1960s, while getting a record deal was big, getting a deal with EMI – the leading record company in the UK – was huge. They had artists like Gerry and The Pacemakers, Helen Shapiro, Billy J Cramer, the Dave Clark Five and, of course, The Beatles. In those days, EMI presented artists with a standard contract that was *printed*, thus discouraging thoughts of changing it. To many, EMI was regarded as a major institution. Nobody tried to change their printed insurance policy with Prudential or the printed conditions of a Barclays Bank overdraft. Naive artists and equally naive advisors just checked the blank spaces in EMI's printed contracts, where the basic royalty rate was inserted, and artists eagerly signed the forms.

Not only were the basic royalty rates very low, but the small print in the contracts reduced them even further. Royalties were paid on 90 per cent of sales, because historically records had once been made from very breakable shellac, and there was an allowance made for broken records. The contracts were not changed when records began to be manufactured with more durable vinyl. Also, royalties in overseas sales were halved – an echo of music-publishing practice. No royalties were paid on stocks of records sold after they were deleted from the current catalogue … and so it went on. All recording costs were deducted out of the pitiful royalties that were paid, even if the record companies used their in-house studios. An artist had to sell an awful lot of records to get a meaningful cheque. Later on I realised that the value of a hit artist had an ever-greater benefit to a record company than the immediate profit. In the sixties, a large proportion of sales were through independent record shops. Record companies had sales reps who called on the shops on a regular basis and if the salesman had a hit record, it was easier to persuade the owner to take other records that were not such certain sellers. The shop owners had to settle their accounts if they wanted new releases, so a hit artist got the record company's bills paid *and* attracted other artists to the label.

Mickie believed that Allen was a bit of a joke, making ridiculous promises that he could not fulfil, but I had been impressed by his knowledge and his lack of fear in taking on 'the big boys'. I returned to Grosvenor House to meet Allen again. This time he was dressed and had dropped the pipe prop. He explained more about the power of artists. At that time EMI did not have their own company in the USA. They licensed their product to MGM Records, a subsidiary of MGM Films. 'The Animals and Herman's Hermits are the only two artists MGM have that sell any records. You're keeping MGM Records alive.' It sounded ludicrous. MGM! MGM who made all of those musicals that

I used to go to watch at the Astoria cinema opposite my dad's sweetshop. It was unbelievable.

By now I could see that confronting EMI with the knowledge of their chicanery would certainly get their attention. However, as I reminded Allen, Mickie had entered into binding agreements with EMI, which they had no legal obligation to change. This did not seem to be of any concern to Allen at all. He offered to take nothing from any deal made for Mickie if he did not get him the million dollars, and a 20 per cent commission if he did. I told him that I would not permit Mickie to enter into any written agreement at this stage, and that I would have to attend all meetings.

I told Mickie that Allen had agreed to a no-win-no-fee deal, and that I would be at all the relevant meetings. Mickie agreed that Allen should go ahead.

I wanted to know Allen better. He was a fascinating man, clearly extremely bright, and his analysis of the music business made absolute sense to me. I invited him and his wife Betty to dinner at our home. Marsha cooked a great meal and the four of us got on extremely well. We laughed a lot and Allen and I found some common ground in our upbringing. We were both from very modest Jewish family backgrounds and had found our way into the music business via accountancy, but our childhoods were very different. My brother Roger and I were brought up by loving parents, and our financial circumstances were no different from our friends' and did not seem to us to be a hardship. Allen was one of four children. His mother had died when he was nine months old, his father could not cope with a baby and Allen, aged barely a year, was sent to live with his grandparents. When

he was four he and his sister Naomi went to Newark's Hebrew
Orphanage and Sheltering Home for five years, until their father
remarried and was able to take them back. Understandably, this
experience would have a lasting effect on Allen and I believe it
was the breeding ground for his exceptional drive and ambition.

We definitely struck a bond and the next day Allen called
to thank us for dinner and said that the four of us should go
to dinner. 'Your town, you choose a restaurant.' Marsha's father,
Jack Bloom, used to take us to Les Ambassadeurs, a very expensive members' dining club off Park Lane, where they had dinner
dancing (it *was* fifty years ago). The club was housed in what
used to be the home of a Rothschild and it reeked of elegance.
If I wanted to impress Allen, and I did, this would do it. I asked
Jack to arrange a booking at Les A. Always keen to advance my
business career, he promised a great table and generously offered
to charge the bill to his account. I declined, explaining that the
Kleins were reciprocating our invitation to dinner at our home
and therefore would pay for the evening.

On the way to the restaurant, Marsha made me promise
not to pick up the bill. 'He's the rich guy with his suite at the
Grosvenor House and it was his idea that we go to dinner. We
have entertained him at our home and obviously it's his place to
pay for us. Don't you be a big shot, we can't afford it.' I promised
not to pay.

Meanwhile, Betty was having a similar conversation with
Allen. She had made enquiries about Les A and had been told
it was the most expensive restaurant in London. She was not
sure that Allen had enough money to pay for their suite at the
Grosvenor House and they certainly couldn't afford dinner for

four at Les A. 'The Myers wouldn't be so bad-mannered as to choose the most expensive restaurant in town and expect us to pay. Don't be a big shot, we can't afford it.' Allen promised not to pay.

As arranged by Jack, we were ushered into the restaurant by William, Les A's famous maître d' who, no doubt on Jack's instructions, fussed over us and seated us at the number one table by the dance floor. Once again we had a fun time together, and when the meal was finished and it was time to call for the bill Marsha was furiously kicking me under the table to make sure that I did not call for the bill. On the other side of the table Betty was similarly abusing Allen's knee. There was an embarrassing few moments while I carefully avoided the waiter's eye.

Suddenly Betty said, 'Allen, let's dance.' Allen hated dancing but before he could protest, she dragged him away. Not sure what to do, I looked at Marsha.

'Don't you dare call for the bill,' she said with wifely authority.

'Right,' said I. 'I'm going for a pee.'

Thinking how clever I was to have outwitted Allen, I delayed my return until I could hear the song finish, waited for a few minutes to give Allen a chance to return to the table and call for the bill, then sauntered back to our table. But no. The band had started a new song and Allen and Betty were *still* dancing. The waiter rushed over to pull out my chair and I had no alternative other than to ask for the bill. Betty told me that she looked over Allen's shoulder, saw me pay, and gave Allen permission to stop dancing. On the way home Marsha asked me why the hell I paid, to which I replied. 'Allen could dance all night, how long could I pee for?'

This was a story that we all told time and time again whenever we were asked about how we first became friends. It was also the story I told when I spoke at Allen's funeral in July 2009. We had been friends for forty-five years and I owed him much. Allen's last few years were cursed with Alzheimer's and it was heartbreaking for me to see this giant of a personality mentally waste away.

In 1964 I was excited at the thought of going with Allen to EMI to see if he could get Mickie his million-dollar deal. Mickie was still dubious and nervous that Allen would spoil his relationship with EMI, but having spent time with Allen I was confident that he would pull it off. Ron Tudor, EMI's managing director, and Clive Kelly, the company's in-house head of legal affairs, greeted us politely.

'Would you like some tea?' asked Clive.

'No,' snapped Allen, 'We don't want tea.'

I was shocked by his rudeness; it was a bit like refusing to shake Clive's hand. I was expecting a little warm-up before the main event but Allen went straight for the jugular.

'Mickie's not going to make any more records for you.'

'I beg your pardon?' said Ron.

Allen repeated it again more slowly. 'Mickie is not going to make any more records for you.' Then he added, 'No more records from The Animals or Herman's Hermits.' The two executives could not have been more shocked if Allen had stood up and peed on the carpet.

'But we have a contract with Mickie,' said Clive, definitely a little red-faced.

'You may or may not have a contract, that is for a court to decide, but you're not getting any more records.' He paused. 'Now we'll have a cup of tea.'

This was the essence of Allen's standard negotiations. Even with a binding contract a record company could not enforce personal services. They could stop an artist recording for any other company, but they could not make the artist record for them. Even if they could, they would have no control over the quality of product they had forced the artist to record. It was a huge bluff, but it made no sense for a record company to call it. If they wanted to keep the artist, they simply had to pay more, which they could easily afford to do.

I subsequently used the formula with great success many times myself when renegotiating clients' contracts or doing a deal for my own company Gem. I was a little less brash, substituting 'My client is not happy' for the blunt 'You're not going to get any more records'. But the effect was usually the same. After a while I became a gunslinger whose reputation was so fearful he never had to take his gun out. As I walked into some negotiations with major record companies, they would produce a Laurence Myers draft contract that I had negotiated for a previous artist. It contained all the revisions that I required and all we had to talk about was the basic royalty rate and the advance. I learned a lot from Allen, but I worked out for myself what was probably the most important aspect of dealing with major record companies.

We all know that politicians' decisions are for the most part based on what they need to get themselves re-elected rather than what is good for the long-term future of the country. Well, the same premise applies to most of the heads of record companies. They put their personal need to hit their annual targets above the long-term interest of the companies. I was invariably able to negotiate the return of ownership of the copyright in the recordings five years after the contract ended, because the person that I was negotiating with believed that they would be long gone from the company by then. This is something that my grandchildren should really be happy about. The income from the catalogue that I retained has diminished over the years, due in no small part to streaming, but after I go to the Great Recording Studio/Theatre/Film Set in the Sky, they will still have something to thank Papa for, when the royalty statements come in.

Allen indeed renegotiated a deal for Mickie that came to a million dollars, albeit advanced over years and dependent on Mickie delivering artists in addition to The Animals and Herman's Hermits. He tossed aside the EMI printed contracts and agreed a new one line by line. Gone were the spurious deductions from royalties, and the rate payable to Mickie was increased considerably. Mickie had the rights to The Animals' and Herman's Hermits' recordings under contracts made with those artists before I became involved with him. He was in no hurry to pass on to those artists more favourable terms. That could be done when *their* representative told us that 'the artists were unhappy'.

Allen's plan was to be an owner of some of the masters that were the subject of his renegotiations. His greatest ally in achieving this was HM the Queen, or more specifically, Her Majesty's collectors of taxes. In 1964 the highest rate of tax was 83 per cent and in some cases 98 per cent. People who could flee, like Michael Caine and Sean Connery, fled to America, but most people had to make such arrangements as they could to legally minimise their tax liability.

Allen proposed that the rights to artists' recordings would be split between the USA and the rest of the world. He would be the owner of the rights in America. The Animals and Herman's Hermits were re-licensed to MGM on much improved terms and future artists that Mickie would produce were licensed for America to CBS Records. Allen's company would retain 20 per cent of advances and pay the balance to Mickie over a period of years. The rest of the world income was also spread over a number of years, but Mickie retained the ultimate rights through the ownership of the company that we set up to deal with them. It was legally tax-effective and I advised Mickie to do it.

After the deal was struck, Allen's family and mine carried on our transatlantic friendship. On 20 July 1966, Peter – our second son – was born. This was shortly after Betty Klein gave birth to their daughter Beth. We had sent Betty a small but taste-ful bunch of congratulatory flowers. Allen, as ever over the top, sent six-dozen red roses to Marsha in her room at the London Clinic. The nursing staff thought that she was a major film star.

More kindness followed. In 1967, my nineteen-year-old brother Roger was working with me at Goodman Myers and was very involved with a girlfriend. She was nice enough, but he realised that he was too young to get seriously involved. I called Allen who, without hesitation, gave Roger a job in the New York office of his firm ABKCO (Allen And Betty Klein COmpany) for a couple of months, which gave him a reason to break up with his girlfriend. He loved living in New York, and it was a great experience for him. A few years later, he met Lee Spencer Morris, an attractive young lady who was working for a UK country music promoter. I knew that this was real love because Lee was going to work at Midem and Roger asked me to look after her, which I did. Roger and Lee married in 1974.

Allen continued to be a good friend to me until he died. He has been much maligned over the years for his perceived unethical dealings with the Stones and The Beatles. The day before I spoke at his funeral there were adverse comments in lots of the press and a particularly vicious and damning obituary from Ray Connolly in the *Daily Mail*. In my eulogy, I recited my dishons, hons and honours theory and how it very much applied to Allen. Allen had certainly gone through all three of those stages and his honour came when he was inducted into the Rock'n'Roll Hall of Fame. I also told the story of Allen sticking me with the bill at Les A., which got a laugh. The service was attended by hundreds of mourners, including the great, the good and a few of the not-so-good in the music industry. At the end of the service both Yoko Ono, John Lennon's wife, and former Stones manager Andrew Oldham came up to me and thanked me for my comments, saying that I had summed up Allen's character completely.

I know that I have already told you how much of my business success I owe to Allen, but I am saying it again, so there, and it all began with the EMI deal he secured for Mickie.

Now that Mickie was fully financed by EMI, the Rak Records group really started to motor. In addition to continuing with The Animals and Herman's Hermits, Mickie produced records with

Lulu, Jeff Beck, and Donovan. Most of the songwriters already had a publishing deal, but the hope was that Rak Publishing, headed by Mickie's brother Dave, would pick up the rights on some of Mickie's records. Mickie was very smart and he never let the publishing rights influence his choice of songs.

In June 1966, I was asked to conduct an audit of Pye Records, on behalf of The Kinks. The Kinks were currently hot with 'Sunny Afternoon' and 'Dedicated Follower of Fashion', written by Ray Davies. They were, I thought, original songs and Ray sang them in his natural London accent, which I found a delight at a time when guys who spoke broad Geordie sang like they were born in Mississippi. As a fan, I was eager to meet Ray. They say never meet your heroes and avoid disappointment, which isn't always true, but in Mr Davies' case it was. Considering that he had written 'Sunny Afternoon', Ray turned out to be less than sunny. This is something that others have remarked upon. Years later I met with Ray again to discuss the possibility of him writing a stage musical and charming he was not. Some would call him taciturn; I would call him a miserable bastard but not – of course – to his face.

The Pye audit was most revealing. Amongst other more minor discrepancies, the good old 'payment on 90 per cent of sales' came up. This anachronism of royalty reduction for break-ages in transit, when records were no longer inclined to break, was standard in contracts of the time. What I discovered was that the Pye accounting system took 10 per cent off *all* sales before the income was reported in an artist's account. They then took *another* 10 per cent off royalties payable to each artist. As I mentioned earlier, it was institutional cheating. Most of the record companies were established icons, and the thought that they would be in any way dishonest was outrageous. In more recent years the same could be said about high-street banks.

10. THE GREEK TYCOON

Although this story is more to do with my life in film, Allen Klein was integral to getting *The Greek Tycoon* made as a Hollywood movie made so I will tell it now.

In 1976 I was really in the movie business. My record companies were doing well and I had started GTO Films in 1974. It was a major player in the UK film scene and we always had a big presence at the Cannes Film Festival. Allen had dabbled in the movie business – mainly spaghetti westerns – but we had never tried to do any films together.

Some few months earlier, Nico Mastorakis had been in my office trying to sell me some low-budget, soft-porn films that he had made in Greece. I declined his offer as we did not deal in pornography – obviously a huge mistake. Nico, a small-time writer/producer had had a career as a TV personality in Greece, but I later found out that it was during the time that his country was governed by the right-wing military junta so he was not particularly popular in Greece by the time he came to see me. He asked what sort of thing I was interested in. I said broad-appeal commercial movies. Nico rummaged around in his bag like a travelling salesman and after examining a few scripts produced a film treatment entitled *Onassis*. 'What about this?'

He wanted to write and produce a film of the life of shipping magnate Aristotle Onassis and needed seed money to get
the project under way. He had, he said, a commitment from
Anthony Quinn to play Onassis. My disbelief was obvious so
Nico asked me if I would like to speak to Quinn directly, right
now, and get his confirmation. Of course I would! Right there
and then, Nico made a call to Rome. In no time I was talking to
Anthony Quinn who – having convinced me that he was indeed
that Anthony Quinn – confirmed that, subject to script, director
etc, he was eager to make this movie.

I had not so long before this read Willi Frischauer's
wonderful and fascinating biography of Onassis. Onassis – a
charismatic figure who had been the richest man in the world
– had died in March 1975, so he was still very much of interest to the general public. I looked at Nico's treatment, which
was obviously stolen from the Frischauer book. Nico insisted
that the information was the same because Ari, as we were
both now calling him, had told them both his life story. Nico
explained that when he was a journalist he had 'interviewed
Onassis extensively'. As I recall, Nico confessed that the
interview was him with a group of other scrambling photographers snatching a paparazzi-type photo of the great man
and being removed by bodyguards before he could get a question in. Internet research reveals that Nico smuggled himself
onto Onassis' yacht as a musician and hid a camera behind his
guitar strings while Onassis was entertaining Teddy Kennedy.
He was discovered and thrown off the boat. Nevertheless, I
was interested. I just knew that we mere mortals are fascinated
with the lifestyles of the rich and famous, and Onassis was as

rich and famous as they came. I doubted that Nico could write the script, but thought that finding someone who could would not be a problem.

The idea was that we would take Quinn to the upcoming Cannes Film Festival and – with the help of Bobby Meyers, a well-respected film salesman – we would create enough pre-sales of the movie to get it financed. The budget for promoting the film at Cannes was not big. Nico had already met with important sponsors in Greece: the Epirotiki cruise line, the Metaxa liquor company and the Greek tourist office who, between them, would provide at no cost to us 'the most spectacular party ever thrown' at Cannes. All I needed to finance was travel and the publicity campaign. Believing this would not cost more than ten thousand pounds, I went to Athens with Nico to obtain confirmation from responsible authorities that what he had told me was true. And it was. It was all very plausible.

Epirotiki had Cannes as a stopover on their scheduled route. Their five hundred passengers would disembark for an evening ashore and we would promptly board the passenger-free vessel for our party. As the ship provided catering three times a day already, our party guests would not be a problem. The tourist office loved the idea of a film showing the glamour of Greece. They promised to give us goody bags for our guests with ouzo, brochures, food samples and worry beads. They could not do enough. We met with Mr Mataxa of Mataxa spirits fame, who promised to provide enough ouzo for us to fill the swimming pool. I could see the headlines, as film starlets cavorted in my ouzo-filled pool. It was all just wonderful and did not impact at all on my ten-thousand-pound budget.

Back in London, I spoke to Quinn's agent and said that I wanted to contract Quinn before I went to Cannes. No problem, they said, but I would have to pay 10 per cent of Quinn's fee up front. This was thirty thousand pounds. I was now completely carried away. In for ten grand – in for forty. I sent the cheque. I then found out that Quinn's agent also represented Jacqueline Bisset. Jacqui loved the idea of playing Jacqueline Kennedy and – subject to script and director – she would also commit to the movie. Yes, she would go to Cannes with us to promote the movie. As with Quinn, I would have to put up 10 per cent of her fee. So that was another fifteen thousand pounds from my already-busted coffers.

Nico was in Athens where he arranged for well-known Greek actress Irene Papas to commit to play Maria Callas. There would be no upfront fee for Irene but we would have to pay for her first-class travel and accommodation for the film festival. Nico also arranged for a bouzouki band to come to Nice from Athens, courtesy of Olympic Airlines. We would only have to pay for the overnight stay of eight musicians. 'Why not?' I said.

By the time we set off for the festival I was in for around sixty thousand pounds, which is probably half a million pounds in today's money. I had to mortgage my house to cover it. This was one of the few secrets that I ever had from my wife. The festival had to be a financial success or I would have to sell my family's home.

Thankfully, once we arrived at Cannes, our project was a talking point for those in the trade and the party on the boat was the hottest ticket in town. Invitations were delivered by foot soldiers to hotels. They would ask (bribe) the concierges but – huge mistake – we did not put the names on the actual invitation cards, only on the envelopes. The concierges sold the invitations (why didn't I think of that?) and I was obliged to send out a further few hundred invitations properly addressed. There were now some eight hundred invitations in circulation.

Allen Klein was in Cannes for his own business and inevitably I received a call from my friend and mentor. He asked me if he could get involved in the film but I said no. Allen would not be capable of being a partner, he would have to run the whole deal, and I was determined not to abdicate control of this golden opportunity to break into big-time movies. I was honest with Allen about my thoughts on this and he was fine about it. He asked if he could read the script anyway and was surprised to learn that I had not got around to having one written.

There is a golden rule in filmmaking that the three essentials are: the script, the script, and the script. I was aware of this but before getting around to it I had lined up the stars, the stars, and the stars. I was the shmuck, the shmuck, and the shmuck who – like Sinatra – would do it My Way. In my defence, I would say that I had been spoiled by my reputation in the music business. If I had gone to a record company with, say, Tom Jones, they would have given me the deal knowing that I would find the right material and producer. But this was the film business and very few producers could get the finance for a film without a good script, director and cast attached and I was fairly unknown to Hollywood studios.

As if there was not enough going on for me in Cannes that year, I had to deal with Angie Bowie, who called me from London to ask if I could put her up for one night. She was David Bowie's wife so I could hardly refuse. My head of distribution Bill Gavin was staying in a suite at The Majestic hotel and agreed to share with her. Angie arrived with eleven suitcases and ran up a phone bill the size of the national debt. She asked me if I could arrange for her to be the date of someone famous for a red-carpet film screening, which I could not.

Anthony Quinn arrived the day before the party. His Italian lawyer and one of his many agents were in town and Anthony suggested that Nico and I had dinner with them. He suggested the Moulin de Mougins – one of the finest and most expensive restaurants in the whole of France – and asked if my office could make the reservation. I said that it was impossible to get a reservation at the Moulin de Mougins during the festival as people booked from year to year but he said that he was a friend of the owner. Sure enough his name got us the reservation.

It was a fun evening. The restaurant was packed with people I knew and I rather enjoyed the kudos of sitting with one of the biggest stars in the world. Anthony was a great raconteur and regaled us with wonderful stories of the golden age of Hollywood. He carried on with his stories after we had finished dinner and – as entertaining as this was – it was getting late. With the big day ahead, I wished that he would call for the bill so that I could go home. The head waiter came to the table and informed Mr Quinn that his car was here. Mr Quinn stood up, thanked me for dinner and swept off with his guests leaving me with a bill which I remember could have paid for the dining room suite in my unfinished and now heavily mortgaged home in London. I subsequently also got the bill for his car.

I had sent Bill Gavin's wife Jane to travel with the cruise ship from Naples to supervise the onboard arrangements en route. On the morning of the party, a distressed Jane called me from Naples with news from the captain. Firstly, the guests on the boat would have to stay onboard unless I paid twenty dollars a head shore supplement. If they remained, the maximum number of guests allowed to attend my party would be two hundred and fifty. I had sent out eight hundred invitations! I had written confirmation from the owners of the boat that I could invite five hundred people and told Jane to inform the captain of this and that I refused to pay any shore allowance.

We had planned that the ship's tenders – smaller boats used to transfer goods and people to and from shore – would collect my guests from the jetty of the Carlton hotel. This was printed on my eight hundred invitations. But the captain said now that the tenders could not be used at all. Only tenders licensed by the Cannes municipality would be allowed. I was given the name of the man I should contact in Cannes to discuss this, a Monsieur Davide, from Havas Travel. I had written confirmation from Epirotiki, the boat's owners, for using the boat's own tenders and told Jane to inform the captain that I would ensure that the bill from Havas was sent to them.

Pretty sure that Havas would not send the bill to anyone other than me I rehearsed what I was going to say to Monsieur Davide. '*Bonjour, Monsieur Davide, je m'appelle Laurence Myers et peut-être que je ferai une grande soirée ce soir,*' etc.

I telephoned Monsieur Davide on the dot of nine that morning. '*Bonjour, Monsieur Davide, je m'appelle Laurence Myers et peut-être* …' He interrupted me immediately and in perfect

English said, 'Ah. Mr Myers, I was expecting your call. You are
the gentleman who is obliged to hire our tenders this evening.
Time is short, I suggest you come and see me immediately.'

I jumped on my little Honda motorbike and drove like a
TT rider to see the man. A thanksgiving turkey riding his
motorbike to the butcher. On the way, I tried to estimate what
this was going to cost me. This was the Cannes Film Festival,
where a Coca-Cola cost a week's wages and the local sport was
ripping off festival attendees. By the time I hurtled in to see
Monsieur Davide, I was near hysterical. Trying not to sob at his
feet I maintained a calm exterior. Monsieur Davide had already
worked on the '*petit problème*' and gave me the '*grande image*'.
The cost of the tenders was six thousand pounds for taking
two hundred and fifty people to the boat from the Gare Maritime (not the Carlton's jetty), and he had strict instructions
to take no more. Then there were the buses that I would need
to take the people who would be following their invitations'
instructions to gather at the Carlton jetty to the Gare Maritime, a mile or so away. That was another thousand pounds. So
a total of seven thousand pounds needed to be transferred from
my bank account before a single tender pulled away from the
shore. Wishing to be helpful, Monsieur Davide would accept
a telexed confirmation from my London bank that the transfer
had been made.

Back at my apartment, I called my bank in London and
persuaded them to send the money from my already overdrawn
account. I then summoned a council of war, attended by my
partner Nico Mastorakis, Bill Gavin, and Dennis Davidson our
PR. It was impossible to change our arrangements at such short
notice and anyway Nico had telexes confirming the boarding

arrangements that had been agreed with the ship's owners. The telexes were in Greek – obviously Greek to me – so Nico telephoned Athens and tried to resolve the issue. Nobody at the shipping line would take his call. The rest of the day was spent sending costly foot soldiers around all of the hotels with costly (everything at the Cannes Film Festival is costly) flyers informing guests that the departure venue had changed.

I had lunch with Anthony Quinn and Jacqueline Bisset who – having no knowledge of the '*l'heure des crises*' that I was dealing with – chatted happily about the project as I sat with a fixed and foolish grin on my face, counting in my head the cost to date of the 'free party'.

In the afternoon the bouzouki band called from Rome. The free tickets provided by Olympic Airlines were only valid for the Athens–Rome leg of the trip and I would have to pay for the Rome-Nice leg. By now I was simply nodding at any requests for money, provided they could be met by my credit cards.

At eight o'clock in the evening, my stars were in the bar of the Majestic hotel, drinking the finest champagne my money could buy. Eight hundred people were lining up at the entrance to the Gare Maritime singing, 'Why are we waiting?' in an assortment of languages. The invited TV cameras and paparazzi were waiting on the dockside and patrolling the waters in hired boats ready to board the ship pirate-style. Bill Gavin was at the Gare Maritime, offering the captains of the tenders obscene bribes to take all of the guests out to the ship. Monsieur Davide was grabbing the money from their hands and giving it back to Bill, who gave it back to the tender captains as soon as his back was turned. Allen Klein was asking if he could bring a couple of extra guests to the party. Of course he could!

Originally, the cruise ship was due to arrive in Cannes at five in the afternoon. We then received a message saying that it would not arrive until 7 p.m. It did not. At 7 p.m. I was standing at the edge of the quay, scouring the empty horizon. I might have thrown myself into the sea had I not been wearing my new white film producer's suit. At 7.15 p.m. the ship arrived. Too big to dock in the port, she moored close by.

I hurried the advance party onto the first tender out. This was Quinn, Bisset, Papas, the bouzouki band and me. Everybody wants to be a star in their own country and Nico was heavily engaged with the Greek press. We arrived alongside the ship where there was a proper boarding platform manned by smart sailors. I felt a little better. I was first up the ladder. My first sight was the deck beautifully decorated with fairy lights and a vast spread of party food. I felt a lot better. My guests would party 'till dawn' as stated on the invitations.

My second sight made me feel worse. A prominent notice at the top of the boarding ladder stated 'ALL SHORE VISITORS MUST BE OFF THE BOAT BY 10.30 P.M.' There was a man with lots of gold on his uniform nearby, repeating the message, over and over again. 'What does this mean?' I asked. He read the notice out slowly as if I was a child.

'Oh no,' said I. 'I have a contract. My guests will be dancing 'till dawn.'

'Fine,' said he, 'but they'll be dancing in our next stop, Marseille.'

Jane, my representative, came to greet me. I am not a great drinker but, on this occasion, I was in desperate need. I asked her for a drink. She did not look happy. 'Laurence, there is no drink.'

'Of course there is,' I snapped. 'You told me you saw it loaded on.' She explained that our ouzo, wine and brandy was indeed on board but held in a bonded hold. Because the ship had arrived so late, French customs had closed and it could not be released from the bonded hold without them.

Eventually the ship's purser appeared and told me that the ship's bar could be opened at discount prices and charged to me but – huge but – he could not keep out the passengers, all of whom were eager to join my stars. I would be buying drinks for five hundred holidaymakers and as many of my guests who could fight their way onto the ship.

As I was desperately trying to deal with the escalating disasters, the bouzouki bandleader had been following me around, trying to get my attention. He informed me that there was no power on the bandstand and as they needed amplification nobody would hear them. Nico was still busy giving interviews to the Greek press, so could not help me. The bandleader said that he was an artist and refused to play. Remembering Peter Grant's great line to Led Zeppelin's drummer, I asked if he could play in a wheelchair, and he huffed off.

So this was the situation thirty minutes after the party started. The guests who had managed to get to the ship were fighting to get up the narrow ladder, just as the guests who were on the ship, fearful of ending up in Marseille, fought to get down. I was having to pay a bar bill for several hundred cruise guests. The only press that had made it onboard were Greek and a local TV crew. The band were playing silent bouzouki music. The PR man for the cruise line was trying to make Quinn wear a branded T-shirt (which was one part of the contract that they had remembered!) and in the process ripped Quinn's shirt. Quinn then – not unreasonably – refused to do any interviews. Jacqui Bisset and Irene Papas sensibly hid themselves away and I realised that Allen Klein was one of the hundreds of guests who had been stuck at the Gare Maritime, unable to join the party.

PR man Dennis Davidson, who was more used to Cannes Festival party debacles than I was, actually got together *the* photo opportunity. QUINN THE GREEK (actually born Mexican of course) WAS GOING TO DANCE AGAIN. We were about to invoke that iconic dance scene in *Zorba The Greek*. The TV and photo press stood by and the unamplified bouzouki band strummed with their bloody, torn fingers as loudly as they could.

Quinn was in fact a terrible dancer with little sense of rhythm but he was a pro and knew that this was the shot everybody wanted. He stood up and – looking around – said that he could not dance alone. He looked at me and said, 'Hey, kid, come and dance with me.' I grabbed Jacqui Bisset and we joined the man. Nico, who had been nowhere to be seen during the earlier dramas, suddenly appeared. Just then, the whole thing seemed worthwhile. Here was I, the boy from Finsbury Park, about to be beamed around the world in my white producer's suit dancing with Anthony Quinn and Jacqui Bisset. The dance began, everybody started clapping, and I was smiling like the cat that got the cream. Then somebody shouted 'Whoopa!' in true Greek style. Then everyone shouted 'Whoopa!' and a glass of red wine came hurtling through the air, all over my white producer's suit. I have the photo. It was an appropriate end to the party. I wanted my mummy.

Notwithstanding the fact that the party was later described in one of the trade papers as the Greatest Disaster in the History of the Cannes Film Festival, we had created a great interest in the project. The next day, Allen Klein once again asked if I needed any help. Once again, I declined. I had a hot property and was determined to run with it myself.

A month or so later, me and my newly cleaned white suit went to Los Angeles where we were installed in an expensive bungalow at the Beverley Hills Hotel. Not any old expensive bungalow at the Beverley Hills Hotel, but the super-expensive Bungalow 5: the one with a dining room and two or three bedrooms. Such was the interest in *The Greek Tycoon*, I actually had appointments with the heads of most of the major Hollywood studios. The meetings were cordial, but brief. They all said the same thing. Nice cast – come back when you have a script and a director. I was shattered. I, of course, knew that these elements were absolutely vital to the making of a good film but I had naively believed that the cast was so strong, the studios would trust me to get them right. Dispirited, I tried some of the smaller studios and distributors but with no success. Everybody wanted to see the script and be sure of the director. By now I was desperate. There was a young Englishman working in LA called David Blake who worked for Cinema Shares, a two-desks-and-an-empty-filing-cabinet type of operation based in New York. I asked him if there was any point in meeting with his boss in New York, but he was quite certain that this would be a waste of time, so I had no idea what my next step should be.

I really was in serious financial trouble. I had literally bet my house on this project and the options on Quinn and Bisset would soon evaporate, making my investment worthless. I decided to go home via New York for no good reason other than I did not

want to immediately face the problems that were waiting for
me in London. I checked out of the Beverley Hills Hotel. As I
closed the door of Bungalow 5 behind me, I heard the telephone
ring. Thinking that it could save me tipping the bell captain, I
went back to answer it. It was Allen Klein asking how I was
doing. The last thing I wanted was an 'I told you so' from my
mentor so I told the first lie that came into my head: 'Great, I'm
flying to New York to make a deal with Cinema Shares.'

'Never heard of them,' said Allen. 'If you don't go with a major,
I'd like you to go with me. Whatever Cinema Shares are giving
you, I'll give you a dollar more.' Not wishing to give me a chance
to refuse him, as if I would under the circumstances, he rang off
and I nearly fainted with relief. I was close to Allen until he died
some forty years later, but I never told him of my deception.

Allen was nervous that I would meet with Cinema Shares
and he had his driver meet me at the airport in New York and
whisk me straight to his office, where he immediately asked me
what my proposed deal was with his 'rival'.

'First,' I said, 'I get my investment of seventy-five thousand
pounds back.'

'Of course,' said Allen. 'What else?'

'I get it back very soon,' I said.

'Yes, yes, what else? What is your deal with Cinema Shares?'

'Well, first I get my money back.'

'And then?' said Allen

I, of course, had never even spoken to Cinema Shares and had
given no thought to anything beyond getting back my money. 'I
can't deal with you as I would with them,' I said, 'What do you
think is fair?'

Allen laid out a proposal but – such was my relief – that I did not even absorb it. I just nodded a lot as the blood returned to my veins. In the event, his offer was fair. He gave me my seventy-five thousand pounds back and the film got made, scripted by Mort Fine and directed by J. Lee Thompson.

As expected, Allen took over the running of the project but – as he personally financed the production and the golden rule was He Who Provides The Gold Makes The Rule – this was his entitlement. Universal Studios had expressed a serious interest in the film and I begged Allen to do a deal once shooting started but he figured we would do better when the picture was finished. By that time Allen was in for eleven million dollars, which I knew he could not afford to lose. I persuaded him not to wait until the film was fully edited as he would have to stand by the film he had made. He took my advice and we showed Universal a rough cut – an assembly of the scenes without the final music, sound effects, etc. Universal went for it. We shook hands with the studio before Allen and I celebrated by going to Nathan's on Broadway and each eating two of their famous hot dogs.

It was not a great film. We claimed that the film was not about the Onassis family but a Greek ship owner called Tomassis who married the widow of a fictional American president. The film anyway had the usual disclaimer that 'All the characters are fictitious', but we were chary about upsetting the Kennedy and Onassis families, so we made a bland film where all of the characters were nice, which, of course, they were not. The film was released in 1978 but did no real business. Years later, *Dallas* and *Dynasty* proved my theory of the commercial value of stories about the rich and nasty.

I never received a penny profit from the film but I still have the poster with my name on it, and I still have my house.

The other benefit of the whole debacle was that when I was in LA Jacqui invited me to lunch with her and her then boyfriend Victor Drai at her home in Beverley Hills. She was a most charming and unassuming host and after lunch we all swam in her beautiful pool. The next film that Jacqui was going to appear in was *The Deep* – remembered by many because she spent a lot of the film in a wet T-shirt. Jacqui was finding it hard to swim underwater, a requirement for her part in the film. She asked me to help her practise by putting my arms around her and holding her underwater, which I did. I don't remember what we had for lunch.

11. PIRATE RADIO AND THE STAR-CLUB

In the 1960s, pirate radio was booming in the UK. Operated from ships outside of territorial waters and so beyond regulatory control, they filled the gap left by the BBC, which had a limited output of pop music. Radio Caroline had made a fortune and Mickie Most and I were convinced that we could do the same in Germany. The idea was brought to Mickie by Henry Henroid – a wonderful cockney character who had spent years working as a road manager for Don Arden without being hung out of a window or smacked.

Henry's job was to look after American acts that Don brought over to Europe and he had wonderful stories about his tours with Gene Vincent. Vincent was a notorious hellraiser, despite having a steel sheath around one leg following a near-fatal motorcycle accident. 'Now 'e was a bleedin' lunatic. You should 'ave 'eard 'im when there was a full moon. I had to smuggle the bastard out of the 'otel in a laundry basket and his bleedin' leg wouldn't fold in.' Henry also toured with Little Richard: 'I was wiv 'im on the plane when he saw the bleedin' light and got religion. He got down on 'is knees in the middle of the bleedin' aisle, 'allelujahrin' to God, and renounced his material possessions. I copped 'is gold watch in all 'is tomfoolery. Lovely man.'

Henry had looked after many of the acts that Don had booked into the Star-Club in Hamburg, the place where The Beatles famously honed their craft. Henry got to know Manfred Weissleder, the owner of the club, well. The Star-Club was in the red-light district of Hamburg and Manfred, who – according to Henry – was involved in soft pornography and all manner of shady deals, was open to any kind of business. Either Henry or Manfred – both claimed the honour – had come up with the idea of starting a pirate radio station under the Star-Club banner, broadcasting from a ship to be anchored outside German territorial waters off of the coast of Hamburg. Henry told Manfred that he could 'raise the readies no prob' and came to see Mickie and me.

Henry and Manfred had already done some spadework. There was a German rum importer who was keen to come in on the deal. He owned a ship moored in Flensburg, a fishing town in the north of Germany, which was being used as a dormitory for imported Turkish labour. Telefunken, the enormous German electronics company, were, it seemed, keen to do a deal for the necessary broadcasting equipment.

I did some preliminary research and it seemed that there was no German law that would inhibit the venture so Henry and I flew to Hamburg. We stayed in a hotel that Henry knew near to The Reeperbahn, where the Star-Club was situated. The Reeperbahn, the centre of Hamburg's red-light district, is a walled-off street near the docks. It is lined with bars, dance clubs and brothels, and the Star-Club was one of the most successful operations. Manfred, eager to attract the custom of the young merchant seamen who frequented the area, had started booking English rock groups. Much has been written about The Beatles who, fuelled by amphetamines and God knows what else, played their fourteen-hour shifts alternating with one or two other bands doing the same. When I was there the policy had not changed, although the now-famous Beatles had not played for about three years. I saw lots of bands, the most memorable of whom were Freddie & The Midnighters. I had a drink with Freddie between sets and he was like the ball in a pinball machine, pinging from flipper to flipper and lighting up whatever he touched. I thought that he was on some sort of speed but later this zaniness found him fame back in England as the comedian Freddie Starr. All the bands played similar sets of American rock'n'roll standards and it seemed as though finishing with 'Walkin'The Dog' was obligatory.

Henry introduced us to Manfred in his best cockney German: '*Das ist Herr* Myers, *dein Geschäftsführer von dein Animals und das 'Ermans 'Ermits.*' I was not the manager of The Animals or Herman's Hermits, just a business advisor, but it seemed to impress Manfred, who had his thriving porn-film business and no doubt many other enterprises which in the UK would not have gained him a knighthood. He was in fact your basic dodgy geezer. He was, however, a shrewd dodgy geezer and recognised the financial potential of a pirate radio station.

We drove to Flensburg, where the rum importer's ship was moored. For six months I'd owned a half-share in a rarely functioning twelve-foot speedboat so I was, of course, the expert in all matters maritime. We climbed onboard and it seemed to me to be big enough compared to the photos I had seen of Radio Caroline's vessel. Being the maritime maven, I demanded to see the engine (this from a man who cannot change a lightbulb or a car tyre). I was invited downstairs – they call it 'below' – where the smell from the dormitories was, as Henry put it, 'absofuckinglutely reels' (reels of cotton: rotten).

Back on deck, I dug my heels into the planking a couple of times and pronounced that the ship had passed my preliminary survey. We returned to Hamburg for a meeting with executives of Telefunken. As Henry had indicated, they were prepared to barter the supply and fitting of all of the required equipment in return for favoured advertising.

The next day Manfred went on national television in Germany where, by use of graphics showing sweet little white-dot radio waves beaming from the radio mast of a ship, he demonstrated the proposed reach of the station. By the time we got back to his office his phone was ringing off the hook from people interested in taking advertising. We went back to London in a happy frame of mind. In just three days we had lined up a ship, the equipment and a line of probable advertisers.

My interest in Mickie's music companies was 10 per cent but in recognition of my efforts in this venture, Mickie offered me 25 per cent. Henry Henroid would also have 25 per cent ('Tasty, tasty,' said Henry) and Mickie, who would be overseeing the programming, would have 50 per cent. We would follow Radio Luxembourg's example of taking song-publishing rights in return for special promotions. We were going to be very rich. Then it occurred to me that we should get a proper survey of the boat, find out the specifications of all required equipment and obtain advice on the legalities of the operation. The cost of this preparatory work was considerable, so clearly we were going to become very much poorer before we became very much richer. Fortunately, before we actually spent any money, I received a call from Manfred saying that he had been informed that the German government would vigorously oppose our scheme. I explained that – subject to verification and further research – the law was on our side. He explained that Telefunken and the Rum Man were not prepared to take on the government. Also because of his own 'rather specialised business interest' he was reluctant to do so himself. Bearing in mind that the FBI got Capone on tax evasion, and presuming that the German taxman had seen one of the relevant movies, I could see he was right.

I thought about taking the project forward on my own. I imagined myself standing proudly on the bridge of my own pirate radio ship, an Englishman once more defiant against German aggression. I then imagined a periscope cutting towards me through the waves and forgot the whole thing.

There is no doubt that my involvement with Mickie was the key to my later success in the music business. I was Mickie's consigliere at a time when there were no other accountancy firms specialising in the world of popular music, a relatively new industry. Many of the artists in Mickie's musical circle became clients of Goodman Myers. The most important to me personally was Mike Leander, a young writer-producer who, in 1970, would have an absolutely life-changing effect on my career.

Mickie was sixty-four when, tragically, he died in 2003 from a form of cancer relating to asbestos, which had been liberally used in the walls of recording studios. We had drifted apart over the years, but for some time he had been very much part of my life. I was very moved when I learned of his death.

12. TETRAGRAMMATON RECORDS AND TINY TIM

I had first met Greg Smith when he was an office boy for some theatrical agents who took temporary office space at Goodman Myers' Albermarle Street premises. In 1968 he became the London representative for Tetragrammaton Records, a new-ish record company in Los Angeles. Tetragrammaton was planning to open London offices and Greg kindly recommended that I should represent them.

They flew me out to Los Angeles first-class to meet up – always a good start. Then they put me up in a very nice room at the Beverley Hilton and even provided a hire car for my use. Tetragrammaton was a strange name for a record company. It is the Hebrew theonym (name for God), a translation of which is used by observant Jews who do not wish to say 'God' aloud. Now you know too.

The driving force behind the company was Roy Silver who, with his partners Bruce Post Campbell and Marvin Deane, ran a very successful management company in LA. They managed Bob Dylan, Joan Rivers, Richard Pryor and other stars. Bill Cosby was Roy Silver's personal client and I suspected that Mr Cosby was the major financer of the Tetragrammaton record company.

The offices on Canon Drive in Beverly Hills were astounding, a low-built block nesting amongst lush trees, surrounded by a parking lot that looked like a sales agency for Mercedes. My meeting was with Roy Silver himself, a charismatic man with an extraordinary personality. I thanked him for the extremely generous travel and hotel arrangements but he brushed my words away, indicating that he had merely asked his secretary to make the necessary bookings. There was clearly no ethos of budgetary control in the company coming from the boss.

The label had two successful artists. Deep Purple were doing well with their debut album *Shades of Deep Purple*, the single 'Hush' from the album having made the Top 10 on the American charts. The only other successful act they had was Tiny Tim, whose novelty recording of 'Tiptoe Through the Tulips' – sung in a high falsetto – had made the Top 20.

Commenting on the number of staff, and noting the number of Mercedes in the parking lot, I asked Roy how the company could afford such a large overhead out of its relatively modest success. Roy said his LA accountants were dealing with that and he only wanted to talk to me about the cost of setting up in the UK. I went through some figures but he was obviously not focusing on what I was saying. I had the distinct feeling that he had given no thought as to why I should be brought over at great expense. On the way out he introduced me to Tiny Tim, a very strange-looking young man. His American mother was the daughter of a rabbi and his Lebanese father was the son of a Maronite Christian priest. Mr Tim had managed to parlay his falsetto one-hit into something of a career. Other than the dubious honour of meeting Tiny Tim, the trip was a waste of my

time and Bill Cosby's money. Tetragrammaton never opened a
London office, and predictably went bankrupt in 1971.

Roy Silver was, however, a naturally talented chef of Chinese
cooking. Later on, in 1976, when his showbiz career was somewhat in tatters, he opened an eponymous restaurant, which
quickly became a very popular hangout for the LA glitterati.
The Chinese food was excellent – he only used kosher chickens
– but the real draw was that if you were a friend – and he had no
enemies – he dragged you into the cloakroom and encouraged
you to help yourself to cocaine from an extremely large jar that
he kept behind the coats. Predictably, his restaurant followed his
record company into bankruptcy in 1982. Not the last restaurant
to disappear up the owner's nose in a cloud of white powder.

As with most LA restaurants, where you sat at Roy's was an
important statement of status. I was once there as a guest of an
important film agent who, of course, had been allocated an appropriate 'I am an important film agent' table. During the course of
our meal Tony Curtis came into the restaurant. Mr Curtis must
have been well into his fifties at the time and arguably well past
his box-office prime, but I was excited beyond belief to see him
in the flesh. When I was a teenager I wanted to look like Tony
Curtis, as did any boy my age that did not want to look like Elvis
or Marlon Brando. Apart from the fact that as Jewish boys we
were both circumcised, Mr Curtis and I had very little in common.
Tony Curtis was slim, handsome and looked fantastic on screen.
Laurence Myers was overweight and did not even look good in
his wedding photos. Anyway, Curtis was now sitting a few tables
away from me in the company of a very attractive blonde lady
and I could not take my eyes off him. My host was sitting with

his back to the focus of my attention and he asked me what I was looking at. In reverential tones I told him that I was looking at Tony Curtis. He did not even look round. 'Tony Curtis? Can't get arrested.'

I was shocked at his callous attitude. 'But it's Tony Curtis, the one from *Some Like it Hot* and ...'

My host turned around, looked at him, turned back to me and said, 'Look where he's sitting. I told you, he can't get arrested.'

I love LA but I regret to say that the incident was, and no doubt still is, typical of the town. When you're hot you're hot and when you're not you're relegated to a 'not hot' table. Many years ago there was a wonderful sketch on *Saturday Night Live* which, for me, sums up the LA view of showbiz status. It went something like:

Chevy Chase, playing a snotty maître d' is standing at his greeter's desk. John Belushi, playing an actor, asks if he could have a table for two. Chevy Chase, without looking up says, 'No. Go away.'

'I'm an actor,' says Belushi.

Chevy Case points to a long line of people standing patiently against a wall. 'Go to the back of that line.'

Belushi meekly does as told. After a while Chevy Chase goes over to him. 'You working?' asks Chevy Chase.

'Yes.' He gets moved up a couple of places.

'Speaking part?'

'Yes,' says Belushi.'

He gets moved up a bit more.

'How many lines?'

'Four lines,' says Belushi.

He gets moved down the line.

And so it goes on, with Chase moving Belushi up and down the line until the famous producer Aaron Spelling, playing himself, comes in and gives Belushi a big 'Hello', at which point the Chevy Chase character physically removes a couple of diners by the scruff of their necks and ushers Belushi to a good table. It is one of the funniest sketches I have ever seen and I urge you to try to find it on YouTube.

Saturday Night Live was, and remarkably still is, a huge and important TV show and in 1978 I was privileged to go and see the live taping, which was a great experience. I had gone to New York with John Goldstone, the producer of the Pythons' *Life of Brian*, Eric Idle and Terry Gilliam to try to help them to find the money to finance the film after EMI Films suddenly pulled out. Allen Klein had put up the money for my film *The Greek Tycoon* and he was my best shot. He read the script, but did not think it was funny. I admired Allen for many things, but not his sense of humour. Eric Idle is a really nice guy and even though I didn't get the film financed, hanging with some Pythons was a great few days in New York. John and Eric took me along to the after-show party that *Saturday Night Live* always held after the broadcast, at No. 1 Fifth Avenue. I got to rub shoulders with the cast, and actually chatted a little with John Belushi. I think of that privilege whenever I watch *The Blues Brothers* on TV.

In 1979 George Harrison put the money up to make *Life of Brian*. By then I owned GTO Films, a film-distribution company, and John Goldstone really wanted me to distribute the film and offered very favourable terms. Unfortunately, Bill Dunn, the American schmuck who was then running GTO

Films for me, did not like the film and did not feel he was the
right person to do it. He was an idiot for turning it down and
I was a bigger idiot for not replacing him with someone with a
sense of humour.

13. THE LATER SIXTIES – SHOWBIZ, HERE I AM!

Another client I got through my growing reputation as accountant/nanny/psychiatrist to the songwriters was Geoff Stephens, born in north London but then living in Southend. He was trying to earn a living as a song-writer and comedy writer and had some of his sketches accepted by the BBC.

In 1964 he discovered Donovan, later to become a huge international star. Geoff told me he was walking along the front in Southend with Peter Eden – a pal who was also trying to get involved in the music business – when they saw a young man in blue denim and a cap, carrying a guitar. They stopped to chat to him and he played them a couple of songs. His music was very folky, and he was clearly a huge Bob Dylan fan, but he had a certain quality that encouraged Geoff and Peter to sign him for management. In 1965 they produced two albums, *What's Bin Did and What's Bin Hid* and *Fairytale*, for Pye Records. Both albums were folk-influenced. The first album included Dono-van's original recording of 'Catch The Wind,' which was released as a single and made No. 4 in the UK charts. The Pye albums were not particularly successful, probably because Pye was a crap record company. Geoff and Peter decided that they were not natural record producers and they brought Donovan to meet Mickie Most, which was when I met Geoff. The first album that Mickie produced with Donovan was *Sunshine Superman*, a change of direction away from folk and a huge hit.

Inevitably, Donovan sought new management and Geoff concentrated on his songwriting. His first big success was writing 'The Crying Game', a big hit for Dave Berry. It was a very classy song and in 1992 inspired director Neil Jordan to make a film of the same name. Geoff wrote that one by himself, but then concentrated on lyrics, and collaborated with a variety of composers, writing great songs like 'There's a Kind of Hush' for Herman's Hermits, 'Semi-Detached Suburban Mr James' for Manfred Mann and 'I'll Put You Together Again' for Hot Chocolate.

In 1966, Geoff came into my Regent Street office and played me a record called 'Winchester Cathedral'. He said the record came about because he was tinkling on his piano with a half-developed song. It was going to be about a guy being despondent about a girl. He got the second half of the first line, '... You're bringing me down', but couldn't come up with who was bringing his protagonist down. There was a picture of Winchester Cathedral on his wall and, as many composers do, rather than get stuck on a line he carried on writing the song with the dummy lyric, 'Winchester Cathedral, you're bringing me down.' A bottle of vodka later he had finished the song in the style of Rudy Vallee, a twenties' megaphone crooner. He went into the studio with John Carter, a multi-talented singer and composer who replicated the twenties' vocal sound. The record cost Geoff three hundred and eighty pounds. In sober mode he was not at all confident that he could get a novelty record released and asked me if I wanted to put up half of the money and own half of the record.

As fond as I was of Geoff, I had no wish to piss away a hundred and ninety pounds on a piece of nonsense. As Geoff often reminded me after the event, I didn't even decline grace-fully. I just laughed.

There was no group so Geoff made up the name The New Vaudeville Band. The record went to No. 4 in the English charts, was No. 1 in the US charts for four weeks and sold over three million copies. Geoff made so much money from the record that, on my advice, he became a non-resident and went to live in Switzerland. I try to never think about 'if onlys' but that one was quite hard to put aside.

The New Vaudeville Band was soon a household name, but there was no band to cash in on the success. Peter Grant was still the head of Rak Management without much to do. Manager and producer Simon Napier-Bell had asked Peter to take over the management of The Yardbirds, who were struggling finan-cially in spite of their undoubted talent, but that hadn't worked out. The Yardbirds split up and Peter needed to find an act to manage. I asked him if he wanted to put a band together, manage them and exploit the success of 'Winchester Cathedral'. Peter did not pretend that he liked the record, but he pulled it off brilliantly until the public tired of the novelty. As a 10 per cent owner of Rak Management, I earned a little from The New Vaudeville Band, but nothing compared to 'if only'.

Probably as a consolation, Geoff allowed me to write the lyrics of a New Vaudeville Band B-side. My song was called

'Uncle Gabriel' and I wrote it under the name of Peter James – the names of the two children Marsha and I had had by then. The A-side was 'The Bonnie and Clyde'. The record sold very few copies, probably just two, to Peter and James. It is so rare that even I don't have a copy.

Peter Grant then put together Led Zeppelin based around ex-Yardbird Jimmy Page and John Paul Jones, a first-choice session musician who had played on Yardbirds recordings. John Bonham joined as drummer and Robert Plant was the charismatic lead singer. You may recall from my Don Arden story that Peter was not averse to using the threat of physical violence and his management style reflected this. There are many stories about Peter's use of intimidation, some apocryphal, but I was in the room when he resolved a dispute with John Bonham, the Led Zeppelin drummer, by threatening in a voice to be believed: 'Listen you c**t, can you play drums from a wheelchair?'

As a shareholder in Rak Management, I enjoyed a small financial interest in Zep's early career. Once, when I was in New York, Peter asked me to bring back a very large amount of cash. I was staying at The Americana hotel and I carefully placed the money in one of the safety-deposit boxes that were situated in the wall behind the reception desk. I was leaving the next day so that only gave me about eighteen hours in which to lose the key. Eighteen hours was enough, and when I went to check out the next day they had to call the safe company to break open the lock. The considerable cost of this was of course charged to me but was a small price to pay for not having to face Peter Grant and tell him that I had left his cash in a wall-safe in New York.

Whilst still in practice I took over the management of The Tremeloes. They had started off as the backing band for Brian Poole, but had since gone out on their own. It was well after 'Silence is Golden' and they were no longer making hit records, but they had done very well and their financial affairs needed sorting out. They were also the publishers of 'Yellow River,' a song that they were going to record themselves but gave to a band called Christie, who had an enormous hit with it. I licensed it to Yellow Pages for an advertising campaign for six thousand pounds. It was probably far too little, but it was hard to get a guide. I liked the boys immensely, especially Alan Howard and Chip Hawkes, and I was sorry that I could not revive their recording career, but they were very sensible in accepting that they were a pop band and their time was over. They were very bright and carried on in the music business, writing, producing and managing other bands.

Most pop artists had a three-year career. Typically, a band would put out four singles a year and then a best-of album. Containing all twelve tracks. The reason for this was that pop artists appealed to early teens and pre-teens. As the kids grew into their later teens, their musical tastes changed. This is, of course, a generalisation and I could do an analysis of the charts to prove my point but, to be honest, it would be a lot of work that I do not want to undertake, so just take my word for it.

14. THE SOCIETY OF DISTINGUISHED SONGWRITERS – THE SODS

As you may have gathered, I had a passionate admiration for songwriters. In the early sixties few artists wrote their own material. Top artists of the day like Tom Jones, Shirley Bassey, The Hollies, Cliff Richard, Adam Faith, Dusty Springfield and even Elvis Presley depended on songwriters for their ongoing success. The Beatles were the real start of the singer/songwriters movement and now of course it is rare to find a successful artist who does not write their own material.

America had Goffin and King, Leiber and Stoller, Barry Mann and Cynthia Weil, Neil Sedaka and others, most of whom were Jewish – as were Irving Berlin, the Gershwins, Jerome Kern, Oscar Hammerstein, Sammy Cahn and most of the other writers of the great American songbook. There must have been something in New York bagels.

In the UK there was a coterie of successful songwriters, many of whom wrote with each other, swapping writing partners as might be expected in London's swinging sixties. I thought that the artists whose careers they had started with a great song did not always appreciate how much they owed to that writer. I knew many UK songwriters well and I devised a scheme whereby, as a condition of a new artist being given a song that became a big hit, the songwriter would have some sort of interest in the artist's subsequent career. More importantly, as part of my scheme, leading songwriters would pool a part of their income in a company owned by them – and me, of course – thus sharing in each other's success. The high-earning managing partner of the company would also, of course, be me.

Just before I left my accountancy practice in 1971, I invited some of the hottest songwriters in London to a dinner: Tony Macaulay, Mike Leander, Geoff Stephens, Don Black, Bill Martin, Barry Mason, Les Reed, Mitch Murray and Peter Callander. If I listed the songs that they had written between them it would take up the rest of this book. Don Black concentrated on films and theatre, working with Andrew Lloyd Webber, John Barry and many other of the best composers around, collecting Oscars, Tony Awards and an OBE on the way. I find it annoying that the contribution of lyricists is often forgotten when songs are credited. *Sunset Boulevard* is known as an 'Andrew Lloyd Webber Musical' but it would not have worked so well without the lyrics and book of Don Black and Christopher Hampton. Bert Bacharach's 'songs' may never have come to light without the genius of Hal David's lyrics. Similarly, Elton John and lyricist Bernie Taupin.

At great, unaffordable expense, I booked the private room at the fashionable trattoria Terrazza in Soho. Every one of the invitees turned up and found my carefully prepared document, explaining my brilliant scheme, on the table in front of them. They all looked through it, some of them more carefully than others, and all promised to take it home to study. I quickly realised that my scheme was a non-starter. These were all ambitious young guys with great faith in their own abilities and they were not ready to be unionised. My scheme was quickly forgotten and they got down to eating and drinking ... and drinking ... and drinking some more. I did not try to keep up with them. I kept myself unamused, totting up the cost as my guests ploughed through the restaurant's expensive wine list.

After the meal someone suggested that we should go somewhere and play poker. I had drunk enough to think that it was a splendid idea. In 1967, we had moved to a flat in St John's Wood and I invited them all back there, where they added to the expense of the evening by cleaning me out at poker. Some of the writers had never met before and socially it was a great evening. Mitch Murray had such a good time he thought that they should all meet on a regular basis. He came up with the idea of forming The Society of Distinguished Songwriters (The SODS) and all of those who were at my dinner joined. There would be a King Sod and other offices. The membership of SODS has since expanded rapidly. Lionel Bart, Andrew Lloyd Webber and Tim Rice, Abba's Bjorn and Benny, Queen's Brian May and many other leading songwriters were later inducted into the society. They would meet on a monthly basis and, once a year, have a SODS' night bash at a grand hotel when the members invited family and friends. I went along to the first of these, where Mitch Murray was the first King Sod. Marsha and I were invited to many SODS' nights thereafter and they were great fun. The SODS themselves performed a cabaret that was always entertaining and the food and wine were of the highest order. The society is still going and quite rightly now dominated by a new generation of songwriters, but I have not been to a SODS night for many years.

15. TONY MACAULAY

Unquestionably my greatest contribution to the song-writers' cause was my orchestration of Tony Macaulay's case against his wicked publisher Schroeder Music.

When Tony first came to me for management he was contracted exclusively to Pye Records for his services as a producer. Using the technique I had acquired from Mr Klein, I told Louis Benjamin, the head of Pye Records, that Tony would no longer be making records for them. Louis did not put up much of a fight, and in return for a very reasonable ten thousand pounds, Tony was free.

For his songwriting, Tony had signed for an advance of fifty pounds exclusively to Schroeder Music Publishing. It was a small firm owned by the American husband-and-wife team of Aaron and Abby Schroeder. The contract was patently unfair. Tony could not place a song with any other music publisher, the Schroeders had no obligation to pay Tony any sort of retainer and they had no obligation to actually do anything with the songs that Tony was obliged to give them. He had made them a great deal of money with songs that he had written with John Macleod including 'Baby, Now That I've Found You', and other hits which he produced for The Foundations.

The traditional split between a songwriter and the publisher was 50/50. This harked back to the days before songs were recorded and publishers had to promote the sales of printed sheet music. They would try to get the songs sung by popular artists, in the hope that the public would want to buy a copy. The publisher would also employ people to sing the songs at a piano inside shops selling sheet music. A publisher's hard work justified his 50 per cent. Almost every home had a piano, and a popular song could sell thousands of copies and make a decent sum to be divided between publisher and writer. In order to get a song exploited in a foreign territory, the UK publisher would license the song to a local publisher in the foreign territory. The local publisher was obliged to work as hard as the original publisher to get the song known in their own country, sending the other 50 per cent of their income back to the original publisher, who would then divide the 50 per cent between himself and the writer. This was all perfectly fair until songs could be exploited on gramophone records and radio, at which point sheet-music sales became just a tiny part of income derived from hit songs.

In the sixties, unscrupulous publishers still applied the 50/50 formula even if they had their own company in the foreign territory. The Schroeders licensed Tony's copyrights back and forth between their own companies to contrive that Tony and John shared 12.5 per cent of the income on foreign sales, as opposed to 50 per cent. The Schroeders also held on to royalties in each country so that the writers might have to wait for years for foreign income to filter through. Other publishers, including some of the majors, also indulged in this practice.

Aaron Schroeder was himself a songwriter who in the past had written songs recorded by Frank Sinatra and Elvis Presley. Abby was the businesswoman who ran the company and she was not at all interested in my threat that Tony would not write any more songs for them. Under the then UK law, the contract was binding and she was both unpleasant and immovable. I discussed the problem with my American lawyer Normand Kurtz. Normand was a passionate man who railed against injustice. Such a contract would not be upheld in the USA and he urged me to take the Schroeders to court in the UK. Nick Kanaar was our UK lawyer and he recommended that I go to see Robert McCrindle, a barrister who was England's leading expert on contract law. Mr McCrindle told me that Tony's contract was indeed unfair *but* binding as English law now stood. If we wanted to get Tony out, we would have to change the law. He really fancied our chances of doing this and would have been delighted to take the case, but he was about to retire and, as the case would take months if not years to run its course, he advised me to find another barrister.

I recommended to Tony that he should sue the Schroeders. John Macleod was on the same unfair contract but he was too meek take them on and Tony decided that he would bear what might be the considerable cost of such an action himself.

The music business is replete with contract disputes and I had become somewhat of an expert in the field. One of the most important things that I had learned was that often it is the best prepared, not the virtuous, who win the day in court. I went to QC Morris Finer. He was under fifty, a young man by legal standards. I made it a condition that I could call him directly, unheard of when protocol demanded that a barrister could only be seen in the presence of the instructing lawyer. I even had his home telephone number. I drove everybody mad with detail and when the case started I sat behind Mr Finer in court, frequently handing him notes on points of the proceedings. I called councils of war with Morris and Nick on a regular basis to discuss strategy.

The Schroeders' lawyer was the notoriously outspoken Oscar Beuselinck. He admitted to me that he had told his clients that they would lose but they ignored his advice. He was right.

We won the case with Macaulay's costs awarded against the Schroeders. Our jubilation was short-lived because they appealed. We won the appeal and once again our costs were awarded against the Schroeders. They appealed yet again, this time to the House of Lords, then the highest court in the land in the days before the Supreme Court. There they lost yet again, with costs awarded against them once more. Not only did they lose the future copyrights of a great writer, their intransigence cost them several hundred thousand pounds in legal fees.

The House of Lords ruling is rather wordy but just in case any of you are interested I am setting out a summary below. It is easy to skip if you are satisfied to know that, as a result of this case, music publishers were obliged to be more transparent and fairer in their dealings with writers.

In 1974 five of England's most senior law lords held that the Schroeders' standard form agreement could not be justified as moulded under the pressures of negotiation, competition and public opinion. Macaulay had no bargaining power. The defendants purported to be able to arbitrarily decline to exploit the plaintiff's work in which event the plaintiff's remuneration under the agreement would be limited to a £50 advance payable hereunder during the five-year period. The defendants' power to assign precluded the argument that the restrictions would not be enforced oppressively. The defendants had failed to justify restrictions which appeared unnecessary and capable of oppressive enforcement.

Morris Finer, our QC, came to the celebration party at our offices and let his wig down a little. He later told me that he had allowed my unconventional approach of dealing with him directly because he admired my enthusiasm and passion for the case. In the seventies Morris successfully represented The Beatles against Allen Klein. He went on to be Sir Morris Finer, a senior judge.

Tony was free from the Schroeders but unfortunately was not returned his copyrights. To do this, the Schroeders would have to have been guilty of fraud as opposed to being dishonest exploiters of young talent. Macaulay v Schroeder became the test case that enabled many writers to escape from unfair contracts, including Elton John.

Nowadays, established singer/songwriters can get as much as 90 per cent of the income, and the copyright in the songs reverts to them after relatively few years. This is because – other than executing the paperwork necessary to register the copyright with the various collection bodies – there is little for the publishers to do. Led Zeppelin's Peter Grant made deals with publishers where the writers got 100 per cent of the money and the companies paid huge advances for the privilege of being the band's publisher and the right to hold on to the money that they collected for a few months until they accounted to the writers. Eventually music publishers just became bankers for writers.

In the 1980s, George Michael's UK publisher Dick Leahy, my ex-partner in GTO Records, asked me to assist him in the negotiating of a new deal for George's non-UK songwriting services. His contract with Warner Music was about to expire and just about every international publisher wanted to sign him. The competition to sign him drove the price so high that I could not see how the publisher could ever earn its money back before the copyrights reverted to George. Eventually Warner Music paid the price to retain him.

Tony Macaulay was one of the best UK writer-producers of his era. He co-wrote and produced a string of hits, including 'Build Me Up Buttercup' with Mike d'Abo; 'Let The Heart-aches Begin' with John Macleod for Long John Baldry and 'You Won't Find Another Fool Like Me' with Geoff Stephens for The New Seekers. He is a very intelligent man, very driven and wanted to be involved in every aspect of his records. He used to help plug his own records in answer to his complaint that one wasn't selling, I told him that I couldn't get a machine gun and make people go into a shop to buy his records, to which he replied: 'Why not?' He was a complex man but had a great sense of humour as he demonstrated when the guitarist on one of his records was unhappy with his solo. The record had gone to be pressed and Tony, with his tongue firmly in his cheek, told him that the only way the guitar break could be changed was if the guitarist plugged his guitar into the pressing plant and replayed his bit as each record was pressed. According to Tony, the guitarist offered to do it!

Tony desperately wanted to be a star artist himself but was smart enough to realise that he was a lousy singer. He was very demanding of my time and attention and when I started GTO Records in 1974 I diplomatically asked him to find another manager. His attitude changed and he became cold. But I will always be grateful to Tony because he co-wrote and produced 'Love Grows (Where My Rosemary Goes)', Gem Production's first release in February 1970, very soon after I started the company. A huge hit, it was like going to the casino for the first time and having a big win. This of course can be dangerous but I managed to continue on a winning roll for some time. Anyway, it was 'Love Grows (Where My Rosemary Goes)' that set Gem on the path to success, so thank you, Tony.

16. MUSIC PUBLISHERS, FREDDY BIENSTOCK AND ELVIS

For those of you who are interested, this is how a song actually earns income for the publisher and songwriter. For those of you who are not interested, skip the next couple of pages.

Still with me? Good. There are three sources of revenue from copyrighted music.

Mechanicals. This is pretty straightforward. Any company that wishes to manufacture a record is legally obliged to get permission from the copyright owner to use the song. There is a statutory rate, which is the royalty that legally has to be paid by the manufacturer. The current UK rate is 8.5 per cent of the price charged to a record dealer. More songs are downloaded than physically bought and the online site is obliged to pay the copyright holder a royalty on every download. In the USA the mechanical rate is paid per track – so the more tracks on an album, the greater the cost. British albums were usually twelve tracks and, until UK artists were powerful enough to insist that their albums were released as recorded, the US record companies used to drop two tracks to save money. The current rate is 9.1 cents per track, so by cutting out two tracks the record company saves 18.2 cents on each album sold. The Beatles sold about one hundred and eighty million albums. You do the maths.

Performance royalties. This is a little more complicated. The songwriter assigns the right to collect income from public performances to the Performing Rights Society. The board of PRS is mainly made up of songwriters. Television and radio companies pay PRS a substantial fee for the right to broadcast music. Live music venues have to pay a fee. Even a shop that plays music that its customers can hear is obliged to pay the PRS a fee for doing so. Fees vary depending on the size of the potential audience. Over many years, the PRS have developed an algorithm by which they distribute the considerable amount of money they have collected between the songwriters.

'Points' are awarded for chart positions and plays on radio and TV. For example, a Saturday-night, prime-time TV show will accrue more points than an afternoon chat show. A big hit song can earn its writer several hundred thousand pounds over a number of years. In 2017, PRS announced record figures including payouts of £527.6 million to its members. It was the first time it surpassed half a billion pounds. To put it in context, Noddy Holder and the bass guitarist from Slade earn around a million pounds a year from 'Merry Christmas Everybody'. Writing a perennial Christmas song is the holy grail for song-writers. Irving Berlin was the first to do so with 'I'm Dreaming of a White Christmas', a song which he anecdotally wrote in ten minutes.

In the days before the public bought records, a publisher would distribute sheet music to bandleaders and end-of-the-pier concert parties, to encourage them to use the song. A bandleader was obliged to file a report listing all the songs that they had played. Many put down songs that they had written themselves, even if they had not played them.

Similar societies to the PRS all over the world collect performance income in their own territories and, after deducting a fee, pass it over to the PRS. Obviously, the allocation of PRS income is somewhat arbitrary but over the years it has been refined to the satisfaction of the songwriters.

Synchronisation fees. This is now a huge revenue earner. If a film or TV commercial uses a song, the producers negotiate a fee with the publisher for the copyright-holders, who can take home a seven-figure sum. I recently saw a TV documentary that purported to list the top ten earning songs. 'Happy Birthday' predictably is the highest at thirty million pounds and 'White Christmas' is next. In terms of pop music 'You've Lost that Loving Feeling' is the highest at No. 3 and 'Yesterday' is next. Obviously the longer a copyright is around the more it can earn and some more recent hits may well be up there in the fullness of time.

At a time when very few so-called publishers actually understood the intricacies of the business Freddy Bienstock was a proper exception. Most importantly he knew how to maximise income from the less obvious revenue streams. Freddy spent twenty years learning about his trade. He ensured that those who were supposed to pay did so. In the sixties and seventies, the publisher also took responsibility to 'plug' a song on radio and TV. Unlike some of his contemporaries, my friend Freddy was an expert in copyright law, to the point that he spotted a rather obscure court ruling which enabled a writer's estate to claim back a copyright years before its natural expiration. Freddy's companies own the copyright of important songs from the biggest hits of rock'n'roll to standards from the great American songbook. Freddie died in 2009, leaving his family a company that I am sure is worth many hundreds of millions of dollars.

In the same way as a lot of amateurs jumped on the property development bandwagon of the sixties and seventies, almost everybody in the music business – including me – started a publishing company. There was no real skill required. The key was to persuade writers to sign a copyright over to your company and then sit back and watch the money come in. The records went out and the publisher collected the income generated. The way publishing developed, copyright owners could contract with major publishing houses to administer and collect on their behalf at a small cost. All you needed was a bank account.

Had I been the publisher of the artists I managed, I could now have a single filing cabinet holding copyrights that, without my lifting a finger, would have generated enough income to keep me and my descendants in a luxury lifestyle until the copyrights expired. But most of the writers I knew had existing contracts with publishers, and in any event, I had decided that I could not be all things to all people and had elected to concentrate on management and records. I did have a 50/50 publishing company with Freddy, mainly B-sides or album tracks that we had picked up via our recording activities. There was one decent copyright, for 'The Pushbike Song', acquired for the company by my partner David Joseph, of whom more later.

As a general rule, copyrights become PD (in the public domain) seventy years after the death of the last living writer of a song. This may vary from country to country. If someone makes an arrangement of a PD song, the copyright in their version belongs to the arranger. 'The House of the Rising Sun' was a traditional American folk song, but Alan Price was credited as the arranger on The Animals, recording and he therefore earned the royalties.

Freddy Bienstock was the last of the old-school independent publishers. Born in Switzerland in 1923, his family lived in Vienna before moving to New York just before the outbreak of the war. Freddy started work in the stock room of Chappell Music in the Brill Building. He worked his way up to being a song-plugger before going to work for publishers Hill & Range, where one of his jobs was to find songs for Elvis Presley to record. In 1966, Freddy bought their UK subsidiary and changed the name to Carlin Music. He was also partner in Elvis's music publishing company. Although Elvis was not a songwriter, his manager Colonel Parker made it a rule to get the company the publishing of every new song that Elvis recorded. Freddy ran the company, and Elvis had such respect for him he would ask his opinion on almost everything that he recorded.

After 'Hello,' the next thing that Freddy said to a talented songwriter was 'I can get you an Elvis cover.' In fact sometimes this even preceded 'Hello.' I used to tease him incessantly about this. If we were in a restaurant I would nod to the waiter and say: 'He can get you an Elvis cover.' Most of us hang our gold discs on a wall. Freddy would have needed the Great Wall of China to hang his and he only had one gold disc on his office wall. It was a gold disc I had specially made for him with 'I can get you an Elvis cover' on the plaque.

Geoff Morrow, a good friend of mine who I managed as part of the writing team Arnold, Martin and Morrow, had several songs recorded by Elvis thanks to Freddy. One of them, 'Let's Be Friends', was the title song of an Elvis album. The team also wrote 'Can't Smile Without You' for Barry Manilow, a huge hit which is still the high point of Barry's act. Our business paths crossed again when Geoff started writing for theatre. Geoff is now an extremely successful businessman.

I went with Freddy on three occasions to see Elvis's opening night in Vegas. Elvis was inclined to coast a little on his Vegas dates, but not on the opening night, which was always an occasion with a celebrity-packed audience. On one trip, Marsha came with us. She was not an Elvis fan so I should never have married her, but when he took his bows after what was an unforgettable performance, she was on her feet screaming his name with the rest of us.

Freddy had a very clever way of dealing with the dissolution of publishing partnerships. He asked the partner he was splitting from to divide the copyrights into two lists, and Freddy decided which of the lists he wanted to retain. It is a brilliantly fair way of dividing assets, which I have since used myself. The other effective way is for Partner A to name a price and Partner B to decide whether he wants to buy or sell at that price. When I decided that we should administer our own copyrights, it was necessary to 'divorce' from Freddy's Carlin Music. At the time,

Keith Potger, one of the original Seekers – a hugely successful group from Australia – was running our publishing company. Keith made up the two lists and Freddie chose the one that included 'The Pushbike Song', the only song that was of any real value. Some people are gifted with musical talent; some people are gifted with brains. Keith could play the guitar and sing. I should never have put him in the ring with Freddie. It was like putting Julian Clary in the ring to fight Mike Tyson.

17. THE ROLLING STONES

I am not trying to compete with the many excellent books written about the Rolling Stones, some of which I have researched (if a writer gets facts from one book it's called 'plagiarism'; if he gets facts from lots of books, it's called 'research'). I will restrict my history of the Stones to stories in which I was personally involved.

In my brief career as a partner in a firm of chartered accountants, nothing was more exciting than Goodman Myers being appointed as accountants to the Rolling Stones. My only previous encounter with the Stones was when they and The Animals were both appearing on a TV show called *Ready Steady Go!* The show was shot in a TV studio in London, and I was in with The Animals, who were sharing a dressing room with the Stones. Eric Burdon grabbed Bill Wyman's camera while the Stones were performing, dropped his trousers and had Chas Chandler take a photograph of his own not inconsiderable appendage. Eric then put the camera back exactly where he had found it. In those days one sent one's films off to be developed, and God knows what problems Eric's prank caused Bill Wyman.

Needless to say, I didn't mention the subject of Eric Burdon's cock when, in 1971, Bill came to see me about an album he had produced with The Walker Brothers' John Walker (whose real last name was Maus). John, Scott (Engel) and Gary (Leeds) split in 1968 – although they would reunite in 1974, when the brilliant talent-spotter Dick Leahy signed them to GTO Records, the record company that we owned together. We had a huge hit with the single 'No Regrets' and the album of the same name. More about GTO Records later. Scott was the real singing talent of the Brothers and after their break-up nobody wanted to release a solo album by John. When Bill came to see me it was to ask if I could place the record for him in Japan where The Walker Brothers had huge success. He hoped I could get him an advance of ten thousand pounds.

The Japanese generally never attended the Midem music festival, but I agreed to take the album to see what I could do. There were rumours of a Japanese guy being seen in Cannes and I eventually tracked him down. He was leaving early the next morning but when I mentioned John of The Walker Brothers he agreed to meet with me at 7 a.m. Now, you should know that a lot of Midem business is conducted in the late-night bars and that night I was at The Martinez hotel bar until the early hours of the morning. I dragged myself out of bed and met my Japanese contact for breakfast at the five-star Carlton hotel, a place he had suggested. There was a lot of exchanging business cards and bowing which went on too long because I did not know the etiquette of who should bow last. Eventually we sat down.

'Are you staying here?' I asked.

'No.' He mentioned a hotel on the outskirts of Cannes that I had never heard of. This should have been a clue. He ordered a huge breakfast. 'I will not eat on the plane.'

I ordered a large breakfast too. I was very bleary-eyed, but as the discussions progressed I perked up considerably. The guy said yes to everything.

'The royalty will have to be 16 per cent.'

'Yes.'

'You will pay an advance of twenty thousand dollars.'

'Yes.'

'In addition to the royalty you will pay me a commission of 2 per cent.'

'Yes.'

This was too easy for words. Bill was going to be delighted with me. I had got him double his hoped-for advance and even got the Japanese to pay my commission. I stood up and leaned forward to shake hands.

'So we have a deal?'

'No. I must report back to my superior in Tokyo.'

I sat down again and he left, leaving me to pay the outrageous price of breakfast for two at one of the most expensive hotels in Cannes.

Needless to say, I never heard a word from the gentleman again. I later learned that in Japanese culture 'Yes' means 'I understand' not 'I agree'. Make a note of this if you ever meet a Japanese person for an early-morning breakfast meeting.

Andrew Loog Oldham left school at sixteen for a menial job with Mary Quant (who almost single-handedly invented the fashion of London's swinging sixties). He then got a job in a PR company, a world that he loved. In 1961 he became a freelance PR, at one point doing PR for the fast-emerging Beatles. He and Tony Calder, another freelance PR guy, started Image, a PR company specialising in pop music.

Andrew often visited The Crawdaddy Club, a popular venue where the Rolling Stones often played. The audience reception was extremely enthusiastic, almost at Beatle level, and Andrew was impressed. Image PR was not making him any money and he decided that he wanted to manage the Stones. Concerned that his lack of knowledge might put them off signing with him, he did not approach them that evening. He went to see Eric Easton, a well-respected theatrical agent, and persuaded him to come and see the band perform. Easton was also impressed. Together they approached Brian Jones, the founder and leader of the Stones, who agreed that that Easton and Oldham would manage the Stones. They charged 25 per cent of the band's earnings. Mick and Keith were underage so Brian signed on behalf of the band. It was 1963 and Andrew was barely *twenty years old*.

Andrew and Eric made the Stones huge in the UK. They had half a dozen hit singles, a number-one album and their tours sold out but they were nowhere near as successful in America, where The Beatles were a phenomenon and The Dave Clark Five, Herman's Hermits and Freddie and The Dreamers were all huge. the Stones' comparative lack of success was a problem and Andrew struggled to find an answer. In the spring of 1965, he was in New York on Stones' business. He had fallen out with Eric Easton and, in partnership with his old PR partner Tony Calder, was planning to start Immediate Records in the UK, a venture that he found more exciting than his management endeavours. He was due to have a breakfast meeting with J. W. Alexander, a partner in Kags Music, Sam Cooke's music publishing business.

He was hoping to get a rebate for the Stones on the royalties paid to Kags for the use of 'It's All Over Now', which was Kags' copyright. There was no reason why Mr Alexander should agree to this after the event, but Andrew thought that he would try.

Sam Cooke's manager, Allen Klein, was also sitting next to J.W. and Allen later told me that he had had his eye on the Stones for some time and was shocked at how young their manager was. Andrew's request for a rebate on 'It's All Over Now' was dismissed out of hand, but they carried on chatting and Andrew told him of his plans to start Immediate Records. He also intimated that he was not getting on with Eric Easton. Allen's main objective was to get to the Rolling Stones, but smart man that he was, he never brought them into the conversation. He offered to help Andrew get distribution deals for Immediate Records. His parting shot to Andrew was, of course, 'I can get you a million dollars.'

Allen called me to ask me if I knew Eric Easton, which I did not. He told me what had happened with Andrew, and his belief that he would soon be managing the Stones with him. I knew that Mickie Most knew Andrew, but Allen did not want to ask him to help snare Andrew. It was important to Allen that Mickie believed that he was getting most of his attention. I understood this, as I was in a similar position myself. Allen asked me to 'be aware' and keep him advised of any information that came my way that would be helpful to his cause. I was a little amused at Allen's Machiavellian style of operating and admiring of his dedication to getting what he wanted. Inevitably, Allen usurped Easton as Andrew's partner. Easton sued Allen and got a court order freezing the band's back-royalties.

After long litigation, Allen paid him off with two hundred thousand pounds in September 1971.

At the time that the Rolling Stones business took up residence in my office, Brian Jones had still been the leader of the band, but in title only – it was clear to everyone, including Brian, that this was changing and that Mick was now The Man. Andrew arranged for Allen to meet with Mick and he did his thing, successfully gaining the singer's confidence. Allen then met with all of the Rolling Stones at the Hilton hotel on Park Lane and they enthusiastically agreed that he should become co-manager of the band with Andrew.

the Stones' business had been run out of Easton's offices, and as this was clearly no longer viable, in January 1967 we gave them some space in Goodman Myers & Co.'s offices in Regent Street. Stephanie Bluestone, the Stones' general assistant, moved in with us to run their office. We hosted them for a few months until they set up their own office in Maddox Street, but those few months were an exciting time in the history of the Stones, and I was privileged to be at the heart of it: this was the period in which Allen renegotiated their Decca deal, Mick and Keith famously got arrested for drugs, and the band firmly established themselves as the 'bad boys' of rock. Brian Jones was confirmed to no longer be the band's leader and some months later died in the swimming pool of Cotchford Farm, his house in Essex. The inquest recorded death by misadventure, arising from Brian's abuse of drugs and alcohol, but there are many other theories still around which dispute this, including murder. If this is of interest to you, the internet is full of conflicting 'maybes'.

The Stones were signed to Decca Records, via Impact Sound, a company owned by Andrew Oldham and Eric Easton. Decca paid Impact a royalty of 8 per cent and Impact paid the Stones 6 per cent. Andrew and Easton also took 25 per cent of the Stones' 6 per cent in their capacity as managers, leaving the band with 4.5 per cent. Clearly the Stones did not have a great deal and the whole mess had to be sorted out.

A meeting was arranged with Sir Edward Lewis, owner of Decca Records. The main Klein party consisted of Allen and myself with Andrew Oldham and all five Rolling Stones. We went to the meeting at Decca House in two Rolls-Royces that Allen had hired for the occasion. He believed in arriving in style.

Sir Edward, Bill Townsley (Decca's MD) and people from his legal affairs department greeted us. Allen, Andrew Oldham and I (the good guys) sat at the boardroom table and the Stones stood around behind us, looking sullen and angry, as had been rehearsed. Without preamble, Allen turned to each of the Stones and asked if he was authorised to speak on their behalf. As rehearsed, each said 'Yes,' and then, as also rehearsed, they trouped out. Sir Edward was clearly dismayed by the pantomime he had just witnessed. His previous negotiations had been with Eric Easton, a businesslike gentleman. He looked at Andrew.

'Is Eric not coming?' Andrew, who had also been rehearsed, did not speak. But Allen did.

'Eric doesn't play in the band. You can speak to me.'

Allen was purposefully aggressive. He wanted Sir Edward to know that he was difficult to deal with and had no wish to be liked. I could see Sir Edward struggling to maintain his composure. 'Very well, what is it that you want, Mr. Klein?'

Allen demanded copies of all of the Stones' royalty statements and contracts, including the draft contract that Eric Easton had negotiated for future renewal. Sir Edward went red enough to double as a traffic light. I do not know what he said because I do not speak splutter but I suspect that he did not wish us a 'good day'.

I later reviewed Decca's proposed contract, negotiated by Easton and it was clear that it contained all of the unnecessary royalty deductions that were standard record-company practice, and committed the Stones to Decca for up to five years. The contract provided that the Stones would get an advance of the equivalent of $300,000 recoupable against all royalties including pipeline royalties. These are royalties on past recordings recently sold around the world, but not yet included in quarterly accountings. I could see that Decca were offering to pay the Stones an advance out of their own money.

Allen negotiated a new deal for Impact Sounds with Decca that guaranteed the Stones $1.25 million for a one-year contract, with more advances for any extensions. $600,000 was to be paid on signing. Andrew agreed that the Stones' royalty from Impact Sounds was increased to 7 per cent and they would pay no management commission on record royalties. Allen's cut came out of what would have been Eric Easton's share and, as he said to Mick, 'I have made you rich and it hasn't cost you a cent.'

As mentioned before, UK tax was at a punitive level and, as with the Mickie Most/EMI deal, it made sense for the Stones to get their money paid over a number of years. Allen, somewhat craftily, structured the spread in such a way that he ended up being the owner of the Stones' recordings for the US and Canada, paying them 80 per cent of the royalty income arising. He also made a deal to be the publisher of Jagger and Richard's songs, giving them 70 per cent of earnings as opposed to the standard 50 per cent. He gave them a writer's advance of a million dollars, an astonishingly large amount even if it was payable over twenty years, to shelter the advances from UK taxes. With success, the spreadable advances went up to three million dollars. Any sums they earned above the advances were to be paid at the end of the twenty-year period.

The net result of these two deals was that Allen had legal control of the vast monies that were generated by the Stones' record sales in America, subject to paying them the contractual advances. In later years – after he had ceased to manage the Stones – they launched several legal attacks on Allen and his company ABKCO, trying to wrest ownership of the master recordings and music copyrights away from him. All the attempts failed and ABKCO still owns the American rights to all of the Stones' hits recorded in the sixties and the copyright in the songs.

Allen was even smarter. Record contracts traditionally provided that the company would own recordings made by the artist 'manufactured out of vinyl' – the current practice – 'or by any means now invented or to be invented in the future'. Allen pointed out that as nobody knew what the economics of unknown future production would be, Decca could only have the rights for vinyl, which was the existing medium. Decca, too weary to fight for a future contingency that might never happen, agreed. This meant that when cassettes and later CDs replaced vinyl, the record company had no rights to the product and his company ABKCO, as the owner, was free to control manufacturing and distribution of the recordings. He arranged for the Stones' records to be distributed in the US by Decca subsidiary London Records, but ABKCO Records became the Stones' de facto American record company.

The relationship between Andrew Oldham and the Stones had been deteriorating for years. There was no question that his faith and flair had launched them but his perceived desire to be famous in his own right had caused the Stones to believe that he was more interested in his own celebrity than theirs. In 1968, he sold his interest in the Rolling Stones to Allen for $750,000. Now there was not even the pretence that Andrew was involved with the career of the band that he had made famous, and Allen had total control of the second-biggest band in the world. The biggest band was, of course, The Beatles and it was still Allen's firm ambition to manage them.

One of my first jobs as the Stones' accountant was to prepare the figures for their past tours for submission to the UK Inland Revenue. These were not the hundred-million-dollar world tours that they undertook in later years. In early January and March of 1964, they did two tours of one-nighters that I had to report on. The January tour was fourteen dates in twenty days and the March tour was thirty dates in thirty days. The accounts I prepared showed that the Stones made very little money from the tour. Brian claimed expenses for the use of his own car and the rest of the boys travelled in a beat-up old van, squeezing between Charlie Watts' drum kit and the instruments. They were one of eight acts that each did about twenty minutes. They played two shows a night and a comedian told a few jokes as the acts changed over. For one 1965 tour, the comedian was Ray Cameron, father of Michael McIntyre, now one of the most popular comedians in the UK. Ray went on to write for *The Kenny Everett Video Show* and in the seventies I produced *Bloodbath at the House of Death*, a spoof horror film starring Kenny that Ray directed.

Mickie Most had toured with the Stones as a performer on a 1963 tour when the crowd-pullers were American acts The Everly Brothers, Bo Diddley and Little Richard. Like most UK pop stars, Mickie's act was a pale imitation of American rock acts in general, and the Stones used to play Bo Diddly songs at their gigs. Mickie and the Stones were both low down in the pecking order. The second tour was largely with UK acts: Marty Wilde, Dave Berry, and The Swinging Blue Jeans. the Stones were not popular enough to close the show.

I had to go through the accounts with each of the Stones to clarify certain expenditure. Mick, Charlie and Brian were very vague but Bill Wyman had kept meticulous records, down to how much of the room service charges were for him in the room he shared with Brian. Bill was always the keeper of records and he never threw anything away. His book *Stone Alone* is full of minutiae of his life with the Stones, and is well worth reading.

There was no tax liability but the man from the revenue demanded a meeting, which was quite unusual for such a small turnover. I duly attended the tax office in Soho Square on crutches, having damaged my ankle on a trampoline in the garden of Mickie's new house in Totteridge. I overplayed my limp, hoping that sympathy for my plight would help me in the meeting. The man from the revenue showed no concern whatsoever about my condition but expressed great interest about an item of cash disbursement described as 'sundries'. It was a very small amount and it became clear I was only there because the young man from Her Majesty's inspector of taxes was clearly a Stones fan. I told him that the cash was used by the band to buy tickets to their own performances – to give to girl fans who would scream. I had made this up, but I swore the guy to secrecy and he passed the accounts, no doubt happily believing that he was in on a Rolling Stones secret.

The bank account for the tour had all of the Stones as signatories. In those days, banks returned cheques that had been issued on the account. Once I completed the audit there was no need to keep them so, in accordance with standard practice, I threw them out. Can you imagine what a cheque signed by all of the Rolling Stones would fetch at a memorabilia auction today? Who knew?

During the time that the Stones were run out of the Goodman Myers offices, Allen Klein seldom visited England. He spent his time and energy berating London Records for not doing a better job, and berating concert promoters for not treating the Stones as superstars. It was working. Les Perrin, an established UK PR person, dealt with the considerable media issues. The Beatles were perceived as the 'good boys' and the Stones were cast as the 'bad boys' and Les, following a pattern set by Andrew Oldham, did a brilliant job maintaining the Stones' image as being rebellious and anarchic on both sides of the Atlantic and beyond. Parents disapproved, so of course the kids loved them.

The Stones were technically rich but Allen was holding their money. When he received the big advance from Decca, he opened American bank accounts in the boys' names, depositing fifty thousand dollars for each them. There were tax implications if they brought the money into the UK and exchange control regulations, which made it illegal to have bank accounts abroad. Easton had sued the Stones and Allen, tying up pipeline royalties from Decca, so one way or another the Stones had yet to directly benefit from their impressive new deals.

I would talk to Allen often, and warned him that his lack of attention to the financial needs of the London office was causing great resentment. His response was always words to the effect of 'I'm busy making the Rolling Stones bigger than The Beatles. I'll deal with these little problems later.' the Stones' financial needs were real. Assured by Allen that they were now rich, the boys started to spend money but, as they could not bring any funds back to the UK that Allen had deposited for them in their American bank accounts, they were as good as broke. The UK exchange control regulators attacked the Stones for holding money abroad, and I had to get them out of trouble by explaining that the accounts were opened in their names but the signatory was Allen Klein. As a consequence, they were then obliged to bring the money over to the UK.

In the meantime, Allen had given vague assurances that if they needed money he would get it to them. the Stones office had to deal with calls for money from the boys as well as from general creditors. The fastest form of international communication was the telex machine. You could dial up any telex number and anything typed your end would instantly appear on the machine at the other end of the line. With a secretary manning each machine it was possible to have 'conversations'. Goodman Myers had such a device and Stan Blackburn, the Stones' long-time bookkeeper, was constantly sending telex messages to Allen's office in New York, asking for money. Allen foolishly did not even acknowledge the requests. Eventually I sent a telex to Allen saying, 'Does my telex have bad breath?' which prompted him to call me. I explained the situation, and he started to take the requests more seriously.

When Allen did concentrate on keeping the Stones happy, he did so with style. I was in New York in August 1965 when The Beatles played Shea stadium, a legendary concert. Allen decided that we should take the Stones to see the show and spent hours trying to get permission for our party to arrive by helicopters and have seats in the dugout. This could not happen so we did not go at all.

Determined to take some public attention away from The Beatles – a lost cause if ever there was one – he rented a huge boat and took the Stones on a cruise down the Hudson River and I was lucky enough to still be in town so I joined them. Whenever we passed another boat Andrew Oldham stood at the prow, his long hair streaming in the wind, preaching to anyone that could hear him that he was Jesus and that this was how He had decided to make His second coming. My great memory was the Stones' non-stop playing and replaying of Wilson Picket's recent release, 'In The Midnight Hour'. They just loved that record, as did I.

After the Stones set up their own offices in Maddox Street I frequently went there to discuss their affairs. Mick had set up a small teepee tent in the middle of the office, which he used when he needed to be shut out from the general hubbub. Jo Bergman, a powerhouse of a lady who was by now running the Stones' office, told me that he spent hours in there talking to a young American guy who had walked from Heathrow airport into London to see him. The young man, who clearly had mental issues, believed that Mick was some sort of messiah. Mick showed extraordinary patience and compassion in dealing with such people. He was also patient with intrusive fans. I once had to have a meeting with him while he was waiting for a plane at what is now Kennedy airport. I was not travelling, so we could not go to a private lounge. We found a quiet table in the public area and settled down to discuss some important matters. A drunk American redneck came over to us and rudely interrupted us.

'Hey, Mick, my girlfriend wants your autograph.'

Mick was in mid-sentence and politely held up his hand in a 'give me just a moment' gesture. The guy wasn't having that. 'I don't even know why she likes your shitty music. You too big for your fans?'

Mick did not say a word. He signed the piece of paper that this rude pig had stuck under his nose. The rude pig walked away without a thank-you, and Mick carried on with his conversation. When I expressed my surprise, he shrugged and said, 'It happens all the time. If I react, there could be a fight and it won't be that arsehole's name that makes the headlines.'

One of the things on the agenda was a pension plan. Mick had considered going into the insurance business when he left the London School of Economics. Ellis, my partner, had a good connection with a blue-blood firm of insurance brokers and Mick actually asked Ellis if he could effect an introduction 'just in case'. Ellis would of course have been delighted to do so, but Mick soon created his own insurance policy via his talent, and the introduction never took place. Mick is a very smart man, which is why he is still singing rock'n'roll in his seventies.

In February 1967, following an anonymous tip-off, the police – armed with a search warrant – raided Keith Richards' home Redlands in West Sussex. Mick and Marianne Faithfull and some other friends were Keith's houseguests. George Harrison and his then-girlfriend Pattie Boyd had popped in but left before the police arrived. It was a major raid with carloads of coppers. Mick and Keith were very polite and cooperative. Marianne, who was upstairs at the time of the raid, appeared at the top of the stairs covered in a rug, which she dropped revealing her naked body shouting, 'Search me!'

The police found four amphetamine tablets – which actually belonged to Marianne – and some hash in the possession of a friend known as Acid King David. Mick, ever the gentleman, claimed that the tablets were his to protect Marianne. In March, Mick and Keith were informed that they would be charged with offences against the Dangerous Drugs Act. I went with Allen and a small army of lawyers to the Chichester court, where the charges were put to them. They were released on bail pending trial and I have a photograph on my wall of a very young-looking me, peering over the shoulders of Mick and Keith, laughing on the steps of the court.

The offences were not serious but Allen and I did not take the charges lightly. If the boys were found guilty of drug charges it could affect their entry into the United States. It was clear that the Stones were going to be constant targets for the police, and indeed Brian Jones' flat was raided on the evening of the day they were charged. Jagger and Richards seemed to think that it was all a hoot, but they followed Allen's advice and went abroad to avoid being hounded by the press until they were obliged to appear before a Chichester judge.

On the 27 June Mick was found guilty of possession of four amphetamine tablets and a day later Keith was found guilty of allowing cannabis to be smoked on his property. They were both sent in handcuffs to Lewes jail to each serve a month's sentence. Released on bail the next day, they appealed and Keith's sentence of one year in jail was overturned. Mick's sentence of three months was also reduced to a conditional discharge. There was a public outcry of support for Mick and Keith. Even *The Times* weighed in, with illustrious editor William Rees-Mogg writing an eloquent leader column in their defence, headed 'Who breaks a butterfly on a wheel?' Brian was also sentenced to jail but on appeal was fined a thousand pounds and ordered to seek professional help.

The Stones were now trophy targets for police forces all over the world. Keith's excellent autobiography *Life* is, amongst other things, a fascinating record of the ingenious ways he managed to get his heroin as he toured the USA, in spite of the district attorney of each state being determined to be the hero who caught him. He makes the interesting observation that he survived the drug itself because he was rich enough to buy only the purest-quality heroin and cocaine. In spite of, or maybe because of, my proximity to serious drug-takers I have never been tempted to try it and I have no idea if there is any truth in his claim.

Because I was a sympathetic ear, Brian Jones would sometimes come in to see me. He was now very aware that he was no longer the leader of the Rolling Stones, nor was it musically the band that he had started. Brian was a true blues fan and wanted to play the music of his heroes. His relationship with the rest of the band was not helped when it was discovered that he had made a secret deal with Easton/Oldham to get five pounds a week more than the other band members when they had first signed with them for management. Brian had started a blues band with the still semi-pro Mick and Keith and, from his point of view, the deal he had signed with Oldham and Eastman led to their ultimate success. Without him there would never have been the Rolling Stones, but he was never invited to write a song for the band and now he was not even wanted at recording sessions.

Brian spoke very quietly and would ramble on, often incoherently, about what he perceived was the injustice heaped on him by the world in general and by Mick and Keith in particular. Keith had stolen Anita Pallenberg, his girlfriend. (Keith famously commented, 'Shit happens in the back of a limousine.') I am not sure why Brian confided his woes in me but I suspect that he did so with anyone who was prepared to listen. Even though his woeful condition was self-induced, I felt very sorry for him.

The housekeeper at Brian's home at Crotchford Farm had my home number as one of the people to call in the case of an emergency. On 3 July 1969 I got an early-morning call from her to tell me that Brian had drowned in his swimming pool. It was the middle of the night in New York, but I called Allen to tell him the news and he was extremely distressed. I was personally very saddened by Brian's death. He was only twenty-seven years old and it seemed to me that there had been little joy in his life, other than his music, and even that had been tainted when the purist blues band that he started was taken in a more commercial direction by Mick and Keith. There was no indication if Brian's death was an accident or suicide, and much has been written since. I personally believe that his death – like that of so many of his contemporaries – was due to the mind-altering drugs that were too fashionable and too freely available to those who could afford them in the sixties.

Apart from my professional relationship with the Rolling Stones, I am to this day a fan. They are, in my view, the greatest rock'n'roll band ever. Mick is astonishingly fit and contrary to that discussion that we had some fifty years ago, he *is* still singing rock'n'roll. Many of their current following were not even born when the Stones had the big hits that the fans demand to hear today.

18. RUPERT LOEWENSTEIN COMES ON THE SCENE AND THE STONES BREAK WITH KLEIN

On the day that Brian Jones died in July 1969, Mick went to a white ball at the Holland Park home of Prince Rupert Loewenstein. Antique dealer Chris Gibbs had introduced them in 1968. Chris thought that Rupert might be of use to sort out Mick's money affairs and Rupert then met with Mick a few times to generally discuss this possibility.

As can be deduced from his full title, Rupert Louis Ferdinand Frederick Constantine Lofredo Leopold Herbert Maximilian Hubert John Henry zu Löwenstein-Wertheim-Freudenberg, Count of Loewenstein-Scharffeneck, was an aristocrat, from minor Bavarian royalty. He was educated in England and was a partner in Leopold Joseph & Sons, a prestigious boutique merchant bank.

Mick had become disenchanted with Allen's obsession with The Beatles and his apparent neglect of Stones' business, and appointed Rupert as advisor to himself and the band. Rupert and his wife Josephine were fixtures in the upper echelons of society and introduced Mick and Marianne to their world, which

Mick rather enjoyed. Mick now became familiar with Antibes, Mustique, St Barths and other watering holes that were once the exclusive haunts of the beau monde. Now these places are frequented by tattooed footballers, girls called Tracy and Cheryl, and even people like me.

Rupert kicked out the UK and American lawyers that had been put in place by Allen and brought in a new team of his own, choosing those who would help him analyse and review the band's legal affairs. I escaped the cull and worked closely with Mrs Stacey, Theodore Goddard's highly regarded tax lawyer, helping her restructure the Stones' tax affairs. The rate for high earners was still about 90 per cent and Mrs. Stacey advised the Stones that they should become non-resident, which they achieved by moving residencies to the south of France.

I got on well with Prince Rupert. The only Prince I had known before was Prince Monolulu, a black racing tipster who used to go to race meetings dressed in exotic Zulu chief garb shouting, 'I got an 'orse.' On Sundays he used to try to sell his tips at the Petticoat Lane market where I had my market stall and he occasionally bought sweets from me. Keeping a straight face, I once asked Rupert if he knew Prince Monolulu. He searched his memory for African aristocracy that he had known and said he did not. Before he became involved with Mick Jagger, Rupert was only interested in classical music but he very quickly became enamoured with rock and pop. He sent me demo tapes of a band called Gypsy and I promised to go to their next gig. Some days later my secretary handed me a priceless message that said, 'Gypsy are playing for the Prince tonight.' It was like something out of a Franz Lehár operetta: I did not go to the gig, but I kept the piece of paper for years.

I warned Allen that Rupert was amassing forces against him, but he did not seem to be unduly perturbed. The way Allen had structured his deals with the Stones' recordings meant that he did not need the goodwill of Mick Jagger or any of the Stones for ABKCO to continue to benefit from their recordings. the Stones' share of income had not changed, but by buying out Oldham and Easton, ABKCO effectively received 50 per cent of the income on every record sold. The three-year deals that Allen negotiated with Decca were about to run out and I told Allen that Prince Rupert's influence was becoming stronger and the Stones might look to him to negotiate a new deal. Allen's ego was his downfall. He was sure that all he needed to do was spend time with Mick to reclaim his loyalty. He tried, but it was too late. the Stones appointed Rupert as their new manager. Allen went into in denial, but as much as he tried to convince himself to the contrary, he was out.

Rupert and Allen both reached for their legal guns. They ultimately came to a preliminary settlement but there was an orgy of lawsuits between Allen and the Stones. As they say in the biz, 'Where there's a hit, there's a writ,' and here there were lots of hits, so the litigation went on for twenty years.

Allen's reign was the golden years for Stones music, producing classic hits like 'The Last Time', 'Paint It Black', 'Ruby Tuesday' and 'Satisfaction'. Stones fans still demand to hear these old hits and none of the records that Jagger made as a solo artist have had any real success. Allen's son Jody now presides over ABKCO on behalf of the Klein family and the money still rolls in.

Prince Rupert negotiated the new deal with Decca, which – with Allen out of the way – gave the Stones all of the royalties. In

America he negotiated a profitable new deal for future recordings with Ahmet Ertegun, the charismatic head of Atlantic Records. I have written earlier about my close relationship with American publisher Freddy Bienstock. Freddy's wife Miriam, a formidable woman who became a good friend of my own wife, started Atlantic Records with Ahmet. She had introduced me to him some years earlier and I got to know him and his brother Nesuhi quite well. Rupert had asked me to advise him in his negotiations with Ahmet, but I felt that helping move them to another record company was disloyal to Allen who was still a close friend, so I diplomatically declined his request.

Allen broke the Stones in America and his deals made them financially secure. Rupert made them personally very rich. He successfully guided all aspects of the Stones' careers until 2007, since which time Mick has effectively managed the band. the Stones' live performances became huge money-makers, and even at an age when they are all entitled to a bus pass, their world tours gross about half a billion dollars. It's a long way from the few thousand pounds from their UK tours in the early sixties, and a long time since that meeting at Kennedy airport when Mick said to me 'After all, Laurence, I'm not going to be singing rock'n'roll when I'm sixty.'

In the same way that I had gained knowledge about the music business, Ellis Goodman, through his clients, had gained knowledge and expertise in the whisky business. We both quit our practice in 1971, but, for years after, we kept a 50/50 interest in each other's work. In all of the years that we were together, we never had a written contract, never exchanged a cross word and we are still close friends.

It's hard to be good at something you don't like and I hated being a chartered accountant. The statute of limitations is six years for a simple contract, so I can now confess that my advice to clients was not always sound. I used to come home to my wife and say, 'Thank God I'm not a doctor, I might kill people.' Aware of my shortcomings, I relied a lot on the knowledgeable people around me, but it is not easy to keep on saying, 'Just got to pop to the loo,' to a client so I could nip next door to a colleague and ask their advice. I remember on one occasion when I was obliged to advise 'Yes' or 'No' to a client there was nobody around to ask, so I gazed out of my office window looking profound and thinking that if a bus goes by before a taxi I'll say 'Yes'. There was a 50/50 chance of being right, and I've acted on worse odds for myself. Another problem for me was that professional etiquette at the time prevented me from going after other accountants' clients. You had to wait until the client approached you, and it was difficult for me to meet people in the music business that I believed needed my help and not be able to say words to the effect, 'I can get you a million dollars.'

Roger, my brother, at the age of twenty-three replaced me as a partner in Goodman Myers & Co. and he continued to look after the Rolling Stones. Roger left the practice in 1974 to go into business with Tony Visconti, producer of Marc Bolan and David Bowie. They started a company called Good Earth. Tony was married to Mary Hopkin, the sweet-voiced girl who had a surprise hit in 1968 with 'Those Were The Days', produced by Paul McCartney. This came about because Paul's friend Twiggy had seen Mary sing on *Opportunity Knocks*, a UK talent show, and brought Mary to Paul's attention. Paul had the song 'Those

Were The Days' in his head for years. He had heard it sung by
Gene and Francesca Raskin, an obscure American cabaret duo
who worked at the Blue Angel, a small club in Mayfair that
Marsha and I occasionally frequented. He instantly fell in love
with the song and thought that he might record it himself. Well,
the Blue Angel did serve alcohol.

Paul spotted that Mary's voice was perfect for 'Those Were
The Days' and he signed her to Apple Records to record it. The
result was a No. 1 record in the UK, sales of 1.5 million copies
in the US and only 'Hey Jude' kept it off the No. 1 spot in the
American charts. It was the magic combination of that voice
and that song that had interested McCartney. They subsequently
made a few records together, which did not work, and he called
in Mickie Most, (small world), who produced a couple of
records including 'Knock, Knock, Who's There?' for Great Britain's entry in the 1970 Eurovision Song Contest. Mickie told
me he couldn't stand being in the studio with Mary, and Apple
brought in Visconti, who made an album that was closer to her
folk roots. The album got no support at all from the now disar-
rayed Apple Records, and she left the label.

The Raskins cabaret duo never wrote another successful song,
but financially they did not need to and they retired, very rich, to
Pollença – a small village in Majorca. Mike and Penny Leander
had a house in Pollença and they and the Raskins were part of
small circle of expats. Marsha and I often stayed at the Leanders'
house in Majorca, and one year Penny Leander, who loves to
cause mischievous fun, told the Raskins that their friend Laurence
'the important record company man' was their houseguest.
As a result, wherever we went to dinner, the Raskins would

unexpectedly appear to play and sing their current summer song 'When Manolo Played Guitar (In the Café by the Sea)'. There was usually a crowd of us at the table and we all had to stop eating to listen to what was a terrible song. For all the wrong reasons, I had 'When Manolo Played Guitar' in my head for years,

Roger and Visconti's Good Earth made records with Mary and Judie Tzuke. They managed Argent and were agents for The Average White Band. Then Roger started a promotions division, bringing James Brown, Jerry Lee Lewis and Chuck Berry to Europe. Roger never mastered promoter Don Arden's trick of hanging difficult artists from windows and he shortly moved on to what would be a spectacularly successful career in the restaurant and hotel business. In 1978, with his friend Alan Lubin, he opened Peppermint Park in London's Covent Garden. It was an American-style diner/soda fountain, revolutionary at the time, and it really took off. It became even more famous after a party that I gave there for *The Buddy Holly Story*, a film that I distributed through GTO Films. Guests included wild-man Keith Moon, The Who's drummer, who died at his home the next day, and the press was full of photos of Keith and Paul McCartney at the party with their wives.

Roger later started the Café Rouge restaurant group, building it to a chain of 130 restaurants before selling it to the Whitbread pub group. He then, with some partners, started the Punch Tavern group, one of the largest pub owners in the UK. Punch went public in 2002 and Roger cashed in and moved to St Lucia, where he and his wife Lee own The Sugar Beach, one of the best hotels in the Caribbean.

The three generations of our families are all very close, which is one of the great joys of my life.

19. THE JEFF BECK BAND AND ROD STEWART

In 1967 Mickie produced 'Hi Ho Silver Lining' for Jeff Beck. It was a great song written by Scott English and Larry Weiss, two highly successful Americans. Larry Weiss wrote 'Rhinestone Cowboy' and in the seventies I did a deal with him to develop the song into a film. At the same time I also did a deal to make Elton John and Bernie Taupin's 'Bennie and The Jets' into a movie. I got close, but neither of them got made into films.

One of the many curses of being a film producer is that you often *nearly* get films made and it keeps you in the game. There are lots of other curses, too many to mention here, but if you get the chance, have a look at the 2002 documentary *Lost in La Mancha*, the story of Terry Gilliam's doomed attempt to get a film based on *Don Quixote* off the ground. At the time of writing, he had finally completed it as *The Man who Killed Don Quixote* and it was awaiting distribution.

Singer/songwriter Scott English (along with Richard Kerr) wrote 'Mandy' for Barry Manilow. Scott actually recorded it himself in under the title of 'Brandy', and had a modest hit with it. Arista Records owned the rights to Scott's recording for America and when Clive Davis, the legendary boss of Arista heard it, he changed the name to 'Mandy' and gave it to Barry Manilow to record. Scott told me that he was initially pissed off that his own version was not put out, but when he received his writer's share of the multi-million-selling Manilow version, he felt better.

Scott came to live in London and we became quite friendly. He was a very funny guy who said that he wanted to write a song called 'Don't Fuck Around with Love', which appealed to my sense of humour. In November 2018 I had dinner with Scott after not seeing each other for some forty-five years and it was great to catch up. He told me that he had sent an unfinished version of 'Hi Ho Silver Lining' to Mickie Most and Mickie had asked him to finish it. He told Mickie that he thought that the song was crap and he did not want to finish it. Mickie, who knew a hit song when he heard one, summoned Scott to the office, called in his secretary and made Scott dictate some lyrics there and then. Scott assured me that this was the reason that the song had lines like 'Flies are in your pea soup baby, they're waving at me.'

I was in the studio when Mickie was mixing 'Hi Ho Silver Lining' and he asked me what I thought of it. I told him that I loved it but thought he should drop the guitar solo in the middle. This is why I am not a record producer.

Jeff Beck went on the road as The Jeff Beck Group with Ronnie Wood on rhythm guitar and Rod Stewart as his singer. I was the accountant. The band members were Jeff's employees and, like any other PAYE employee, a payroll tax had to be deducted from their wages. They were paid on a performance basis and, as there was not a gig every night, the band's wages varied from week to week. The plan was that each Monday Jeff would give us money to place in our clients' account, to cover the band's previous week's wages. We would then calculate the statutory deductions for tax and provide cheques for the band members.

Rod wanted his cheque on a Friday and he would come to Goodman Myers's office to collect it. The problem was that Jeff's Monday payment into the Goodman Myers client account drifted later and later into the week, to the point where I would be phoning Jeff on a Friday to tell him that Rod Stewart was in reception waiting to be paid. I explained to Rod that we could not be expected to pay him if we had not received the money and maybe he would like to come back on Monday. Rod assured me that he would not like to come back on Monday; he would like to wait at our offices until he had been paid. Jeff, being a musician, was not an early riser and Rod would hang around our reception, chatting up our pretty receptionist whilst waiting to be paid. Eventually a roadie would turn up with the amount due to each of the band members, and we would quickly calculate Rod's wages after tax and give him a cheque.

One Friday, my partner Ellis had a prospective client, an important city type, coming to see him. Every time Ellis passed through reception he saw this tall, lanky lad in tight tartan trousers, sprawled out in reception with his feet on our reception coffee table, disturbing the nice piles of business magazines that Ellis had set out to impress the prospective client. He asked Rod what he was doing. Rod explained that he came in to see me on Fridays to collect his wage cheque. Ellis, fearful that his prospective client would be deterred by such an untidy and unwholesome sight, popped his head around my office door to ask me to have this person removed. I was not in my office so Ellis went back to reception and politely asked Rod if he would kindly remove his feet from our coffee table, go away and only come back when he had a proper appointment. Rod, who is actually quite a gentleman, apologised and left. Throwing Rod Stewart out of your office was not a smart move. Who knew?

20. THE BEATLES AND APPLE CORP

When Brian Epstein died in 1967, Allen Klein was so convinced that he would become the manager of The Beatles, he even put a date on it: the end of 1968. To many this seemed like wishful thinking and Chris Most bet him a thousand pounds that it wouldn't happen.

Fast-forward to January 1969, and Allen Klein had his first meeting with John Lennon, who asked him to look after his business affairs. The following evening he met with all of The Beatles, when Ringo and George asked him to look after their affairs as well. Paul vociferously declined. Allen was now effectively managing three-quarters of The Beatles. It was a month later than the date of his bet with Chris Most, but she wouldn't let him off. I suggested that she should only claim a quarter of the bet, but she insisted on full payment, which I thought was rather mean of her.

At the time, Paul was engaged to be married to Linda Eastman, the daughter of a prominent New York lawyer who had extensive interests in both art and the music business. Linda's brother John was a partner in the firm. The Eastmans loathed Allen, no doubt because when Brian Epstein died they fancied taking control of The Beatles affairs themselves. The Eastmans were from a very uptown background and they made no attempt to hide the fact that they looked down on Allen, regarding him as a Jew with no class. This made Lennon, who was very conscious and proud of his own working-class background, an even stronger supporter of Allen. There were vicious confrontations between Allen and the Eastmans and eventually it was agreed that Allen would look after The Beatles' business affairs and the Eastmans would become their American attorneys.

Brian Epstein had run the management of The Beatles and his other artists through a company called NEMS. He had named the company after North End Music Store, which had been opened as part of the family's thriving furniture store in Liverpool, where Brian had his office. There was often a crowd of excited teenagers waiting to get into the Cavern Club, a short walk away from Brian's office. Intrigued, he went down into the small basement space to see what all the fuss was about, and the rest, as they say, is history.

His elder brother Clive had taken over the running of NEMS after Brian's death. Clive was thrown in at the deep end to a world which he had no knowledge of and in which he had no real interest in, and The Beatles were left without anyone to give them direction and guidance. It was no secret that the Apple finances were totally out of control. The news of the profligacy had reached New York and that was when Allen got on a plane to London.

No doubt flushed with their new 'freedom', the four lads from Liverpool had decided to start their own company, which they called Apple Corp. Allen asked me to go to their offices to prepare a report on the company's current financial position and make recommendations for its future running. The Beatles' wanted Apple to be a company that any creative people could come to – not just musicians – to get financial support. Lennon described it as, 'Artistic freedom within a business structure'. You are already wincing, and you are right.

They had taken over a beautiful period building at 3 Savile Row. It was on its roof that they famously gave their last performance in 1969, filmed by Michael Lindsay-Hogg. Although totally unannounced, the word quickly spread and the surrounding rooftops soon filled with lunchtime office staff who could not believe their luck. The streets became blocked with traffic as passers-by stopped to look up to see where the music was coming from. The Savile Row police station was a couple of hundred yards away and the police reluctantly asked The Beatles to stop so that order could be restored to the West End streets. Unfortunately, I was installed in the Savile Row offices too late to witness this historic event.

I started my investigation and what I learned was astonishing. Under the Apple brand, the boys started a record company, a film company and a music publishing company, all to be run by them out of the Savile Row offices. In the basement was the workshop of Alex Mardas, who at The Beatles' expense was developing amazing inventions that could never work. He installed a 'state of the art' recording studio, which also never worked. They opened a fashion boutique in Baker Street, which I had often passed on my way to work. The building was painted with psychedelic designs and looked amazing and the shop was stocked with the tie-dye and Indian-influenced fashions of the day. Clothes flew out of the store, most of it stolen by staff and customers. There was no control whatsoever and the shop was closed after six months, with The Beatles instructing that any stock left should be given away. An experienced American music executive called Ron Kass had been hired to run Apple Records but he had not managed to exercise much control and one of the first things that Allen did was fire him.

The Beatles themselves seldom turned up at the offices, other than George Harrison, who was sequencing his new album. It was a time when unreleased records were sampled on individually recorded acetates which could not be played too often without loss of quality and George sat alone in a room for days surrounded by piles of acetates of each song, trying to decide the running order. The acetates would have cost a fortune but George only played each one once, selecting a fresh one for each play. John once came into the office where I was working. He had no idea what I was doing there, and I explained that I was trying to find out what had happened to The Beatles' money. Anxious to find a reason to spend time with him, I started talking to him about my preliminary findings, but he did not seem to be interested, surprised or concerned. He just said, 'Really?' and wandered out again.

I did get to spend time with Lennon when Marsha and I had dinner with Allen and Betty and John and Yoko at the very plush Le Gavroche restaurant in Mayfair, Allen's favourite haunt. Yoko, who had yet to become the self-confident lady of later years, mostly clung monkey-like to John's arm and communicated with us by whispering in John's ear. John was very relaxed and chatted away about his early life when he, Paul McCartney and George Harrison played skiffle music in a group called The Quarrymen.

I told him that when I was about sixteen I had played in a skiffle group myself. I had to admit that sadly I wasn't on guitar (which would have required me to buy a guitar, which I could not afford, and learn three chords) but rather the lowly washboard. Skiffle as a musical force never took off in America, and John and I had to explain to Allen that it was a usually played by a few guys who knew three chords on a guitar, accompanied by a tea-chest bass player and someone creating a beat with thimbles on a washboard. Skiffle repertoire was mainly Lonnie Donegan songs or folk songs borrowed from American heroes Pete Seeger or The Weavers. The skiffle craze only lasted about three years in the mid-fifties and Allen was surprised to hear how many other early English pop groups had been inspired, including the Stones and the UK's first young pop idol, Tommy Steele.

Lonnie Donegan outgrew skiffle and became a wide-appeal entertainer. Coincidentally, when I wrote this in March 2018, I had been on the set of *Judy*, the film I am producing about Judy Garland, starring Renée Zellweger in the title role. In the scene I was watching, Lonnie Donegan was standing by to go on stage instead of Judy Garland at The Talk of The Town, a popular London cabaret club in the sixties. Miss Garland was going through a terrible period of addiction to drink and prescription drugs and was incapable of reliably turning up. Lonnie was a big enough star to appease the audience in her absence. Sadly, Judy Garland died of a drug overdose a few months later.

At the dinner, John discussed the problems that he was having renovating Tittenhurst Park, an early Georgian mansion near

Ascot that he had recently bought as a home for himself and Yoko. The house was Grade II-listed, and he could not get the permissions that he needed to make sweeping changes, including removing most of the walls. In that wonderful Liverpool accent, he told us, 'I can't see the point of having separate rooms to sleep in, eat in, fuck in and piss in.' Considering his predilection for 'bed-ins', it was maybe more than an idle thought. In the meantime, he and Yoko were living in a caravan parked in the seventy-two acres of ground that came with the house. He ultimately had to compromise but he did put a lake in the grounds without bothering to get planning permission and an unauthorised recording studio where he recorded some important albums for The Plastic Ono Band. When he moved permanently to America in 1971, he sold the house to Ringo, who had more traditional taste. I once went to see him there, and it was indeed beautiful.

John's most memorable remark of that unforgettable evening at Le Gavroche was about the time he was leaving school and his headmaster advised, 'Stop spending so much time playing the guitar, Lennon, you'll never make a living with that.'

The cost of running Apple's Savile Row operation was ridiculous. Many of the mainly overpaid staff made free use of Apple Corp's account with a minicab company to take them to and from work. The company had an account with a wine merchant, which was also cheerfully abused by staff. There was no semblance of discipline and staff came and went at their own convenience. The Beatles were paying for the good time that was being had by all. My report showed how and where substantial savings could be made and, armed with the specifics, Allen waded in and sorted out the mess.

I ran into Ron Kass again – the guy Allen had fired – in the mid-seventies. He was by now husband No. 3 for Joan Collins, who I met socially from time to time. One evening, we bumped into each other at the Tramp nightclub and I mentioned to Joan that we were planning to rent a home in Los Angeles for a month in the summer. She suggested that I rented hers. I had been to her London home, close to where we lived in Highgate, to pick up our son who had been to her own son's birthday party, and it was not a modest place. I had never been to her home in LA but I remembered that Sue St John, a mutual friend who was close to Joan, telling me it was spectacular. It was certainly big enough to take my family and I would be sleeping in Joan Collins' bed, so it sounded a great idea. Joan asked me to 'be a darling and talk to Ron about the business side'.

Joan was pretty broke – this was before she made *The Bitch* and *The Stud*, and a long time before *Dynasty* – and Ron asked for four thousand pounds, a very reasonable sum, *in cash*. As further enticement, Ron offered to throw in the two cars that they kept in LA. Then, in what he clearly thought was a clincher, dropping his voice to a conspirator's whisper, he promised to speak to Walter – the all-powerful maître d' of the Polo Lounge at the Beverley Hills hotel – to make sure that I had Joan's booth whenever I went there. You may recall that one's positioning in a fashionable LA watering hole was vital to one's prestige in town. The red leather booths at the Polo Lounge were up there with the window tables at Spago, and Ron assured me that Joan was always afforded the *No. 1 booth*. This was an offer I clearly could not refuse. And I didn't.

I went to the house a couple of days before my family arrived to make sure that all would be in order for their arrival. Ron's sister was staying and she showed me around. The house was in Bel Air, a very exclusive gated community. It was close to the house that was used in the filming of *The Beverly Hillbillies*, a popular comedy TV show about a country man who strikes oil on his land and moves his family to Beverly Hills. Most of the people who live in Bel Air have struck oil in some form or other and there is no social housing on the estate.

Ron's sister left and I turned on the TV. There was a remote, something that we were yet to get in England, and I clicked the button and sank into a couch the size of a small ocean liner to watch TV. The TV did not go on but the doorbell rang. Fighting my way from under the cushions I went and opened the door. A mountainous security guard in uniform, a huge gun at his hip, blocked the ever-present Californian sunshine out. He asked if the owners were at home and I said no, I was alone. He asked me for the security code, which I did not have. He asked me some other security questions, none of which I could answer, but I did offer to give him Joan's telephone number in London. He got on to his walkie-talkie and I thought he was going to call for back-up. I had visions of being read my rights, cuffed, and placed in the back of a 'black-and-white' by Starsky and Hutch. Disappointedly after listening to his walkie-talkie, he told me to 'have a nice day' and drove off.

I went back to my couch and tried again to turn on the TV with the remote. The doorbell rang, it was the BFG again. My TV remote was not remotely connected to the TV. It was a panic alarm connected to the Beverly Hills security patrol. Who knew?

The house was indeed spectacular, if suited to a particular taste. Huge, its roof-height living area dotted with silver lamé faux-palm trees, the place had more glitz than Ziggy Stardust's make-up box. There were photos of Joan everywhere and for Marsha's arrival I had carefully arranged a large photo of Joan by my side of the bed, with a single red rose next to it. She was so amused I discovered another spare bedroom.

We had a great time there. We had a big party for Marsha's fortieth birthday, which was a huge success. I told all my LA friends that we could 'do lunch' at my reserved booth at the Polo Lounge. They were very impressed.

21. MIKE LEANDER – THE MAN WHO ENCOURAGED ME TO CHANGE MY BUSINESS LIFE

I think that Mike Leander really understood my frustration at being an accountant, in a career I did not really enjoy. He had started his own working life in a solicitor's office but his first love was music, so he gave up law after a year and got a job as an office junior for a small music publisher. He had a natural gift for orchestration, which he studied in his spare time at Trinity College London. He tried his hand at songwriting and production, without much success. When he was twenty, Dick Rowe of Decca Records gave him a three-year deal as a musical director. Dick famously turned down The Beatles, a fact that has become synonymous with his name. His home electricity bill was probably addressed to Mr Dick Rowe-Turneddownthebeatles Esq.

Dick Rowe was by no means the only one who passed on talent. About twenty years ago, Jocelyn, a close friend of ours, had a holiday home in a small village in Tuscany where her Italian neighbour had a son who was a singer. Jocelyn told the neighbour about her friend Laurence, the *'grande uomo nel mondo della*

With Marsha at our engagement party, 1960.

Left: Marsha and me on holiday in Acapulco, 1974. *Right:* With Marsha at our son James's wedding, 2018.

With Allen Klein, my music business mentor in the 70s.

Marsha and me with Mike Leander, the man who persuaded me to go into the music business full time.

Mike Leander and Marianne Faithfull at Decca, 1964 (photo: Gered Mankowitz).

Left: Wearing my trademark cowboy hat in the mid-60s. *Right:* A young me looking over the shoulders of Mick and Keith at Chichester Crown Court after their drugs bust. (Photograph copyright Alamy images)

Tony Defries and Tony Macaulay on either side of me at a Gem celebration, 1970.

Tony Burrows, lead singer of Edison Lighthouse, receiving a Gold Disc for 'Love Grows (Where My Rosemary Goes)' from songwriter Tony Macaulay (*left*) with co-writer Barry Mason (*right*).

With Larry and Michael Levene and The New Seekers at an Arcade Records presentation.

With Nicky Chinn, the man who brought me The Sweet.

Top row: D.J. Ed 'Stewpot' Stewart, Andy Scott of The Sweet, Gary Glitter.
Bottom row: Three members of Springfield Revival and Brian Connolly of The Sweet.

Left: David Essex and me in the late 1970s. *Right:* With Tony Macaulay, Geoff Stephens, Johnny Johnson and Anya Wilson, a record plugger.

Above: With Alan Price. *Below:* Top row: Me, Glenn Wheatley, Senior V.P. GTO Inc., and my partner David Joseph. Bottom row: Three GTO Inc. artists and Eileen Bradley, V.P. GTO Inc.

With Dick Leahy on my boat 'Ziggy Stardust' making the GTO deal.

Left: With Phil Daniels, who starred with Ray Winstone in the GTO film *Scum*.
Right: With Hazel O'Connor, who starred in the GTO film *Breaking Glass*.

With D.J. Alan 'Fluff' Freeman.

Left: Signing the Gem Records deal in 1978, with RCA's Bob Summer. *Right:* Dancing with Anthony Quinn at *The Greek Tycoon* film launch party on a boat in Cannes.

musica'. Suitably impressed, the neighbour asked me if I wanted to manage her son Andrea, who was struggling to earn a living as a cabaret singer in Tuscan holiday resorts. I responded '*Grazie* but no *grazie*,' because, as I said to my wife, 'what am I supposed to do with a blind Italian opera singer?'

It gets worse. In the 1970s, Norman Sheffield and his brother had a management company within his Trident Studios group of companies. Norman asked me if I wanted to buy the management company, whose main asset was its contract with a band called Queen. Norman claimed that he wanted to concentrate on the studio, which was his core business. I had heard rumours that the band were unhappy with the Sheffields and if they had come to me of their own accord I would, of course, have been interested. But I was sure that the band would not want to be 'sold on' as part of a company, I was up to my ears with my existing successful artists, and I did not think that it was worth pursuing. My only regret is that, had I pulled it off, I would have featured in the huge hit film *Bohemian Rhapsody*. I would fancy George Clooney to have played me, but I fear that they would more likely have cast Danny DeVito.

In 1988 I got to know Brian May a little. He was a regular after-show visitor to the delightful-in-every-way Anita Dobson who, at the time, was starring opposite Adam Faith in *Budgie*, the first musical that I ever produced. Brian was about to get divorced from his first wife and Anita did not feel secure about her future relationship with him. This is when I learned that the duties of the producer of a musical extended to reassuring your lead actress that she would marry the man she loved, so please stop crying. There was a lovely Don Black/Mort Shuman ballad in the show called 'In One of My Weaker Moments', which Anita told me she sometimes struggled to perform because of her romance with Brian. I would sometimes chat with Brian as he waited for Anita after the show. It was all a bit teenagery, as Anita would later ask me 'Did he say anything?' Brian and Anita made their own record of 'In One of My Weaker Moments' in 1989, which made me very happy. Indeed, they did marry and are still together, the marriage having run a lot longer than the show did. *Budgie The Musical* closed in three months, losing all of the investors' money.

The extraordinarily talented Brian May was a lovely gentle man, unlike Adam Faith who, whilst mildly talented, was a nightmare in so many ways that I could write a book entirely about him. Maybe I will. All right, one story now. He was impossible about publicity. His test was 'Would Marlon Brando do it?' To which my answer should have been, 'Of course not, you schmuck, but you're not Marlon Brando.' Instead I felt obliged to cajole and beg him to promote *Budgie*. We were offered *Russell Harty*, then the top TV plug programme. The show's format was to feature three guests, but Adam would only do it if he had the show to himself. I pointed out that the line-up for the previous week had been Dustin Hoffman, Sting and Dave Allen, to which he replied 'Well they're c***s.' This was just one example of his delusional sense of importance, and even though he was the star of the show, I should have fired him before we opened. It was my first production. A later, more experienced version of me would have done so.

In 1981 Brian Brolly, who was then managing Andrew Lloyd Webber, asked me if I wanted to invest £130,000 in *Cats*. He was quite desperate and offered me the record rights and an interest in all future productions. Comfortable in the thought that nobody would be interested in a musical using the poetry of T. S. Eliot, I said, 'No'. To add to my foolishness, when I went to the opening night I was convinced that I had made the right decision. The show of course has played for years in every major country in the world and those bloody cats' eyes advertising the show follow me round at every airport. *Please* don't tell anyone about this.

Back to Mike Leander. Whilst he was with Decca, Mike Leander worked with the Rolling Stones, Billy Fury, Marc Bolan, Shirley Bassey and many other stars of the day. He released two albums under the Mike Leander Orchestra banner without great success, but to enormous critical acclaim. Jerry Wexler, the revered head of A&R at Atlantic Records, flew Mike over to New York to work with Ben E. King, The Drifters and other artists on the Atlantic label.

At the time I first met Mike, he was working with MCA Records as an in-house producer. He had already written 'Lady Godiva' for Peter and Gordon (with Charlie and Gordon Mills), 'Early in the Morning,' a big hit for Vanity Fare written with Eddie Seago, and a couple of hits for Paul Jones. He had done the fabulous string arrangement for The Beatles' 'She's Leaving Home' for the *Sgt. Pepper* album, the creative work that he was most proud of until the day he died. Mike was executive producer of *Jesus Christ Superstar*, one of the first concept albums and the vehicle that set Andrew Lloyd Webber and Tim Rice on the road to success.

I have a theory about why the *Jesus Christ Superstar* album was so successful. At the time of its release, there was a strong movement amongst young Christians in America known then as 'Jesus freaks', maybe born out of the general hippy philosophy of peace and love. The telling of the story of Christ in such a modern manner had enormous appeal to them and they made the album a huge hit, leading to a Broadway production in 1971. This is not to take away from Andrew and Tim being in tune with the times or the commercial bravery of Brian Brolly, the head of MCA in the UK, in financing the recording.

Apart from this, not a lot was happening for Mike but Dick Leahy, the UK head of Bell Records – a recently formed subsidiary of Bell Records in the USA – was well aware of Mike's talent. Dick, unquestionably one of the best 'record men' of his era, had just had a successful spell as A&R manager of Philips Records and was keen to sign UK artists, including Tony Macaulay. I was by now establishing myself in my career as a manager and both Tony and Mike were clients of mine. There was a deal to be done.

Dick was obliged to go to his New York-based boss Larry Uttal, who had started the company, to do any significant deal. By now, 'significant deal' was my middle name. I negotiated a terrific three-year deal to finance recordings produced by Mike and Tony. Dick Leahy at Bell UK, later my partner in GTO Records, would be our point of contact. Mike had committed his exclusive services to me via Gem and he urged me to quit accountancy and devote my time to the company. Altruistically, he knew that I was unhappy with the accountancy side of my work and that I wanted to leave Goodman Myers. Selfishly, he wanted me to have more time to devote to him. Either way it was a meeting that I had with him towards the end of 1969 that made me decide to make the move. He sat in my office, lecturing me to 'get out from behind that boring desk' and go and compete with the 'old farts' who then dominated the business side of the UK music industry (it was amazing how quickly the years flew and I became an 'old fart' myself).

I went home and told Marsha that because of the deal I had made with Bell Records, I had a unique chance to go full-time into the business. Beth, our daughter, had been born in 1968 and we now had three young children but I recklessly wanted to give up a financially secure future for a leap into the unknown. Marsha, of course, knew how much I wanted to do this, and she encouraged me to grab the chance. I would never have made that leap without her blessing and encouragement. It was only the first of many occasions in more than fifty years of marriage that Marsha supported me taking business risks. My wife really did help me succeed. She smiled at gigs that she hated and graciously entertained people that she did not necessarily like. When I wanted to monopolise the attention of one or two people at a business dinner, I would identify the possible diversions and ask her to 'take them out', which she did without them even being aware of it. Smart and funny, she is an amazing woman, and I am lucky to have found her.

Ellis had given up trying to make me even look like an accountant – I had taken to wearing cowboy hats and boots at the office – and he also supported the idea of me devoting my time to the music business. Happily, for me, and maybe more so for my clients, I quit being an accountant in practice in 1970.

Bearing in mind what Allen Klein had taught me about giving the artist 80 per cent of yours rather than taking 20 per cent of theirs, under the deal that I made with Mike and Tony, Gem Record Productions Ltd would own the records that they produced. They would receive 80 per cent of Gem's revenue from records that they recorded after deducting payments to the artists.

Gem's first release was by Edison Lighthouse in January 1970. It was 'Love Grows (Where My Rosemary Goes)', written and produced by Tony Macaulay with co-writer Barry Mason. Barry's then girlfriend Sylvan Whittingham was credited as co-writer, which later became a general issue as to whether helpful comments by a writer's girlfriend during the writer's creative process entitled her to be a credited collaborator.

Macaulay's brilliant production used Tony Burrows as lead voice to make what was a perfect pop record. Burrows was a talented and versatile singer who could sight-read music and he was much in demand as a session singer. The other musicians on the recording were all seasoned session artists. I later managed Tony as a solo artist, but never got him the success his talent deserved. (I met with him in the course of writing this book and he referred to me as his 'damager'. It was with affection – I hope.)

At that time Tony Macaulay's girlfriend was Anya Wilson, who was working as an independent record plugger. Tony promised her that if she worked on the record and it became a hit, he would recommend that I took her on as a full-time in-house plugger. With the help of Anya, the record got immediate airplay and shot into the charts at No. 12 for the weekend of 24 January 1970. Anya met with Mel Cornish, the producer of *Top Of The Pops*, whose weekly average audience of fifteen million could almost guarantee to make a record a hit. She hoped to persuade Mel to use the record for a routine with Pan's People, a group of sexy and talented dancers who had a regular spot on the show. To her surprise Mel loved the record and did better, offering to put the band itself on the next *TOTP* going out in a few days' time.

This would have been great news had Edison Lighthouse actually existed, but of course Anya could not admit this slight hiccup to Mel. Fortuitously, she bumped into an agent who represented a little-known band called Greenfield Hammer, who immediately agreed to morph into Edison Lighthouse. Macaulay rehearsed them solidly for a day and on 29 January 1970, with Tony Burrows singing lead, they appeared on the show miming to the original track. On that same show Tony also appeared as featured singer with White Plains and Brotherhood of Man. Appearing on the same *TOTP* in three different bands was a feat achieved by no singer before or since. In the chart for the week following the show, 'Love Grows' shot to No. 1. It was the fastest-ever climber to the top spot. It stayed there for five weeks and continued to sell, becoming the 'summer hit' for the year.

Gem's second hit, also produced by Macaulay, was 'Blame It on the Pony Express', a song that that he wrote with Roger Greenaway and Roger Cook for Johnny Johnson and His Bandwagon. It got to No. 2 in the charts in January 1970 and established Gem as a serious player in the world of independent production companies.

I was busy with the hits that Tony Macaulay was producing, working with Mike Leander on his projects, whilst still being involved with Mickie Most's Rak Records, as well as looking after the affairs of my other accountancy clients including the Rolling Stones. My time was clearly stretched. Mickie Most was unhappy that I had left my practice to set up my own production company and he thought that I should give him back the shares that I owned in the Rak group of companies – I had 10 per cent of all his companies in lieu of fees. I hated having to account for the time that I spent on each client's affairs and this meant I didn't have to bill him in the same way. I offered to sell Mickie the shares for the recorded time that I had accumulated over the years. It was about five thousand pounds, a small fraction of what the shares were actually worth. He refused to do this for a long time until reorganising his own affairs forced him to do so.

I had no obligation to stick to my original offer but I did. There was a saying amongst the literati of market grafters: 'If they're gonna hate you anyway, fuck 'em.' The advice was right. Mickie would have disliked me no more had I held out for the six-figure sum that the shares were actually worth, but I have never regretted my decision. I had earned the true value of my shares, but Mickie was my entrée into the music business, and in any event, it was my choice to leave him.

I had been in practice for five years without getting found out. I was known and respected in the music business and I had enormous faith in the talent of Mike Leander and Tony Macaulay. I was thirty-five years old, I had a great family and I felt wonderful.

22. GEM PRODUCTIONS – MIKE LEANDER, TONY MACAULAY

I said earlier that the sixties were a great time to go into the music business. It was, in fact, a great time to go into *any* business.

Post-war, the fifties were austere and grim but the sixties were booming and colourful. Anybody who wanted to work could get a job and if you worked hard you prospered. Most of my friends were lower-middle-class, as was I. We were all state-educated, none of us went to university and, with almost no exceptions, all of us did OK. As a matter of interest, most of us stayed married too. Maybe the two are linked?

As the business grew, I concentrated on music and Ellis continued to build up his contacts and expertise in the wine and spirits business. He had already formed ADP Ltd to take care of our interest in that industry, and he was about to take that company public. Ellis had a 50 per cent interest in Gem and I had 50 per cent of the shares in ADP. He was also ready to fly the Goodman Myers' nest and set up a new office in Sackville Street. In January 1970, I walked about two hundred yards out of my office at 273–287 Regent Street, across Oxford Circus, to the space I had taken for Gem at 252–260 Regent Street.

Nineteen-seventy proved to be a truly amazing year in my career. People spend their whole lives in the music business without being attached to major success. By the end of my first year, I'd had a No. 1 record with Edison Lighthouse, two Top 10 hits with Johnny Johnson and His Bandwagon and had signed David Bowie. A single could sell 300,000-400,000 copies and Gem's end might come to well over ten thousand pounds (about £100,000 in today's money). By contrast, today sales of singles are so low that, even with downloads, nobody makes much money and they are largely seen as promotion for the album.

My offices were about three thousand square feet on the top floor above Dr Scholl's footwear store, about a hundred yards from Oxford Circus. Formally the London headquarters of Warner Brothers' Corset Company, you walked into a space with a large reception and a showroom on the left. I took that as my own office/meeting room, and to the right there was a corridor with four small offices on either side. The initial occupants were Mike Leander, Tony Macaulay and Tony's secretary – a very posh gel called Jane Hickey who went to Fortnum & Mason to buy the office tea supplies. The space was much too big for my immediate needs but ... I had a dream.

I have already mentioned the famous Brill Building in New York, where there were eleven floors crammed full of publishers, writers, song-pluggers and executives who were the heart of the New York music industry. Hits poured out through the windows onto Broadway. I was going to have my own little Brill Building-ette where I would give space to creative people who, in my plan, would create hits that would pour out through the windows onto Regent Street.

23. DAVID BOWIE

I had my new office and the most significant hits that drifted out of my Regent Street windows were created by David Jones, aka David Bowie.

As with the Stones, I have no wish to write a version of David Bowie's life story, only that part of it that relates to my personal involvement. There are dozens of books written about David but I particularly recommend *Alias David Bowie*, by Peter and Leni Gillman, who interviewed me extensively in 1986. Also read *Stardust: The David Bowie Story* by Henry Edwards and Tony Zanetta and *Any Day Now* by Kevin Cann. This last book contains some very specific accounting information that I do not have and the author told me that he had got it from the Gillmans. They told me that they had been given copies of the accounting by the widow of Peter Gerber, who was my in-house accountant until he was seduced away by Tony Defries. In a way I was getting information back that had originally belonged to me. It was very bizarre.

As we all know, success has many fathers but failure is an orphan. David's talent may well have brought him success, but the road to stardom is littered with the bodies of talented people who were never afforded the break they deserved. The financial risk that I took on when David was by no means a star, entitles me to proudly claim to be one of the fathers of his success.

The first manager to be meaningfully involved in David's career was Les Conn, at a time when David Bowie was still David Jones of Davie Jones and the King Bees. I first met Les in 1965 when, as a sometime artists' manager and wannabe songwriter, he was a peripheral figure in Mickie Most's circle of business friends. Les came from Stamford Hill, a Jewish area in north London close to Finsbury Park, where I had been brought up. There were not many north London Jewish boys in the music business, so there was something of a bond between us and, although I was a little younger, I became something of a confidant. Les had not managed to achieve any real success for the King Bees and they had recently amicably parted company.

I later met with Les Conn after the struggling David Jones had become the superstar David Bowie and he never showed the slightest bitterness about what might have been. In fact, he laughed when he told me that David and another young hopeful, Mark Feld (aka Marc Bolan), had painted his kitchen. Les was fond of introducing himself as 'Conn's the name and con's the game' – referring to hype rather than financial misdeeds – and Bowie (who had worked briefly in the advertising industry) was not hype-adverse when it came to advancing his own career. He actually used the name The Hype for a short-lived band that he formed with Tony Visconti and Mick Ronson. He also learned the value of branding, which no doubt influenced his successful self-reinvention during the course of his career.

Les was an extremely easy-going and affable guy, which could be why he never really achieved his potential in the music business. When Les died in 2008 David wrote a very warm obituary acknowledging the important part that Les had played in his early career.

I first met David Bowie, briefly, at the Ivor Novello Awards in The Talk of the Town in May 1970. Tony Macaulay was receiving an award as the British songwriter of the year. Peter Sarstetd won best song with 'Where Do You Go To (My Lovely)?'. Peter would be a GTO Los Angeles-managed artist in later years as one of the Sarstedt Brothers, along with siblings Robin Sarstedt and Eden Kane, the stage name of another brother. David's 'Space Oddity' won the special award for originality and without doubt it was the talking point of the evening. I went over to David and congratulated him on writing not a love song, but a great theatrical song with a story. I also mentioned the fact that he did not sing with an American accent, which I greatly applauded. Actually, he sang very much like Anthony Newley, an entertainer I admired immensely. David freely confessed that he was a huge Newley fan, and I recall that in an *NME* interview in the early seventies, he said 'I was Anthony Newley for a year.' It was not only Newley's voice that David admired. Newley was an actor who could sing and had used mime to great effect in the avant-garde musical *Stop The World – I Want to Get Off*, written with Leslie Bricusse, a show that I went to see three times. I think that I got brownie points from David because of our shared Newley fandom.

Newley was the artist I would most like to have managed simply because I was a huge fan of his talent. He was a great actor, songwriter and a great performer. I was in contact with him in the early nineties about a musical project with Don Black. He once left a message on my home answerphone which started:

'Anthony Newley here, I was very big in the sixties.' Such was my fandom, I kept that cassette for years. He was a great talent and a lovely man. Newley was by then working in UK cabaret venues that, sadly, were a far cry from his days topping the bill at Las Vegas. Joan Collins, who was married to Newley for eight years, once told me that he was the love of her life, but she could not take his philandering. Tony died in 1999, aged 67. It was a great loss to the world of entertainment.

When I met fellow Newley fan David Bowie at the Novello awards, I had no idea that the wheels were already in motion that would eventually lead him to my office. It was Tony Defries who brought Bowie to see me. I will call Defries by his surname in this book, not to be derogatory but because there are far too many Tonys involved in Bowie's story and it will get confusing.

I met Defries when he worked for Martin Boston and Co., a law firm that I had recommended to Mickie Most in his fight with Warrior Records. Defries definitely made an impression on people. He always wore a strange type of frock coat, slightly Dickensian in style. He smoked big cigars, but certainly not the Havanas that he could later afford. He had a huge Afro hairstyle and a slow, rolling gait. He moved slowly, but he thought quickly. Although he was not a qualified lawyer, I thought he was very bright. Soon after I moved into my Gem offices in Regent Street, Defries came to see me. He had left Martin Boston and moved to Godfrey Davis and Batt, a respected firm of lawyers who had engaged him to represent the Association of Fashion Advertising Photographers (AFAP) who were seeking to retain the copyright in the photographs that were commissioned by advertising agencies. He switched sides and decided that models should have a share of the copyright in their photographs. Also, it seemed that the top models were often kept waiting to be paid by their agent and were treated badly in other ways. Defries was aware of the manner in which I had improved the lot of music artists and thought that I might be interested in doing the same for these girls. Why would I not want to meet with some of London's top models? I was soon hosting a dinner at La Trattoria Terrazza surrounded by about ten of the best-looking girls in London.

In essence these girls were all unhappy and desperately wanted to improve their financial relationship with their agents. I explained how I improved the lot of recording artists by threatening to withdraw artists' services and offered to meet with the agents in question and tell them that these girls were not going to work for them any more. I stressed that they would have to back me up by refusing further work until the agencies met what we thought were reasonable demands. We would form an Association of Fashion Models, which of course I would manage. The last time I had hosted a business dinner at the Trattoria was to propose a similar arrangement for songwriters and it had occurred to me that that had not worked out particularly well, but these were beautiful models so, of course ... well, of course.

In spite of the mistreatment, it seemed that all the girls loved their agents. One of the girls said that if they did not work her agency might go broke, to which I replied, 'So be it.' One said that they thought it was a horrible thing to do to the agent; another started crying at the thought of my nastiness and that was pretty much the end of my managing models. Whoever said men were from Venus and women from Mars must have, at some point, tried to help models.

After the models fiasco I did not see Defries again until April 1970 when he came to see me about David Bowie. After leaving Leslie Conn in 1965, the singer was managed by Ralph Horton, a young guy from Birmingham. Horton did not have the money or resources to effectively manage a band and approached Ken Pitt, an established agent, who had brought Manfred Mann his first success. Horton wanted Ken to put some money into promoting David, who was by now performing as Davy Jones and the Lower Third. Ken initially said no, but advised David to change his name to the more distinctive David Bowie. Ken did help Horton with money and advice and gradually became a bigger influence on David himself. In February of 1967, David split with Horton and Ken Pitt became his manager. Ken, in my opinion, did a lot of good advancing David's career. Most of all he was a fan and you cannot successfully manage an artist if you do not admire his or her work. But by 1970 David had decided that it was time for a change of management and I can imagine how Ken must have felt. He had risked money, shown faith and given good guidance.

Artists often leave a manager who has done a good job for them. The reasons are sometimes valid but as often as not it is because someone has whispered in the artist's ear that they are not as rich as they should be or are being taken for granted, neither of which might be the case. There are very few managers, including myself, who do not bear some scars as the result of disloyalty. Mickey Duff, in his day a leading manager of boxers, once advised me, 'If you want loyalty, buy a dog.'

Ken's problem was that David had come under the influence of Angie, the powerful American lady he had married

in March of that year. They met at The Speakeasy Club, a
music-business hangout, about a year earlier. She was with Lou
Reizner, an American record producer and Calvin Mark Lee, a
Chinese-American friend of Lou's – one or both of whom she
was romantically involved with. I am confining my recollections
to matters which concern my relationship with Bowie, but for
those of you who are interested in the fascinatingly liberal sexual
machinations between these characters and many other people
in David's life, I would refer you to *Alias David Bowie* which
deals in some detail with the web of David and Angie's sexual
preferences and relationships.

The introduction of a new wife/girlfriend in a pop star's life is
not always positive. Some ladies think that they can do a better
job of management than the manager. On the few occasions I
was faced with this problem, I encouraged the lady concerned to
test her talent by going out and finding someone to manage. This
issue is best illustrated in *Spinal Tap*, Rob Reiner's satirical but
definitive film on the subject of rock bands. If you are considering
managing an artist I urge you to watch it every night. In the years
after I gave up management I was occasionally tempted to go
back by an artist who I believed had talent that I could nurture.
I would watch my copy of *Spinal Tap*, take a cold shower and go
to sleep – undisturbed by any 3 a.m. phone calls about the artist's
van broken down outside Sheffield (as if there was anything that
I could do about it) or the drummer being arrested for assault,
which was the *good* news because the police had not yet found the
drugs taped to the inside of his bass drum.

Angie, who was very bright, unquestionably had a positive
influence on David's public persona, providing a level of energy

and urgency that he lacked. It was she who encouraged him to do something about leaving a manager he was not happy with. They discussed his dilemma with Olav Wyper, the marketing manager of Philips Records, which released 'Space Oddity', and he recommended his own lawyer. Enter Defries, who drafted a letter to Ken from David, informing him that he was terminating their business relationship on the basis that Ken had not fulfilled his management obligation to further David's career.

Gem had got off to a flying start and the UK music industry was certainly aware of my presence when Defries came to explain that David was free, and that he would like to stop being a lawyer and get involved with managing the star himself. As he had had no music-business experience he did not think that David would go for it, but he had enthused about me and Gem, my hot new management/record production company. Defries offered to bring David up to meet me, on the understanding that he could come and join the company if David signed with us. My experience as an accountant in the music business had taught me that where there's a hit there's a writ and, irrespective of getting involved with David Bowie, I quite liked the thought of having Tony Defries as an in-house business affairs person.

We agreed that Defries would work for me for a salary of thirty pounds a week. I would sign David to Gem and – if everything worked out – I would give Defries 20 per cent of the company and make him a director. It was difficult to define what 'worked out' meant but Defries said that he was happy to trust me to 'do the right thing' and there was no paperwork between us. It is worth noting that I would never have signed David Bowie had Defries not brought him to me, and equally it is my belief that David would never have signed with Defries in a management capacity, had he not been working with me.

Before I committed to sign David I, of course, wanted to get to know him a little and we met a few times to discuss his relationship with Ken Pitt and what his hopes were for the future. My first impression of David was that he was quietly spoken, very gentlemanly and very polite. He was, however, very firm in his ideas about how he wanted to present himself to the public.

Most artists, encouraged by their management, base themselves on precedents. In the fifties, stars like Johnnie Ray, Frankie Laine, Eddie Fisher and their contemporaries dressed like cabaret singers in glitzy tuxedos with lots of white teeth. Elvis set the mould for undulating hips in tight trousers and English pop stars like Billy Fury, Cliff Richard and Marty Wilde happily followed The King. Brian Epstein put The Beatles into cute uniforms. the Rolling Stones were the scruffy rebels – although Jagger was very choosy about his stage gear. By and large, the management's hope was that the artist looked 'sexy' to the teenage girls who were a large share of the record-buying market. Part of that sex appeal meant you shouldn't seem to be gay. Many Hollywood stars disguised their homosexuality or bisexuality, including male pin-ups Marlon Brando, Montgomery Clift and Rock Hudson.

I touched on this issue lightly but David just laughed and told me not to worry about it. He obviously thought that I was too conventional in my thinking, and he was probably right. It was obvious to me that David was very bright, had a clear vision of his stage persona, and he was not looking to be moulded into any of the perceived 'looks' of his predecessors. In fact, he was clearly not looking to be moulded in any way at all. I had to decide if I wanted to sign this self-determined artist who was going to be very different from the norm and was going to stretch my limited resources.

Please understand, this was not Laurence being a shrewd businessman looking to make an adequate return on investment. This was Laurence worrying how he would pay his mortgage and feed his family if he lost too much money supporting Bowie. I liked his songs and admired his being his own man, a pioneer and all that. The problem was that pioneers tend to get arrows up their arses, and financially it was my arse that was the potential target.

I was somewhat encouraged by David's reaction to a sign I had on my desk, which read: 'Art for art's sake – money for fuck's sake'. He picked it up and looked at it and I thought that he would disapprove, but he laughed and said, 'I like that, I'll bear it in mind.'

David only owed one more album to Philips records and his songwriting contract with Essex Music had expired in June of the previous year. Whilst he was signed to Essex Music, Geoff Heath – who ran the company for owner David Platz – brought David a song he had heard at Midem called *'Comme d'habitude'*. The song had been written and recorded by Claude François, a successful French pop star, who was tragically electrocuted at the age of thirty-nine when an electric heater fell into his bath. Bowie wrote new lyrics and called it 'Even a Fool Learns to Love.' It did not really work and eventually Paul Anka wrote new lyrics to the song, now called 'My Way', for Frank Sinatra. The song fitted his persona like a glove, but I personally think that whilst the sentiment is wonderful, the actual lyrics are embarrassingly contrived and I find listening to it quite painful. I don't think my view would bother Mr Anka or indeed the late Mr Sinatra. Incidentally, I feel much the same about 'Strangers In The Night', which to me sounds like a pastiche crooner's song written for a B-movie. Who doobee doobee knew? Certainly not me.

Now to the exciting bit … The end of David's publishing deal with Essex was a perfect time for a new manager to take over. David was by no means a star at this point in time but there was a slight buzz about him in the industry. I was a big fan of 'Space Oddity' and had heard 'The Man who Sold the World', another great song that was not about love.

Defries moved into my new offices at Regent Arcade House and on 1 August 1970 David signed a six-year recording agreement with Gem Productions. He also signed a management agreement under which Gem would take 20 per cent of his earnings. A very standard deal. Defries insisted that there was a key-man clause in the management agreement allowing Bowie to walk away if Defries were to leave Gem. I considered this to be perfectly reasonable, as it was Defries who had brought David in and Defries had no contract with Gem to give him security. However, no record company would accept a key-man clause for a recording agreement, so Gem signed David with no protection for Defries if his star ever walked away from me.

Gem also signed Dana Gillespie, a singer who was an ex-flame of Bowie and now a close friend of his and of Angie. Dana had starred in *Jesus Christ Superstar* and was, I thought, a very talented artist. She was at the heart of the Bowie crowd during the time that I was involved, and has been kind enough to recently meet with me and fill in some background information.

24. THE PLAN TO LAUNCH BOWIE

In 1970 the cornerstone of an artist's career was a record deal. The major companies provided the money to make records, had marketing departments to exploit them and the ability to distribute the physical recordings to record shops. Remember record shops? They were where teenagers would meet on Saturday mornings, crowding into little sound booths to listen to records through headphones.

Music is still the centre of most teenagers' lives but of course owning a record is not, which I think is sad because in the olden days, having a record collection was a big deal. The first album I ever bought was in 1956 when I was twenty. It was Frank Sinatra's *Songs for Swingin' Lovers!* and the cost was more than my weekly salary of about one pound. I made a label with my name on, which I carefully stuck to the album sleeve so that when I took it to a friend's house it would not be confused with their copy. All of my friends had a copy or they would not have been my friend.

I created space in the shelf above my bed for my record collection and it filled *very* slowly – it fact it never really filled at all. When I got married and moved my 'collection' to my marital home it was not very heavy. In a way, it was one of the few downsides of being successful in the music business that I was gifted almost any record that I wanted by the record companies. I even persuaded some of them to put me on their reviewers' list, sending me a copy of every release. The result was I gradually ceased to value having an album/CD in my personal collection and didn't even hold on to them all. If I had kept them for my home I would have had to live in a warehouse.

David Bowie's own record deal was with Mercury Records and it had expired. There was general interest in him from other record companies, but they were not exactly knocking on my door. My initial interest in David was as a songwriter and I was keen to develop this side of his career. Gordon Mills, who managed Tom Jones, was always looking for songs for the Welshman to record and – with no imminent record deal in sight – I sent him demos of some of David's songs, but he did not like them. In the meantime, Tony Defries was busy planning gigs to showcase David to record companies and was also dealing with ex-manager Ken Pitt's claims that David had breached his contract.

The Man who Sold the World was released in the UK by Philips Records in April 1970 and flopped. If anything was to establish David's casual approach to androgyny it was that album cover, dominated by a large image of a blond-wigged David Bowie lolling on a chaise longue wearing a dress designed by Michael Fish, a fashionable designer of the day. David's look on the album was frequently referred to as pre-Raphaelite, but now I find it more pre-Grayson Perry. The album was produced by Tony Visconti who, for whatever reason, did not work with David again until Defries was moving out of the picture in 1974.

The album was free for publishing and was about to be delivered to Mercury Records. This, together with the prospect of a deal with a new record company, strengthened our hand with any potential music publisher. Chris Wright of the highly successful Chrysalis Group had just started a new publishing company. Neither Chris nor his partner Terry Ellis knew much about publishing, and they had appointed Bob Grace, a young man with a good background in publishing, to run it. I knew Chris and Terry well, admired them very much and was confident that Chrysalis Publishing would be an active publisher and not just a banker, as many of the larger publishing companies had become. I called Chris to alert him that David would soon be recording a new album and we would be looking for a publishing deal. It is to be remembered that David was by no means a hot artist at this time. Chris was not particularly excited, but I persuaded him to arrange for Bob Grace to meet with us.

Tony Defries went to see Bob Grace and played him 'The Man Who Sold the World' and some of the unrecorded songs that David had written. Bob Grace was very interested. Nick Blackburn, Chrysalis's money-man, called me to talk a deal. Defries and I decided that we wanted five thousand pounds, and Chris was very much against paying such a substantial advance. He had never imagined giving such a hefty amount to an unproven songwriter but he was swayed by Bob Grace's enthusiasm. Under the terms of the deal that Defries cleverly negotiated in October 1970, once Chrysalis recouped the five-thousand-pound advance, half of the copyright would be assigned to Titanic Music, owned by Bowie, increasing his share of the income from the then standard 50/50 to 75/25 in his favour.

Titanic would not be party to Chrysalis's existing obligations to sub-publish with publishers around the world, for which it would have received substantial advances. Bob Grace was concerned that this was a ploy by Defries to allow Titanic to negotiate separate advances, which if true, was a move that he reluctantly agreed to even though he thought it was immoral. He later said that he was green and allowed Defries to push him into the agreement. Defies always maintained that the purpose of setting up Titanic was primarily to gain David an increased share of his copyright income, not to circumvent Chrysalis's existing contractual arrangements.

David could have been signed to Chrysalis Records then, but according to Chris's excellent autobiography, Terry Ellis did not like the material that David had written for *Hunky Dory*, and Kenny Bell, who ran the record company, thought that David would never make it as a live act. Nick Blackburn is now in the theatre business and I bump into him from time to time. He never fails to rib me about selling Bowie's publishing for a mere five thousand pounds. It is important to realise that in today's money that is about fifty thousand pounds, and Gem's 20 per cent commission at least made a small dent in the money I had laid out on Bowie. David now had four thousand pounds – about forty thousand pounds today – so was now less financially dependent on Gem, and there was now a company other than mine who could give support if needed. David's obligation to Chrysalis was to write a minimum of one hundred songs of which seventy must be commercially recorded.

Bob Grace, a good music man, worked closely with David and the singer had more faith in Bob's creative opinion than he did in that of Tony Defries or me. Bob sent David's song 'Oh! You Pretty Things' to Mickie Most, who recorded it with Peter Noone as his first solo record after parting with the Hermits. I kept well in the background for this, knowing that Mickie would not favour a song submitted to him that had my thumb-print anywhere near it. I subsequently learned that Bob tried to convince David that Defries and I were unproven managers and that David would be better off being managed by him. Fortu-nately, at that time, David had absolute faith in Tony Defries' guidance and resisted Bob's advances. I had sent David to Chrys-alis and it was wrong of Bob to do this, but having been guilty of similar actions myself it would be hypocritical of me to have held this against Bob. There's no business like show business.

Anya Wilson was now employed by me full-time as a record plugger, and she worked on the singles from the album released in the UK, but 'Memory of a Free Festival,' with Marc Bolan playing piano, and 'Holy Holy' weren't successful. 'Memory of a Free Festival' was seven minutes long, making it difficult to get airplay. Radio liked a three-minute single and we later always told stations, if asked, that the length of every song we submit-ted was always three minutes and twenty seconds – whatever the actual length. I even had 3'20" written on the sleeve of the acetate. I will tell you another little secret: A&R men at record compa-nies often felt they needed to contribute artistically and when presented with a record would often say things like, 'The bass needs remixing.' We always agreed with them and would then re-submit exactly the same version in a sleeve labelled 'remix', thanking the A&R guy for his input. It was important to make the record company feel some ownership of the creative process.

About this time, Anya brought a man called Jon Brewer in to see me. He and his partner Robert Patterson were managing a band called Czar whom I quite liked and I thought Jon, in particular, was bright and personable. They used to drive around in an old hearse that at some point was used by the Belgium royal family – presumably when one of the royals was past driving. They had had some experience of putting a band on the road, something that neither Defries nor I were familiar with. Jon's sister Liz, a socialite party planner/publicist, was a friend of Penny Leander, Mike's wife, so I knew that Jon was a 'real' person. As part of my 'Brill Building in London' ambition, I gave them an office on the understanding that they would offer me involvement in any acts that they signed and help out with Gem acts if needed.

I introduced Jon to Defries, and as I recall, he was indeed very helpful in this area. He booked some of David's early gigs and David enjoyed being driven around in the ornate hearse, and the two of them became quite close. Robert left the Brewer/Patterson partnership and Jon devoted a lot of time to helping Defries. He was never on the Gem payroll but has since told me that Defries had promised a financial interest in Bowie's gigs. Jon claims that he was never paid by Defries but he went on to manage Alvin Lee and Gerry Rafferty, so the Gem experience obviously helped him. He produced and published Rafferty's huge hit 'Baker Street', a smart move. Jon is now a maker of important documentaries on music legends, including B. B. King, Nat King Cole and Mick Ronson. Jon has been very helpful to me in filling in some details of his time working with David at Gem.

Mercury Records took David to America in February 1971 to promote *The Man who Sold the World* and it is my belief that, although it did not help record sales, it was an important episode in David's career. Starting in Washington, he toured major cities, frequently wearing one of his Mr Fish-designed dresses. The reactions of outrage from the more conservative press, DJs and public balanced the delight from the thinly scattered outré among them. David finished his tour in Los Angeles, an experience which I believe was pivotal to his career. He was hosted by Rodney Bingenheimer, who at the time was Mercury's main promoter in southern California. Rodney would become a great fan of David and helped promote his career when he later opened a trendy music venue on Sunset Strip in LA. Rodney borrowed a friend's Cadillac convertible and drove David on a tour of radio stations. To David's delight, he was refused entrance to an LA restaurant because he was wearing a dress. In 1973 Richard O'Brien's *The Rocky Horror Show*, about the sweet transvestite from Transylvania, was first staged and demonstrated yet again that the younger public was not disturbed by transgender entertainment. So much for my initial concern, when David first came to my office, that openly incorporating gay imagery could affect record sales.

In San Francisco he was asked to pick some songs to be played as a guest host on a local radio station. He was urged to pick a record by The Stooges, Iggy Pop's band. He had never heard of Iggy but learned that he was the idol of the 'in the know' music media for his outrageous behaviour as much as for his talent. This registered with David, himself no stranger to outrageous behaviour. David was then interviewed by *Rolling Stone*, the hugely influential music magazine. You will read later that it was this article that inspired a group of avant-garde American actors in a play about Andy Warhol to go to see the not-yet-famous David perform in London. They then introduced David to Andy Warhol in New York, resulting in David becoming a gay icon in the Big Apple, which was instrumental in his success.

As *The Man who Sold the World* did nothing in America, Mercury were clearly not passionate about having Bowie on their label and Defries brilliantly negotiated the transfer of the Mercury albums to Gem in return for repaying the cost. I took a deep breath, wrote a cheque for eighteen thousand dollars and the albums belonged to Gem. I subsequently recouped this when Gem licensed them to RCA as part of the deal for future Bowie product.

When he returned to London, David continued to write material for the album that would be *Hunky Dory*. The American trip definitely got his creative juices flowing and I thought that the material that he was writing for this album was just terrific. I particularly liked 'Changes', 'Life On Mars' and 'Kooks', the song he had written for his new baby son.

In June 1971, Defries and I agreed that we would make David's next record without record company finance. Obviously, this was a great risk for Gem, but this would enable us to make a beneficial new deal *if* the record was great when completed. David wanted Ken Scott, a well-respected recording engineer, to help him co-produce the album. I was a little nervous about this because, whilst Ken had engineered for The Beatles, Elton John and many others, he had not actually sat in the booth as a producer.

I will overcome my desire to bang on about Bowie not being an artist in demand at this time, but you must permit me to occasionally do so. The golden rule in business is 'he who provides the gold makes the rules.' Whilst I never berated Defries or David about my increasing financial exposure, they were very aware and appreciative of the artistic freedom that I allowed them. I had seen the magic that great producers like Mickie Most, Tony Macaulay and Mike Leander brought to a recording, but they were producing pop acts who did not write their own songs and were totally reliant on the taste of their producers to pick likely hits written by others. Bowie was an artist with a distinct view of how the songs that he wrote should be recorded. Tony Visconti would not return whilst Defries was around, so I agreed that Ken could co-produce with David. Ken has subsequently admitted that he was very nervous about stepping up from engineer to producer and that both he and David were both unsure that they could do the job, but the more they worked together, the more confident they became that they had done the right thing. They recorded at Trident Studios in Soho, the most in-demand studio in town because it was one of the few with an eight-track desk.

My relationship with David was very comfortable. We would chat about his business life, but I never attempted to socialise with him. I would not have felt at ease hanging out with the habitués of El Sombrero (a gay-friendly club called Yours Or Mine in Kensington High Street which had a sombrero above the door) or participating in the smorgasbord of drugs that were freely available. I did go to his flat in Bromley. He was very involved in the local arts scene and had starred in the Arts Lab at the nearby Beckenham Recreation Ground – a mini-Glastonbury of its time. Bowie's home reflected his interest in music and art. He and Angie had no money to spend on decor but it was furnished in a very quirky and eclectic style. They lived in the huge ground-floor flat of Haddon Hall, a large Victorian villa. Until their professional split, Tony Visconti and his girlfriend shared the flat with the Bowies. In later years, when Visconti was in partnership with my brother in Good Earth, he told Roger that both he and his girlfriend were terrified by the bewildering array of bedfellows that David and Angie invited to Haddon Hall. Gender seemed to have little to do with who did what to whom.

David and Angie once came to my flat in St John's Wood. Angie gave us a small, mirrored duck that was sort of fashionable at the time, which was very sweet of her. David politely expressed an interest how we had done out the place and I showed him around whilst Angie chatted with Marsha. We had only lived there for a few months and I was naturally proud of our new home. David did say all the right things but I could tell that had I rolled back his sleeve I would have heard the laughter. I did not take offence; he would never warm to the middle-class decor of our home, no matter how chic we thought it was.

David and Ken started recording at the beginning of July and were in and out of Trident until August. This was lengthy – I was used to producers like Mickie Most, who got a single and a B-side down in a three-hour session and usually only needed one more session to mix the tracks. But when I went to the studio I liked what I heard and I did not impose any budgetary restrictions.

David booked Rick Wakeman, the piano virtuoso, then a session

musician who would go on to be part of mega-band Yes. Although
Rick was a fabulous musician, David wanted Dudley Moore, the
film star who could easily have had a career as a pianist, to play
piano on 'Life On Mars'. This was a very commercial thought, but
Dudley did not respond to Gem's letter of invitation so the very
fine piano you hear on the final version is Rick's. Four of Dana
Gillespie's songs were recorded for her own album and she also did
a version of Bowie's 'Andy Warhol', but later told me she preferred
lyrics with emotion and her recording didn't work. David's own
take on it ended up on *Hunky Dory*. Dana didn't reach her potential at the time but later developed into a fine blues singer.

There was still little interest in David from record companies, although I was constantly in touch with the right people:
no one was asking me about Bowie. His gigs were sparsely
attended and I could tell from those I saw myself, in truth, that
he was not particularly exciting. This is hard to believe considering the dynamism of his stage act in later times, but in June
1971, after David played the second ever Glastonbury Festival,
he told his small audience, 'I don't do gigs any more because I
got so pissed off with working and dying a death every time I
worked.' His offstage, gentle manner did not really change when
he performed. David really exploded when he could hide behind
a character. Ziggy of course was the most dramatic and remains
the most iconic to this day. I firmly believe that had David not
been so brilliant at reinventing himself he would never have
achieved the almost god-like level of success that he did.

David's study of mime with Lindsay Kemp had taught him
how to put on a mime face and Angie was certainly a huge influence on David's look. It was, however, the brilliance of David to

actually inhabit Ziggy and his later alter egos and deliver the quality of music that enabled him to make such an impact on the world. I also believe that David Jones, the boy from Beckenham, invented a superstar identity called David Bowie who he could call on to be his face to the outside world.

In June, David and Mick Ronson played the first Glastonbury Festival organised by Michael Eavis on the fields of his farm. It was then, by contrast with the world-beating extravaganza it has become, an unambitious event with one stage, but it was still quite important and I was eager to know how it went for my artist. I had to wait until David and Defries came into the office the following day to learn how they had got on.

The pair, along with Angie, Bob Grace and Dana, took the train to the nearest station to the site. They walked to the farm for miles along country lanes. David was due to go on at 7.30 p.m. but the organisation was lacking and he only took the stage at 5.30 a.m, by which time it had poured with rain, creating the unavoidable sea of mud for which the festival is still famous. Understandably there was a very small audience, most of whom were wet and cold – but David and Mick went down well. I think that one of the highlights was when Defries tripped and went sprawling in the mud, David and Bob Grace giggling together like naughty schoolboys. More seriously, Defries told me on his return that he was sure Bob was trying to steal David away from us, which I did not doubt. Bob had been very involved with David's creative path and I am sure that he continued to stress how much more of a 'music man' he was. Jon Brewer has since told me that Bob Grace made a point of telling David that we were pursuing Stevie Wonder and would lose interest in David.

Defries complained vociferously to Terry Ellis that Bob was trying to create a rift between David and us. Terry called to assure me that Bob was just doing his job as David's music publisher. I expressed my doubts and reminded Terry of the law relating to 'incitement to breach a valid contract'. Later, when Terry and I became good business friends, he admitted that my reminder was timely. Five years later, when David's songwriting contract with Chrysalis was up, he did not renew. Under the original deal, Chrysalis retained 25 per cent of the copyright of the songs that David had written during the contractual term, so Chrysalis continued to enjoy a great income stream with no responsibility whatsoever. They took the chance, so good for them.

Having signed a publishing deal that required David to secure commercial recordings, it was now even more important to make a record deal. We needed something to attract some interest from major record companies. The new material that David was writing was exciting and David and Ken mixed down tracks for a Gem promotional/sample album, seven songs performed by Bowie and five Bowie-produced tracks of Dana Gillespie. This was a very unusual step to take and, at considerable cost, we pressed five hundred copies that are known to collectors as *BOWPROMO*. The album was presented in a gatefold sleeve that had a pocket in which we put selected reviews and interviews.

(A word about *Hunky Dory* test pressings and acetates. Research shows that the various acetates that Gem produced at the time are sometimes offered on eBay and other auction sites, fetching astoundingly high prices. A *BOWPROMO* was reportedly sold for ten thousand dollars. I no doubt had copies of them all cluttering up my office, which I would have thrown away when having the occasional tidy-up. Who knew? To add insult to injury, my son James recently gifted me with a replica copy of *BOWPROMO* that was released to mark Record Store Day in April 2017. It was a limited edition of fifteen thousand copies and my son paid fifty pounds for it. I have no idea how the releasing company got the rights to do this. It certainly was not from me. I should probably pursue them but I do not have the energy to take on issues that are not important to me. (It is, by the way, surprising how quickly old age happens.)

We started to line up record companies by sending them the sampler acetates. There was definitely antipathy in the UK. Bowie had created a high expectation with 'Space Oddity' and the failure of *The Man who Sold the World* meant that most record companies in the UK wrote him off as a one-hit wonder. But 'Space Oddity' had done nothing in the USA and it was decided that we should look there for a company to sign David, where hopefully he would have no 'previous' and could be judged on his new material. My New York attorney, Normand Kurtz, arranged August meetings for Defries with RCA, CBS, United Artists and Columbia. I set up a meeting for him with Bell Records. Being pop-orientated, they were not really the right label for Bowie, but because of the already successful deal that I had with Bell for Macaulay and Leander productions, I felt Defries should at least speak to them. The quality of the tracks on the sampler, coupled with Defries's unwavering faith in Bowie, attracted positive interest from everyone.

A few people recommended RCA. They had bought Elvis in 1955 from Sam Phillips, who had first signed him to his Sun Records, a tiny label in Memphis. Elvis had stayed with RCA and Defries was particularly impressed by the staying power because he admired the way Colonel Parker managed Elvis. David felt the same because even though Elvis was now recording some really crap songs amongst his classics, he was in the DNA of every UK artist who ever picked up a rock'n'roll guitar.

Dennis Katz was head of A&R at RCA and saw David Bowie as that weird transvestite guy who made 'Space Oddity', a record that had done well in the UK. He was a good A&R man and listened to the Gem sampler with care and without prejudice. Dennis enthused to Rocco Laginestra, head of RCA, who was not that taken with the material but supported Dennis. He had recently taken him on to find some interesting acts, and Bowie was nothing if not interesting. Rocco was aware that there was no desperation on the part of any other companies to sign David, and Mel Ilberman, his head of business affairs, was told to make a tough deal. He offered Gem $37,500 as an advance for each album and a royalty of 11 per cent of the retail price, excluding any taxes. Eight per cent would go to David, from which we would not deduct management commission, 1 per cent to producer Ken Scott and 2 per cent would be retained by Gem.

When the Rolling Stones signed to Andrew Oldham's company they were paid 6 per cent. Andrew Oldham used to deduct his management commission of 20 per cent, leaving the band about 5 per cent, which was shared between them. Reputedly, when The Beatles had signed to EMI a few years earlier, they were paid one old penny per single, also shared between them. Under my deal with David, he was paid about four pence per single. By any standards, David had a fair deal from Gem. No royalties were to be paid until RCA recouped its advances, which was a standard provision in all record deals.. It was a two-year deal for three albums, with options for RCA to extend with increased advances of $56,250 per album. David had committed to Gem for six years so I would be able to renegotiate with RCA after their term ended or negotiate a new deal with a different company. Clever me!

The advances were not high by RCA's usual standards, who were known to pay advances of a hundred thousand to two hundred thousand dollars for some American artists, but the royalty rates and lack of spurious deductions was fine, and David was keen to be with them. RCA also agreed to pay twenty thousand dollars for the Mercury albums that Gem now owned, approximately the amount Gem had paid for them. There was also an advance of $18,750, 50 per cent of the amount due on delivery of the next album (what would be *Ziggy Stardust*).

All in all, Gem would receive a cheque for around seventy-five thousand dollars from RCA. Aside from the advance on the next album, the money would go towards recouping my initial outlay on Bowie. True to my credo, the albums were to revert back to Gem five years after the deal ended.

About the time that *Hunky Dory* was finished, a play called *Pork* came from New York to London. It was based on conversations recorded by Andy Warhol in his New York studio, The Factory. The play was outrageous, and controversially pornographic. Andy Warhol was played by an actor called Tony Zanetta and the rest of the cast played other characters from Andy Warhol's Factory cabal. *Pork* played at The Roundhouse, a cool venue in funky Chalk Farm, north London, down from Haverstock Hill and The Country Club, where David was performing with Dana Gillespie.

One of the *Pork* company members had read the article in *Rolling Stone* magazine referring to David wearing a dress, so of course the entire company went to see him perform. It was love at first sight. David was invited to go to see *Pork* and a bond was established between all concerned. David and Angie went to see the play nearly every night but, despite the opportunity to see simulated masturbation on stage, I declined his offer to join them. David was hanging out with the *Pork* cast at El Sombrero most nights and he invited them to make themselves at home at my office in the day. Like-minded characters from the dark side or the enlightened side – depending on your point of view – seemed to be drawn to my offices, a corner of which became a mini-outpost of Andy Warhol's Factory.

25. STEVIE WONDER – AN INTERLUDE IN THE BOWIE STORY

One of the people who frequently appeared at the Gem offices in early 1971 was Don Hunter. I cannot remember how he came to us but he was there a lot. He produced a band called Milkwood that we had signed to Gem for management. Maybe he brought Milkwood to us, I don't remember. They did not have any great success, which is probably why I don't remember.

Don was an educated, rich, young white man from Minneapolis who had worked extensively in the studio with Stevie Wonder, co-writing and producing. I think that he was also employed by Berry Gordy, the head of Motown, to look after Stevie on the road in the UK. Don told us that, other than Diana Ross – who was Berry Gordy's great love – Motown treated their artists really badly. Don was very close to Stevie, who, according to him, was deeply unhappy and was thinking about leaving Motown and moving to England.

Stevie was part of a Motown revue that was touring the UK and was hankering after a state-of-the-art Sony music player, which unbelievably he could not afford to buy for himself. Don suggested that we buy it for him and he would bring him in to meet us and say thank you. In Don's opinion we could then start to woo Stevie for management. I thought that this was highly unlikely, but Defries had spent time with Don and assured me that they were really close.

We bought the gift and – to my great surprise – Don brought Stevie up to the office. Defries and I declared ourselves to be fans, which was not difficult because who wasn't? That first meeting was particularly memorable because Stevie felt our faces. He loved Defries's afro hair and we chatted about what we were doing. The fact that I had been involved with the Rolling Stones seemed to impress him and he left saying he would come and meet with us again. Don had obviously been selling us hard because Stevie did return. He told us he had made 'Fingertips', his first hit for Motown, in 1963, when he was about eight years old. Since then his hits included 'Uptight (Everything's Alright)', 'For Once in my Life' and 'My Cherie Amour'. He had done many tours but astonishingly he had no money, was living in a very modest house in Detroit and had no idea how much, if anything, he had coming to him in the future from the trust that Motown told him had been set up for him. He was twenty years old.

Stevie said that he wanted to get away from Motown and Berry Gordy and he felt that the only way he could do this was to move away from the USA. Don had told him that if he signed with us Don would move to London to look after him, and Stevie agreed. As much as I understood the logic behind Stevie's motives, I still did not believe that it would actually happen. I told him that I wanted him to call Berry Gordy there and then and tell him of his intentions. He made the call in private while

Defries, Don and I waited nervously. He came out of the room in tears. He told us that Berry had told him that he was like a son to him and he would never stand in his way, whatever he wanted to do.

I was still unsure and got *Music Week*, the bible of the UK music business, to run an article saying that Stevie Wonder was coming to live in London and was signing to Gem for management. I sat back waiting for a call from Motown's lawyers or a visit from two large gentlemen carrying baseball bats but there was no reaction whatsoever. There was no question, legally, that Stevie was free to leave Motown. He had been signed when he was blind and underage. He was going to be twenty-one in May and could disavow his Motown contracts with absolute certainty. First he would be touring the US and we made plans to take over his management on the day of his birthday. Defries sent Motown the appropriate paperwork, advising them of our plans and yet again there was no response. By the time it had gone out Stevie was in the middle of his tour and there were practical issues to deal with. We wanted to ensure continuity and put money into an American bank account so that there would be no problems when we took over.

Don recommended a Minneapolis-based lawyer to advise Stevie on the new contract, away from the gossip of New York or Los Angeles. The details were finalised and the contract had to be signed. Stevie told us that on his actual birthday he had been given a day off from the tour and was going home to Detroit for a big party organised by Syreeta, his wife. Lots of his friends from Motown would be there and he would feel uncomfortable if we were there too. We, of course, understood and flew to

Minneapolis on the day after his birthday to sign our copy of the contract. The lawyer was then going to meet with Stevie and get his thumbprint of approval.

Stevie, who had enjoyed his generous one-day-off, was back in New York, staying with his crew at The Hilton. We called the hotel and asked to be put through to the room in the assumed name under which he was registered. A voice, not Stevie's, answered abruptly. Stevie was not there. The phone was put down. Don had the room numbers of various crew who were staying at the hotel. He called them one by one and each put the phone down on him. We called Syreeta who said, 'I can't talk about it,' and she too put the phone down. It was obvious to me that Stevie had been 'got to' by Motown at his party the night before and Gem were no longer going to be managing Stevie Wonder. Defries and Don wanted to fly to New York but I was not going to incur any more expense in chasing what I knew was a lost cause. Sure enough, a few weeks later there was a full-page ad in *Billboard* magazine in Stevie Wonder's name stating, 'Motown is the place for me.'

Stevie had gone to Joe Vigoda, a legendary American music-business lawyer who was one of the great characters of his era. He looked like he was dressed by a charity shop and carried his office around in a beat-up old rucksack. He once gave me all of his contact phone numbers; homes and offices in Los Angeles, New York, and other places of interest around America. He took a full page of my Filofax (remember them?). I have no doubt Joe negotiated a fair deal for Stevie to stay with Motown, part of it being a reputed thirteen-million-dollar advance on signing. I'm sure that Joe also secured a bigger financial interest in Stevie's past success and a degree of ownership, which of course we could never do if we had taken him to Gem, a different company. I never really blamed Stevie for what he did, although because of him I missed seeing Arsenal winning the double, a very rare feat in football, and there was a very brief moment when I wished he'd go temporarily deaf, just in one ear.

Some months later, Normand Kurtz bumped into Joe Vigoda and complained to him how badly Stevie had behaved in his dealings with me. Joe said nothing, but a few days later he sent Normand a ten-thousand-dollar cheque for me, together with a brief message of apology on behalf of Stevie Wonder. Normand told Joe that I had spent a lot more than that in the pursuit of Mr Wonder, which was true, but Joe advised us to take the money and run, which I did.

Now that Stevie Wonder was no longer a diversion, all the focus was back on David Bowie. Before Gem was paid its seventy-five thousand dollars under the agreement with RCA, the masters of *Hunky Dory* had to be delivered to the record company and David had to sign an 'inducement letter' to RCA, confirming his formal agreement to his personal obligations under the Gem agreement. In September 1971 David and Angie, together with Mick Ronson, went to New York with Defries. We sent them all over first-class, something none of them had experienced, and on arrival RCA arranged for them to see Elvis Presley perform at Madison Square Garden. David was now beginning to feel like a star.

On 9 September in the RCA boardroom, the *Hunky Dory* master was formally delivered to Rocco Laginestra, the head of RCA. As was their style, David and Angie were both dressed similarly. Both had identical red hairstyles and there was a slight hitch when the RCA head of publicity thought that Angie was in fact David. That resolved, David signed his inducement letter and RCA handed Defries the cheque for seventy-five thousand dollars, made out to Gem. It was quite a moment in my business life and I rather wished that I could have been there myself. Defries called me as soon as he was out of Rocco's office to tell me that he had the cheque. It was obviously a great relief to me personally – in addition to covering recording costs, Gem paid David, Mick Ronson and the rest of the band weekly wages. Not only that, but so far not one of David's recordings had ever recouped its cost, and he was earning a pittance from personal appearances.

Tony Zanetta or 'Zee' as he was generally known, enthusiastically welcomed David and his party to New York. Zee took them to The Factory and introduced them all to Andy Warhol and Paul Morrissey, the film-maker who was closely associated with the artist. After the meeting, Defries called me to say that he thought we could get involved with the distribution of Warhol's films. In Defries's view, Warhol was not exploiting his commerciality and he was certain that he could help. In Zee's recollection of the meeting, Warhol gave Defries no reason to think that he was interested in any assistance.

After a dinner where David and Defries met Lou Reed, the crew went to Max's Kansas City, a New York club where they were introduced to Iggy Pop. The next morning Iggy was invited to breakfast with Defries and David, resulting in Defries soon signing Iggy, a proud heroin addict and general wild-man, as a Gem artist. The Warhol/Reed/Iggy/Bowie relationship was a forge that made David a major talking point within the

New York gay community, who were a very influential force in Manhattan's movers and groovers. It did him no harm at all in advancing his career.

Defries returned to London full of his fantastic trip to New York. He was convinced that we could manage Warhol and Lou Reed as well as Iggy. He brushed aside my concerns that we were taking on more than we could chew. He also became somewhat dismissive of other Gem artists. I became concerned about Defries' enormous belief in his ability to achieve world domination of the 'alternative' music business and began to think that I might not want to bring Defries into my company as a partner. When he first came to see me, I believed that he was hoping to attach himself to my rising star. Now just over a year later, he clearly thought that his personal comet had eclipsed me. We still had a warm relationship but I was wary of the change.

In November we all went to The Rainbow theatre to see Alice Cooper – maybe the first successful rock'n'roll artist to wear character make-up. The Rainbow was previously The Astoria cinema, just across the road from the Astoria Candy Stores – my parents' business, my home from the age of twelve to eighteen and now a very tacky dress shop. I explained to David that I used to live above it and I think he was surprised by my humble origins.

The Alice Cooper show was groundbreakingly great and spectacularly theatrical, but David promised that he could do better. He was already in the studios, recording tracks for the album to follow *Hunky Dory* and there was no doubt that he was influenced by his contact with Iggy, Lou Reed and the Warhol cabal.

Hunky Dory was released in the UK in December 1971. It had a Gem Productions logo on the back, which was dropped without my permission in later pressings and on the CD. I could have taken legal proceedings but it did not seem important to me at the time. My kids, now grown up, have copies of the original, which is enough for me. I have the gold disc that was presented for sales of a hundred thousand copies. I also have a gold disc for the *The Rise and Fall of Ziggy Stardust and the Spiders from Mars*, which was also a Gem production. I have three children and, unfortunately, only two Bowie discs to leave them, so to be fair I will have to work out how many New Seekers, Donna Summer and Heatwave gold discs equal one Bowie. I also have Gary Glitter gold discs, but suspect these would probably be a minus in the equation.

Hunky Dory did not do well on its initial release, selling barely two thousand copies in the first month. RCA London boss Ken Glancy was very concerned at the amount of money being spent on the promotion of the album at the insistence of Defries. To everybody's relief, it had a surge in sales after the release of *Ziggy Stardust*, accumulating sales of three hundred thousand. *Hunky Dory* did get great reviews in the music press and was widely acclaimed by the industry.

Choosing the first single off the album was important and – in a rare nod towards my success at having selected hit singles for other artists in the past – I was asked to choose a track. 'Life On Mars' was clearly a masterpiece but I was concerned it did not have the instant appeal to producers of radio, especially BBC Radio 1, the station that was then vital for exposure to the pop-buying public. I settled on 'Changes', which I thought better fitted the radio-play requirements, and 'Life On Mars' would be the second single. 'Changes' did not make the Top 40 … so much for my reputation as a pop picker.

The album definitely created a Bowie buzz, and the material that David was writing for *Ziggy* excited us all. The relative failure of *Hunky Dory* was a disappointment against that but was not a major setback for me personally. Tony Macaulay was producing hits for Johnny Johnson and Mike Leander was in the studio producing albums for David Essex and Marianne Faithfull, so I was fully occupied on positive projects.

In January 1972, Michael Watts – an important music journalist – came to Gem to interview David for the *Melody Maker*. This was quite a serious weekly paper and I remember standing in the Gem reception afterwards with David, who told me that he had just come out to the writer. He reminded me about my initial concern that being openly gay could affect his popularity with female fans, laughed and said, 'Laurence – we're about to find out.' David's announcement was no great shock, bearing in mind his penchant for wearing dresses and his general lifestyle, but it was hailed as a statement of pride by the gay community and many gay men who were not particularly aware of his music became instant fans. In some quarters, his coming out was seen as a publicity stunt. David had a big UK tour coming up and there is no doubt that the article was a huge help.

Shortly after the article appeared, a letter came to the office. It was in a brown envelope marked On Her Majesty's Service (OHMS), presumably from the taxman, so it came to my desk. It was in fact from a gay man who described in great detail what he would like to do to David and what he would like David to do to him. I still blush at the thought of it. The remarkable thing is that the sender continued sending letters in similar OHMS-marked envelopes almost every day for some months, presumably all written in working hours ... and we wonder why the UK has a trade deficit.

I took Marsha to see David playing in Aylesbury that same month. He still showed no confidence on stage and was frankly disappointing. I remember saying he needed someone to help him create a stage act. A couple of weeks later he played the Imperial College in London. The gigs were chalk-and-cheese – he had now really got into his Ziggy character. He was in front of a small, studenty crowd but I remember 'Suffragette City' bringing them to their feet. I had taken the whole office along to support David. Paul Gadd – soon to be Gary Glitter – came with Mike Leander. After the show we all offered David our congratulations. David was patronising to Paul, which upset me a little at the time.

By now Defries' spending – of Gem's money – was getting totally out of hand. He always insisted on having a large amount of cash on his person so that he could be magnanimous to David and other artists (albeit with my money). At Gem's expense, people were flying back and forth across the Atlantic, studios were being hired and musicians employed. Gem was like an avant-garde musicians' benefits office and, having investigated the profligacy of The Beatles' Apple Corp in my previous life, I clearly had to get my own house in order. Any concerns that I expressed to Defries were met with a shrug and, 'I'm building us the biggest artist roster in the world, Laurence.' My problem was finding the time to properly address this issue. Apart from work-ing with Leander and Macaulay, I was starting to put together

Arcade Records, the compilation company that would become the most profitable business venture I ever undertook.

One of the most important and interesting of Defries' signings was Iggy Pop. David was keen to work with Iggy, who arrived in London in February to collaborate on David's new album. We initially put him up at The Royal Garden hotel in Kensington. Iggy did not like the poshness and I was not mad about the cost. My tiny house in St John's Wood was currently unoccupied as we had recently moved. I foolishly agreed that Iggy and his guitarist James Williamson could move into the house for the rest of their stay. 'What a stupid thing to do,' I hear you say, and you are right, but it seemed like a good idea at the time. Iggy was very charming when I took him to the house – no sign of the wild-man of rock who appeared on stage – and he thanked me most politely for allowing him to stay in my house. He repaid me by leaving burn marks on our carpet where he had made little fires, no doubt to warm spoons for eating soup.

The Rise and Fall of Ziggy Stardust and the Spiders from Mars, to give it its proper title, was produced by David and Ken Scott, and was released in the UK in June of 1972. The album artwork featuring David, dressed in a stunning jumpsuit, was brilliantly photographed by Brian Ward on a rainy night in Heddon Street, a cul-de-sac off Regent Street. It's now full of trendy restaurants, but in 1972 it was something of a seedy backwater where Brian could work undisturbed. Such is the importance of the album, there is now a plaque on the wall where the photograph was taken.

The album was immediately a success in the UK, selling eight thousand copies in the first week and peaking at UK No. 5. The music press had enormous goodwill towards David. They wanted him to produce a great album and *Ziggy Stardust* did the job. The alien had landed and had conquered the world.

It is important to acknowledge the contribution that Mick Ronson made to Bowie's music, not just as one of the Spiders from Mars, but as a general contributor. He was not only a great guitarist who gave Bowie's recordings a distinct sound, he was a brilliant arranger and producer who should have received much more formal credit for his work. Mick was quite an enigma. Very much a salt-of-the-earth northern lad, he was inclined to stand up when I – the guv'nor – entered the room. Classically trained from childhood to play piano and violin, he wanted to be a cellist until, influenced by the distinctive sound of guitar virtuoso Duane Eddy, he switched to guitar. From 1963 he played with a variety of bands in the Hull area, while working as a gardener for the Hull City parks department between gigs. He did a lot of session work and toured briefly with Van Morrison, Bob Dylan and others. In 1970, he joined David as a member of his backing band, The Hype, and was a huge influence on David's music until he left him in 1973 to pursue a solo career.

Mick's arrangements included the lovely string arrangement on 'Life On Mars'. He was also, of course, part of the controversy when David famously simulated fellatio on his guitar on the tour to promote the *Ziggy* album – something that Mick was not happy about. But he was unquestionably one of the great guitarists of his era. He was a thoroughly nice bloke and I was deeply moved when I heard of his death from cancer, aged forty-six, in 1993. Mick was something of an unsung hero and I was happy to contribute to *Beside Bowie: The Mick Ronson Story*, Jon Brewer's excellent film.

Based on the success of the album I had bought a twenty-two-foot motorboat, which I named *Ziggy Stardust*. I thanked David for his 'gift' and he urged me to commission a paint job by George Underwood, a childhood friend and one-time fellow band member. It was hardly a practical idea, and the boat would never have lasted until now, but I sometimes wonder what a boat painted by George – now a successful artist – would be worth these days.

Success was a double-edged sword. On one hand I was delighted that the expectation and hype that had surrounded David had at last come to fruition and that I no longer needed to be concerned about my financial exposure. The downside was that Defries, vindicated in his belief of Bowie's stardom, was paying less and less attention to my advice to concentrate on our other artists. He was now trying to get more deeply involved with Iggy, Mott the Hoople, Lou Reed and various other artists within that circle. David sat on my office floor playing 'All The Young Dudes' for Ian Hunter, the lead singer of Mott. Ian loved it and David produced the single and the following album. With my approval, Tony Defries signed Mott the Hoople to Gem.

My offices were now a home from home for a motley collection of musicians – now including Mott the Hoople – outré hangers-on and arguably weirdos, who sucked up so much of the oxygen of Gem that the other occupants – including me – were made to feel like background characters. I had no wish to fall out with Defries, but clearly I had to make some changes. I had promised him 20 per cent of the company 'if things worked out well' and at some level things had worked out very well indeed, but it was clear that if I did not change my relationship things could work out very badly.

There was no question that if David was to be a worldwide star he had to conquer America. America had by far the biggest market for music. As a generalisation, a US hit sold more than five times as much as a UK hit, and a successful US tour could make ten times as much as a UK tour. Through his marriage to Angie, a US citizen, David was allowed to work in America and it made sense for him to physically establish a base there. Defries was completely in love with the New York scene and had been nagging me to open a Gem office in New York, which he would run. I was unable to contain his extravagance when he was in an office five yards from where I sat, so clearly my chances would not improve if he were three thousand miles away. I was also very much aware that once he was that far away – human nature being what it is – at some point Defries would start to resent being a 'junior partner' and things could well become nasty. I had been increasingly convinced that I could not live with Tony Defries as a partner in my company and the timing of his wish to move to New York suited me very well.

The Defries coterie of artists was still in deficit to Gem. Pay attention to this next bit because it introduces irony into my story. I did not keep copies of my old Gem accountings – who knew? – but Kevin Cann's book *Any Day Now* sets out some very specific balances of Defries-signed artists from around 1972:

Bowie's deficit: £29,062.

Mott the Hoople's surplus: £2,603

Iggy Pop's deficit: £5,767

Dana Gillespie's deficit: about £2,000

I called Kevin Cann and asked him how on earth he had come by this information. He told me that he had been given copies of accountings by Peter Gillman, who with his wife wrote *Alias David Bowie* in 1986. I called Peter who told me that he had been given some files by the widow of Peter Gerber, who was my internal accountant until he was seduced away by Defries. So essentially, the information that I have set out above was generated in the seventies by a member of my staff, passed on to Peter Gillman for the book he published in 1986, and passed on to Kevin Cann for the book he wrote in 2010. I was upset at the time that Defries had approached Peter to work for him without asking me if I minded, but on the other hand – and there is often another hand – I thought that Peter would protect my future interest, so I did not make an issue of Tony's poor behaviour.

Having decided to change my arrangement with Defries, we had to agree a 'divorce' deal. If it came to a fight, in the left-hand corner was David Bowie's contract with Gem, which provided that if Defries left Gem, David could walk away. But – big *but* – in the right-hand corner we had David's obligation to RCA, which was through the recording contract that he had signed with Gem. Even if Gem lost David for management, it would still own his recording services and most importantly, the Gem/RCA contract provided that outright ownership of the albums reverted to Gem five years after the contract ended. Gem would win. Happily, Defries acknowledged my contribution to his position at that time and there was no fight.

Defries had decided to go it alone under the name Main-Man. There was to be a MainMan London and MainMan New York. He had no money so I loaned him forty thousand dollars to finance his New York operation. Gem assigned to MainMan all the rights and benefits that it owned in David and the other artists brought in by Defries. Gem would receive all outstanding amounts due plus 20 per cent of the gross income from all of David's earnings for five years. After the deal was agreed, Defries asked if there was a point at which I would be satisfied to give up my financial interest in David's gross income. Without giving it too much thought I said that if he repaid the loan and paid the deficits on the assigned artists account, plus – a big *plus* – five hundred thousand pounds within eighteen months, I would then give up any future interest. Before you conclude that I was a schmuck to make this deal, a few points in mitigation:

1. Five hundred thousand pounds was an enormous sum of money then and approximately five million pounds in today's terms.
2. David would have to generate two-and-a-half million pounds in eighteen months for me to get five hundred thousand at my rate of 20 per cent, which at the time seemed very unlikely.
3. With the benefit of hindsight, I should have insisted on keeping a 5 or 10 per cent interest in David's future, which I am sure would not have affected the amount I was to get under the deal that I had agreed. It would probably have earned me another five million over the years. Who knew?
4. Read on and I will tell you how I pissed away most of the five hundred thousand pounds opening and running an office in Los Angeles.

Defries now had to make his own deal with David. He had often expressed his admiration for the Colonel Parker/Presley concept

of a 50/50 partnership between manager and artist and he told
me that this is how he intended to operate with David. The
Colonel only had Presley, so I could see how this might work but
I questioned how it could work when you had an office looking
after multiple clients. This was answered with a typical Defries
don't-you-worry shrug. It was no longer going to be my any of
my business, so I did not worry. We will get to the actual deal
that David might have signed with MainMan in Tony Zanetta's recollection of the crisis meeting that he had with David in
1974, a full account of which is set out a little later in this book.

David, who of course desperately wanted a career move to
America, was delighted that I was facilitating Defries' opening
of a New York office. He and Angie came to express their appreciation of all that I had done to help them in the past and what
I was now doing to help David's future.

In August 1972, Defries moved from Gem to a home/office
in Gunter Grove – between Fulham and Chelsea and an almost
fashionable part of London – to plan the American venture. I
felt good about the departure of the Bowie circus. Everybody in
my office clearly felt that I now had more time to spend with
them and the general atmosphere was more 'one family'.

MainMan's New York offices opened on East 58th Street,
with Tony Zanetta, the actor Defries had first met the year before
in *Pork* at the Roundhouse, running the company. Dana Gillespie
also went to New York with Bowie and both she and Zanetta
tell how Defries hit the ground running. He now had what he
wanted – a stable of talented artists who had complete faith in
his apparent Svengali-like ability to progress their careers. He no
longer had an obligation to answer to me and his business ethos

of 'live like a star to be a star' flourished unchecked. This philosophy was not confined to MainMan's artists. Defries obviously believed in leading by example, with cigars flown in from Cuba and general profligacy. His twenty-six employees were allowed to charge any expense they chose to the company account, including – I've been told – cosmetic dental work and plastic surgery. According to Zanetta all, even maids and chauffeurs, had the use of a fourteen-room suite of offices in uptown Manhattan, an Upper East Side penthouse, a duplex on East 58th Street, an apartment at The Sherry-Netherland hotel and a loft on Lower West Side (now part of the trendy Tribeca area). There were also four apartments for the use of clients. Defries lived in a twenty-six-room estate in Connecticut where his customised Cadillac limousine was available to him twenty-four hours a day.

Tony Zanetta told me that David was surprised by the extravagance of the MainMan offices when he arrived in early 1974, but he had complete confidence in Defries' judgement and went along with the set-up. Tony ensconced David in a suite at the very chic and very expensive Sherry-Netherland, which is as nice a place as any to go along with anything. When David toured America, Defries made sure he enjoyed a similar level of high-profile luxury. For instance, most bands when in Los Angeles stayed at The Sunset Marquee, a reasonably priced rock'n'roll hotel, but David and his entourage stayed at the five-star Beverly Hills hotel, very much the haunt of A-list movie stars. I must confess that in later years I often stayed there myself. There is something about breakfasting with Paul Newman and Dean Martin at nearby tables to add a frisson to one's morning – but I was paying the bill with my own money.

Within months the Defries/Bowie honeymoon was over. The catalyst was the Diamond Dogs Tour. Defries authorised a highly-paid West End/Broadway design team to create an amazing set without budgetary restrictions. This of course is like setting kids free in a candy store. The design team created a set that cost four hundred thousand dollars and took thirty men a full day to erect. Madness for a touring set. The rehearsal was a shambles and the tour was a nightmare for the crew. During a break, David would go off to record *Young Americans* with soul and R&B musicians, where he was to catch a bit of roots soul, and decide that he should present himself in a back-to-basics way. He would then dump the set without reference to Defries.

MainMan had debts piling up. Defries lost three hundred thousand dollars producing *Fame*, a play about Marilyn Monroe, which came off after one night on Broadway. The UK bank account was overdrawn and debts were piling up on both sides of the Atlantic. Peter Gerber resigned from MainMan, unable to cope with Defries' cavalier attitude to pressing creditors. Peter died suddenly a few years later from a heart attack. He was in his thirties. At his wife's request, I spoke at his funeral, which Defries did not attend.

Back at the beginning of the Diamond Dogs Tour, Angie had flown to New York, and was summoned by Defries to his penthouse to explain how she had spent a hundred thousand dollars in a year on travel, limos and hotels. He told her to stop and that she must no longer meddle in business affairs. David then summoned Tony Zanetta to his suite at The Sherry-Netherland hotel, furious with Defries for his treatment of Angie.

Henry Edwards related Tony Zanetta's recollection of the meeting in their book *Stardust – The David Bowie Story*. It is quite a long extract, but it is a major event in David Bowie's career. I was not there, but Tony Zanetta was. It happened to him, and I think that his recounting brings it to life. I am most grateful to have received Tony's permission to use it.

David finally came into the living room, dressed in a kimono. Angie snuggled up next to him on the couch. She looked adoringly at him and stroked his hand. The roles they had elected to play with each other that evening were man of the house and loving wife.

David emptied a vial of cocaine onto a mirror and chopped it into lines. Using a hundred-dollar bill, he snorted a line or two. He enjoyed the drug-taking ritual, chopping the cocaine and deciding how big each line should be. He especially liked the fact that he controlled the stash and could decide if and when to offer Zanetta a line. Angela neither took drugs not drank. The cocaine binge between David and Zanetta would last fifteen hours.

Even when he was relaxing, David had an agenda; there was always a scenario, a script to act out, with David triumphant at the third-act curtain. Looking back at that meeting, Zanetta realises that Bowie had several intentions. He wanted first-hand confirmation from an eyewitness of what he had been told was going on in the MainMan offices. He was also engaged in a subtle but deadly war with Defries. Now David wanted to win Defries's right-hand man over to his side; he wanted Zanetta to work for him and not Defries.

'Every day I wake up to face a nightmare,' David began, 'a nightmare I don't understand. I once had a dream, and Tony had that dream. It's a dream we shared.'

He looked knowingly at Zanetta. His dream automatically was everyone's dream, his quest a mission shared by all who knew and loved him.

'But I had to do my part,' he continued. 'I had to create; I had to do my work. I've done my part, haven't I? I've upheld my end of the bargain. I don't understand why he has done this.'

Overcome with confusion, he paused. 'Is this the time to abandon me?' he finally asked. 'Is this the time to abandon the dream? This is the moment that is supposed to be triumphant.' It was impossible not to believe along with him that he was a victim of a colossal betrayal.

'Z, I don't have a dollar in my pocket,' he said incredulously. 'It's ridiculous, laughable, a bloody nightmare. When Tony spoke to Angie like that he was meddling in my personal life,' David declared. 'I don't advise him on the subject of Melanie's [Defries' wife] spending. Where does he come off telling Angie how to spend her money? He's crossed his boundaries with that one. He's in charge of my business, not my personal life or my work. All I know is I don't have the money to give Angie to spend while he has all the money in the world to give to Melanie.'

Angela looked lovingly at her champion. 'I was never so insulted in all my life,' she said sadly. 'He really hurt me.' They cuddled up to each other. They looked so childlike and wounded they could have been posing for an orphanage poster.

Although they slept in separate bedrooms Angela and David had enormous loyalty, neither tolerating criticism of the other.

In the proper mood they could give stunning performances of husband and wife. They acted the roles so well they convinced not only everyone around them but also themselves that they were deeply in love.

'I can't get through to Tony on the phone. I can't see him. He doesn't have time for me or my career. He's too busy getting the price of gold, too busy worrying about how many nights I'm going to play and counting heads. Everything, everything, has a dollar sign on it. It's diabolical!'

There was a pause. He stared at Zanetta. 'Z, I feel very alone. I feel totally defenceless.'

Zanetta was touched by David's surprising display of emotion. He replied, 'I'm willing to do anything I can to help. I can talk to Tony for you.'

'You're the only one I can rely on. You're the only one in that office I can trust, whom I can expect to give me answers about what's going on. I'm financially dependent on Tony. I have no idea what I've got, I don't know what I'm worth. I don't know who's paying for everything. Where's the money coming from for all the projects? Who's paying for the Wayne County film? Who's paying for the Broadway production of Fame? Who's paying for Mick Ronson's campaign? Who's paying for Dana's campaign? Who's paying for the billboards? Half of this company is mine, but I have no say in anything. I don't know what's going out, I don't know what's coming in.'

'David,' Zanetta said, 'your deal is no secret. You are to receive 50 per cent of the profits – after your expenses are deducted – of the monies generated by you and you alone. You own no portion of MainMan. MainMan belongs exclusively to Tony.'

It was as if David had erected a soundproof booth around himself. His look grew determined, and he jutted out his jaw. 'I don't understand,' he said. 'Tony and I are partners, our agreement has always been 50/50.'

'You own 50 per cent of your income after all expenses are deducted. Tony is under no obligation to pay you anything other than your salary and to support you, your family, and your staff. The money you generate is MainMan income, not Bowie income. It remains MainMan income until Tony decides to distribute it. You have given him permission to use this money to develop other acts and to build MainMan. All your money goes to him, and he has total control over it. You have never had any control over your money.'

'I own 50 per cent of MainMan.'

'That's not your agreement. You own no portion of MainMan.'

'I know I own 50 per cent of the company.' Nothing could make him change his mind.

'Surely you always knew what your deal with Tony was?' said Zanetta.

David looked confused. To admit that he had not known the truth was to admit that he had behaved irresponsibly, to admit that he was less than perfect. 'I never understood it,' he said stubbornly. 'I know I own 50 per cent of MainMan.'

Once again Zanetta told him the exact terms of his deal. 'David, it's the deal you made. You could always have renegotiated it; you can still renegotiate it.'

'I own 50 per cent of MainMan, I know I do.'

'If you think Tony's cheating you, hire an accountant and audit his books. See where the money is going. Decide which expenses you think are legitimate.' Zanetta was talking to a wall. David stared silently into space. 'If you have suspicions about anything, hire a lawyer and conduct a full investigation,' urged Zanetta.

Bowie didn't want lawyers and accountants. He wanted to maintain his fantasy that Tony had become involved with him out of love and a belief in his talent, not as part of his empire-building.

It was almost dawn but the cocaine had filled David with speedy energy.

Angela curled up on David's lap and fell asleep.

Later, while Angela dozed, the two men watched the sun rise over Manhattan. Everything seemed peaceful and happy for a few moments. Then David again became crestfallen. 'How did it come to this?' he asked quietly. 'Why did it come to this? It shouldn't have. You know it shouldn't have. I don't understand any of it.'

I met with Angie in May 2017 whilst doing research for this book. She had been invited to London by the filmmaker Jon Brewer to help promote *Beside Bowie*, his film about Mick Ronson. Our meeting was interesting. She is no less of a force of nature than she was when I first met her almost fifty years ago. Angie was born in Cyprus to American parents. She was well educated in Cyprus, Switzerland and England and then went to Connecticut college where she was expelled for having an affair with someone of her own sex. She was, by her own admission, brash and opinionated. She now lives in Atlanta with a long-term partner – male! In some quarters she has been exclusively cast as a bad influence in David's life, which I think is unfair. I have no view of who was 'the bad guy' in their personal relationship, and by conventional standards I think Freud might have given up psychiatry had he taken the case. But I firmly believe that she was extremely important in prompting David to make the initial breakthrough from talented musical artist to chameleon-like, world-famous icon. He was a low-energy individual and she provided high energy for them both.

I first asked Angie why it took so long for David to actually take any action against Defries. The relevant meeting with Tony Zanetta was in the summer of 1974 and it took six months before David instructed his attorney Michael Lippman to start any proceedings. She told me that David was on tour, doing a lot of cocaine and it was a big decision, requiring careful thought. Apparently, John Lennon and Mick Jagger had both advised him that no managers were to be trusted.

Angie told me that Defries was determined to get rid of her as soon as he felt he had a hold on David. Corinne Schwab – Coco – a MainMan employee who had become David's assistant, was also a great influence and was also determined that Angie should go. Coco became David's fiercely loyal gatekeeper for many years. Angie physically split from David around 1977, although they were not divorced until February 1980. By then she was in Switzerland and Angie told me that she was not given enough to live on and was deprived of any relationship with her son Zowie (now Duncan Jones). I asked her if she was proud of his success as a film director. 'Good for him,' she said, 'but David poisoned him against me, and I have not seen him for forty years. I don't know him so it gives me no thrill.' Tony

Zanetta later told me that Duncan, who had been sent by David to be educated in Switzerland, used to visit Angie in school holidays until he was about thirteen. Angie was still very much living a rock'n'roll lifestyle and, in Tony's view, Duncan was not comfortable staying with her. David sent him to be educated at Gordonstoun, the Scottish school attended by the Duke of Edinburgh and Prince Charles, from which time Angie and her son were totally estranged.

Angie told me of the sexual merry-go-round of her circle in the early seventies. David was certainly a busy boy. He had 'fucked countless women, and there were also many men,' said Angie. David had 'fucked Corinne once, to make her feel good'. She said that Defries and Dana Gillespie were also, at some point having sex. Defries had married Melanie, who had met him via Rodney Bingenheimer. Angie said of Defries and Melanie, 'I fucked them both. Well ... not fucked, but ... you know?' In truth I did not know, but nodded, not wishing her to think that I was naive – which in this area I was and am. A middle-class background and the leftover sixties' hippy trippy/free love/do-your-own-thing/let-it-all-hang-out lifestyle had passed me by. She actually said that she had always admired me for being 'the most honest man she had ever known in the music business, with a wife and family that gave stability'. She also said that when the MainMan carnival moved to America she missed my steadying influence, and told David so. She may have just been telling me what I would like to hear, but I liked to hear it, so that's OK.

I did not meet David again until 1975. I had received a call from Mel Ilberman of RCA Records, whom I liked very much.

'Where there's a hit, there's a writ' was manifesting itself in a tsunami of litigation. In addition to the bitter fight between David and Defries, Defries and RCA were also actively engaged in litigation. Following the fallout with Defries, David was trying to get RCA to deal with him directly. Record companies invariably support artists who are in a fight with their manager as, invariably, managers can't sing. In this case, Mel would have been delighted to bypass Defries, but the manager had a powerful legal position which complicated the situation. There seemed to be no hope of David releasing a new album until the legal issues were resolved, a stalemate which could have gone on for years.

This would have been a problem. No matter how big the artist, if the fans' interest is not maintained with a new album there is a danger that they can eventually be forgotten. It genuinely concerned me that David's career would be harmed if this logjam was not resolved. I no longer had any financial interest in David, having happily banked my half-a-million-pound pay-off at the end of 1974, but I had started my relationship with David in 1970 because I was a fan, and I still was.

Even though there were things about Tony Defries' conduct that had upset me, I had maintained a cordial relationship. I knew Michael Lippman, David's new attorney/manager, so I was in a unique position to calm things down. I told Mel that if RCA would host a 'peace conference', I would do my best to get the warring parties together. Negotiations followed that made organising a Middle East summit look like a doddle, but eventually RCA took a huge suite at The Century Plaza hotel in Los Angeles. The Defries camp had a room, the David camp had a room, and RCA and I had a room, the neutral ground, where we met. It had a living area that looked like a forerunner of an IKEA show-room. The two warring parties sat on sofas at either end of the room, which could easily have accommodated five-a-side football. If I'd have had a whistle I would have blown it to start the game.

The essence of my referee's instructions was something like this: 'If you carry on fighting you are going to make some lawyers a lot richer and yourselves a lot poorer. You two have made me a lot of money and it concerns me that you are both wasting time, money and energy fucking up David's career. I have no financial interest in the outcome of this meeting. Both of you have to be prepared to give a little and both of you have to want to resolve the issues. I do not wish to act as any sort of mediator and will not be present during your discussions.'

They agreed to talk and I went and hid in the RCA room with Mel Ilberman. After a long time Michael Lippman came in to see me, looking a little shamefaced. 'I am very embarrassed but David insists that I ask you to sign a piece of paper confirming that you have no financial interest in Defries' affairs any more.'

I was furious, and replied, 'Tell David to go fuck himself.'

I am pretty sure that Michael did not pass on my specific choice of language, as on the few occasions I subsequently ran into David he was his usual polite self. But as Oscar Wilde once famously said, 'No good deed goes unpunished' and in later years when I wanted to get David involved in some theatre projects, my approaches were ignored. Maybe he *was* told of my suggestion to 'go fuck himself' and was returning the compliment.

As I recall, the peace and reconciliation meeting came to a premature end when Mel Ilberman received a call to say that Defries' lawyers had just served another formal notice on RCA, pursuant to his general campaign, that they were not to deal with David's recordings other than through MainMan. But dialogue had, however, begun between David, via Lippman, and Defries, and eventually a very long and detailed settlement agreement was signed giving MainMan a substantial interest in Bowie's future earnings and granting them joint ownership of his album masters (full details of the agreement are set out in the Gillmans' *Alias David Bowie*). The agreement was far-reaching and in 1997 – more than twenty years after their split – Defries was still profiting hugely from David's work.

It was also in 1997 that the star raised fifty-five million dollars – not a misprint; fifty-five million dollars – by issuing 'Bowie bonds'. Put simply, these were loan notes paying 7.9 per cent interest, maturing after fifteen years, secured on his future earnings from his albums. As Defries was half-owner of the masters, David would have needed his cooperation and he presumably received half of the full amount raised, to buy out his interest. Under my Gem deal with RCA, the masters were to revert to my company and that benefit I passed on to MainMan for a lousy half a million pounds. Who knew?

Tony Zanetta told me that the MainMan offices were closed in 1975 and he and many others felt cast adrift. It seemed that he had never had a proper salary working for Tony. He had his rent and credit card paid by Mainman, and was given a few dollars walking-around money. The same had applied to the Spiders' Mick Ronson, bass guitarist Trevor Bolder and drummer Woody Woodmansey.

After a hugely successful tour playing sixty-one venues in seven weeks, the final date was at London's Hammersmith

Odeon in July 1973. Just before they finished with 'Rock'n'Roll Suicide' in front of a star-studded audience, including Mick and Bianca Jagger, Paul and Linda McCartney, Lou Reed, Keith Moon, Barbra Streisand and me, David made an announcement that shocked the audience. 'Not only is this the last show of the tour, it is the last show we will ever do.' The band was over. Woody and Trevor had no idea that they were now out of work. Even Mick Ronson was only told earlier in the day. Like Tony Zanetta in New York, the three Spiders From Mars had never been paid a proper salary. Their expenses were covered generously: Mick was given fifty pounds a week and Trevor and Woody were each given thirty pounds a week. Mike Garson, the American jazz pianist who had been brought in for the tour was paid eight hundred dollars a week, more than the rest of the band put together. After the tour David was taking time off from recording so Mick was also going to be out of work. Defries took Ronson on as a solo artist, but according to Suzanne, Mick's then wife, they didn't have any money until Mick produced the *Your Arsenal* album for Morrissey.

After the Century Plaza un-peace talks, I next met David at the Cannes Film Festival in 1978. David Hemmings was there with David, promoting *Just A Gigolo*. Marsha and I had met David and Prue Hemmings in the summer of 1977, through Mike and Penny Leander. This was when we had been due to go and stay with the Leanders in La Barracca, their villa in Majorca. On arrival, they told us that their house was not completed and we were to stay with David and Prue, who had rented a large house not far away. We had met the Hemmings socially a few times, but were hardly proper friends. The Leanders had not told us of this switch in accommodation until we arrived, because obviously we would not have wished to impose ourselves on people that we hardly knew.

David Hemmings came to prominence as an actor in Antonioni's *Blow-Up*, one of the seminal films of the sixties. He went on to make dozens of films before turning to directing. In addition to being a superb actor, he had a great voice and had started his career as a boy soprano working with Benjamin Britten. He starred in Andrew Lloyd Webber's musical *Jeeves*. He was also a gifted artist and a superb raconteur. Most of all he had a huge sense of fun, as indeed did Mike Leander. They were both inclined to drink *a lot*, which often fuelled their naughtiness. Hemmings, offered a drink, would say, 'Well, it is a warm day.'

The Hemmings made us extremely welcome and we had a great time. David played all day but had enough energy to work late into the night. Though around forty and past the youthful beauty of *Blow-Up*, he was still an extremely handsome and attractive man. I noted that if Marsha needed to get up in the night to go to the lavatory she spent some time fixing her hair and make-up before she ventured out of our room. There must have been something in the Majorcan water because she never got up in the night to pee when we were at home.

David and I did become friends and we also worked together. In 1981 he directed *The Survivor*, a film that I had developed based on a book by James Herbert. Hemmings changed the story so much that James Herbert, quite rightly, never forgave me.

Hemmings and Mike Leander were like brothers. They even looked alike. One evening at Tramp, when Mike was being treated for the cancer that would eventually kill him at the

too-young age of fifty-five, he complained that the chemo had
made him bald. Hemmings roared with laughter, 'Your hair will
grow back, but these won't,' as he took out his false teeth and
slapped them on the table. This in a crowded Tramp club was a
true measure of friendship. Hemmings also died young, at the
age of sixty-two. They had both smoked, drunk and enjoyed life
to excess. Personally, I do not believe in heaven or hell but would
like to think that Leander and Hemmings are together somewhere, along with Peter O'Toole, Oliver Reed, Richard Harris,
Richard Burton and others of that ilk whose way of life we mere
mortals condemned but wished we had tasted.

Just A Gigolo starred Kim Novak and Marlene Dietrich as
well as David Bowie. It was made in Berlin and Hemmings
invited me to come and see him on set. It was 1978, the Berlin
Wall was still up and I jumped at the chance of having a glimpse
of life in the besieged Berlin. I flew into Tempelhof airport feeling very 'spy who came in from the cold' and went straight to
the studio. I had not seen David Bowie for some years and I
was intrigued to see how he reacted to me. I was particularly
excited at the thought of meeting Marlene Dietrich and Kim
Novak, the other stars of the film. I was very disappointed –
David was not on set. Marlene Dietrich had never been on set.
All her action had been shot in Paris and cut in to her scenes
with David.

David would probably not have taken a part in the film had
he not been living in Berlin. He had recorded *Heroes* there,
produced by Tony Visconti, in a studio about five hundred yards
from the Berlin Wall. Hemmings confided in me that other
than his 'close relationship' with Miss Novak, things were not

going well. He was over-budget, he was unhappy with the script – there had been four different screenwriters – and it was not a happy set. Bowie was understandably pissed off because one of the main reasons he had said yes to the film was to work with the legendary Dietrich, whom he never even got to meet.

Anyway, Hemmings took the film to Cannes in 1978 and David was there to promote it. By then I was a regular participant in the festival. Mike and Penny Leander were also there and we all saw a lot of each other. *Just a Gigolo* was a poor film but Hemming's optimism was infectious and we all celebrated its upcoming release as if it had Oscar potential.

There was one memorable night when I took David Bowie and the Leanders to the Whisky À Gogo, Cannes, hip disco. David did not raise his differences with Defries and actually thanked me for his 'great times' at Gem. David seemed quite philosophical when I explained that I could not accommodate his request to get 'my artist' some cocaine. The Whisky was full of music-business people, and I must confess to enjoying the looks of jealousy/admiration as I sat chatting to one of the great glam-rock pioneers I had helped to fame. David took Penny on the floor for a slow dance, and she was not best pleased that Mike did not appear to be the least bit upset. Hemmings was supposed to join us but had been obliged to spend the evening with potential buyers of his film.

Just A Gigolo was released to such universally terrible reviews that it was withdrawn from circulation, causing Bowie to later quip: 'It was my 32 Elvis Presley movies rolled into one.'

That evening at the Whisky was the last time I spent time with David and I am glad that it is such a pleasant memory.

26. POSTCRIPT ON DAVID BOWIE AND TONY DEFRIES

Since I began writing this book, David Bowie has died. I had not seen him for forty years, and it would be hypocritical to say that I was devastated by the news in a personal way, but David had been a big adventure in my business life and I was certainly saddened and shocked by his unexpected death.

What shocked me even more was the effect that David's death had on people around the world. The outpouring of grief was extraordinary, and the worldwide media coverage was equal to that following John Lennon's murder.

I think that it was not David's musical ability, special though it was, that had such a profound effect on his fans and followers. In the sixties, The Beatles and the Rolling Stones had caught the wave of youth revolution and became the symbols of change from the older generations. David had not caught a wave, he had created one. Through his music, performance and lifestyle, he articulated that people should be what they wanted to be, and that conventions were made to be broken. Though forever a chameleon, he was always quintessentially English and when we were together in private, he never appeared to take himself too seriously. He also wrote songs that were not love songs.

I have not seen Tony Defries for some thirty-odd years. He is, I believe, a highly intelligent man. In the 1970s, he predicted that every home in the developed world would have a personal computer for general family use, an outrageous idea at the time. Sadly, after I helped him set up MainMan, I only ever heard from him when he needed my help. Around 1978 he called me to ask if I could assist him in getting a record deal for John Mellencamp, an artist whose name, against his wishes, Defries had changed to Johnny Cougar. I was unhappy with the offhand way that he had dealt with me once he had fled the Gem nest, and I did not feel that this was something that I wanted to do. Mr Cougar had little success under Defries' guidance but subsequently became an important artist when he left Defries and changed his name back to Mellencamp.

About eight years ago, Defries called me again, out of the blue. He told me that he had become a self-taught scientist and had developed a technique that would revolutionise solar-panel heating. He was urgently looking for substantial monies to develop the project and asked me if I could help him find an investor. Still a respecter of Defries' intellect, I did not doubt his ability to come up with something brilliant but had no inclination to be involved with him in business again.

Since the demise of MainMan, as far as I am aware he did not manage any other well-known artists other than those he met during the time he worked with me at Gem and John Cougar Mellencamp,. Maybe he chose not to. According to Wikipedia, Tony Defries lost twenty-two million dollars in an offshore tax-evasion scheme. He was also sued by Capitol Records for copyright infringement – a case that he lost, costing him nine million dollars in damages and costs.

I do not think that Defries behaved particularly well with me but I do not rejoice in any woes that may have befallen him. He brought David Bowie into my business life and, in the early days, before he began to believe his own publicity, he was fun to work with.

27. GTO INCLUDING DAVID JOSEPH AND THE NEW SEEKERS

So, how did I manage to go through the five hundred thousand pounds that I received from the Bowie deal? It is a cautionary tale.

One of the reasons that I was not unhappy that Defries and his entourage were moving out in the summer of 1972 was that I was actively considering a merger with the Toby Organisation. It was a company started by a young man named David Joseph, who had brilliantly taken three boys and two girls, named them The New Seekers and guided them to major success with 'I'd Like to Teach the World to Sing'. This had become a worldwide hit thanks to a Coca-Cola commercial.

David was the opposite of Defries. He was conventional, serious, obviously reliable and a proven success as a manager. I was still aware of my own lack of experience of managing a group on the road, getting the right gigs, arranging tours etc, and I was interested in working with him. He, on the other hand, had negotiated a poor record deal with Polydor Records for The New Seekers and I could see that we complemented each other. At the time he was based in St James Street, London, sharing offices with Slim Miller Entertainments, a successful agency who booked the group's live performances in the UK. David had an interest in Slim's company but his ambition was not to help grow a company involved in cabaret acts. He wanted to be a player on the international pop music stage.

David was born in England but his parents soon moved to Australia. He worked in radio and then became a successful TV producer, marrying Robin, an accomplished and well-known Australian jazz singer who then raised their family. They moved to the UK in 1970 and when we met, he and Robin had three daughters and a dog called Toby – hence the name of his company. One of the reasons I had been outside the Bowie/Defries circle was that I was married with children and in the evenings I wanted to have time to devote to my family while they were happy to spend their leisure time at the somewhat louche Sombrero club. Like myself, David Joseph was a family man. We were not close friends, but we had a lifestyle in common.

The New Seekers were a five-piece harmony group born out of The Seekers, a hugely successful sixties Australian, folk-influenced act led by the amazing voice of Judith Durham. They had a string of hits including 'The Carnival is Over', 'I'll Never Find Another You', and 'Georgy Girl'. Judith left in 1968 and the group broke up. David had the idea of forming The New Seekers and organised Keith Potger – one of the original Seekers – to front the group and to 'resign' once The New Seekers were established. Keith retained a financial interest in David's business.

I suggested that David and I merge our two companies on a 50/50 basis. Even though the skills that David brought to the merger were important, the 50/50 agreement now may seem a

HUNKY DORY (WHO KNEW?)

poor deal on my part, bearing in mind the subsequent success of Bowie, Gary Glitter, GTO Records and others. *HOWEVER* – purposely in *bold* capitals – in July 1972 when I made the deal, David's New Seekers were a star act who had broken through big time, were touring for good money and generating substantial income. They were bigger stars than David Bowie. They were the UK entry to the European Song Contest (a very big deal at that time). My existing artists – Bowie included – had great potential but were an overall drain on my limited resources. *Ziggy* had just been released, and whilst we all thought it was rather special, nobody could anticipate the way it would set his career alight. I felt comfortable working with David and felt that acquiring the Toby Organisation was a safety net for GTO.

The joint company was called Gem Toby Organisation Ltd, which soon became GTO. Keith Potger had a minority share-holding in Toby and was therefore a minority shareholder in the new joint company but, in practice, I was the dominant partner.

Following the success of The New Seekers, David tried the same formula with The Springfield Revival. The original Spring-fields, featuring Dusty Springfield and her brother Tom, had been a big success in the early sixties. Mike Hurst – one of the original group – fronted the new band to get it going. Dusty of course had gone on to have a brilliant solo career, but The Spring-field Revival was not a success, and we lost all of our investment. I did get to keep one of the guitars that we had bought for them, which I call my 'fifty-thousand-pound guitar'. In the same vein, I still have some very costly mementos bearing the name of my various artists and films that failed at spectacular cost. I have a very expensive paperweight from my Broadway production of

End of the Rainbow. It was a play about Judy Garland, which I have since had made into a film starring Renée Zellweger called *Judy*, so maybe I will get some of the play losses back after all. It is no bad thing to keep reminders of one's failures, along with the trophies of one's successes – pride of place in the former category definitely goes to my four-hundred-thousand-pound *Breaking Glass* T-shirt, from the film starring Hazel O'Connor that sent my film company broke.

Hazel wrote and performed the songs in the film. The soundtrack album went to UK No. 5 and two or three of the singles from the album also charted. It was a good film and I organised a double royal charity premiere on two screens at the Odeon Shaftesbury Avenue. Prince Charles attended one screening and Princess Anne the other. Hazel arrived in a military tank – of course! It was the highest promotional budget I had ever committed to a film, but we promoted its punk aspect and the film failed to attract a wide audience.

When she came to the film, Hazel was under contract to a small record company called Albion Records. They had one release with her, which did nothing, and she was working as the company's receptionist to earn some money. Somebody brought her to the attention of film director Brian Gibson when he was about to start on *Breaking Glass*, financed by Dodi Fayed and produced by Davina Belling and Clive Parsons. The pair had produced *Scum*, which had been a hit for GTO Films some three years earlier and gave Ray Winstone his big break. Hazel auditioned for Brian, but it was some time before she heard from the producers that she had the part. John Finch was *Breaking Glass's* male lead and Jonathan Pryce had a smallish part, as a saxo-

phone player. After the film Hazel would have a long personal
relationship with John Finch.

After her audition, Hazel signed an agreement with Albion
as a recording artist and songwriter, for which she was paid forty
pounds a week. Albion licensed her services to A&M Records
– the successful US company – to make and release the film's
soundtrack, which was produced by Tony Visconti. Although
Hazel maintains that she never received any money from Albion
for her work on the soundtrack, the film and the successful
soundtrack gave her great exposure and she was poised to have
a very good career. Hazel was convinced that small-thinking
Albion Records were incapable of helping her find her potential. Tony Visconti presumably agreed with her view because he
declined to produce her on the Albion label and Albion refused
to let her go.

Eventually, Hazel came to me for help. I met with Albion
heads Dai Davies and Derek Savage and tried hard to negotiate a deal under which Albion would have had a significant
financial interest in any record deal that I made for Hazel with
A&M, who were desperate to sign her. Cutting off their corporate noses to spite their corporate faces, they flatly refused to
let her go. I had also introduced her to my old GTO Records
partner Dick Leahy, who now had a very successful publishing
company in partnership with Bryan Morrison, who published
Pink Floyd and other important acts. Morrison Leahy Music
would go on to be George Michaels' publisher and, in 1990,
Bryan would become my producing partner in my stage musical
Matador. Morrison Leahy offered a very generous deal to buy
Hazel's publishing from Albion, but they too were met with a

flat refusal. Eventually Hazel's contract came to an end, with Albion having earned very little from hanging on to an artist who, with some reason, did not want to be with them.

Hazel remains a uniquely talented writer/performer. She still has a career, with a devoted fan base called Hazelnuts but, in my opinion, she never fulfilled her potential because of Albion's intransigence.

The one good thing that happened with The Springfield Revival was that in 1973 they appeared at the Academy Awards ceremony, having been asked to sing a song that was nominated for an Oscar. We all went along and it was a fabulous night. The song, 'Come Follow, Follow Me', was very forgettable as was *The Little Ark* – the film it came from – but the evening was not forgettable at all and I have a photo of Raquel Welch and me up on my wall to remind me. Impressed? Don't be. Bob Levinson, our LA publicist, had offered to introduce me to singer Glen Campbell that night and I facetiously said that I would rather meet Raquel Welch. Later in the evening, Bob came and got me from the really unimportant people annex where we were all sat and – with photographer in tow – marched me through to the main room where Raquel Welch was sitting at a table with other luminaries. He shoved me in against the unsuspecting Ms Welch, clicked his fingers for the photographer to take the picture, said, 'Thank you, Raquel,' and schlepped me away. The whole thing must have taken less than thirty seconds. Without question, the most embarrassing thirty seconds of my life.

David closed his St James office and, together with his wife and three children, moved to a very nice home in Beverly Hills that was bought for them by the company. There was a deal to be done with an American record company for the American rights, but this would in no way meet the expenses of a GTO Inc. office in Los Angeles – as part of my renegotiation with Polydor, I had freed The New Seekers' recording rights for the USA. I suggested that David initially ran our business from his home, but David insisted that we 'do it right' and demonstrate to the industry that we were 'serious players'. He took a suite of prestigious offices in Century Plaza in the heart of Beverly Hills and staffed up, ready to deal with the yet-to-be-discovered stars of tomorrow which he hoped to sign. The company also bought him a Lincoln Continental, which David assured me was the car that 'serious players' drove. In fairness to David, whatever my private reservations were, I did not object to him setting up our LA operation as if it were already a huge success. He thought that if you wanted to be a success in LA you had to present yourself as if you already were. Defries thought that if Bowie was to be a star he should live like one. Same principle.

David was right. I love LA but it is a shallow town where people can, and do, rent a Rolls-Royce for an afternoon so they can arrive at a business meeting in style. Before I bought my own little house in LA I stayed at a bungalow at The Beverly Hills Hotel or the Chateau Marmont and shamelessly rented a Cadillac Eldorado or the like for myself. I kidded myself that I too was obliged to keep up the façade of success, but the real truth was that I just loved briefly living a lifestyle that I could only have dreamed about in my Finsbury Park youth. When I was later in the film business, I sometimes had meetings at the big film studios. I cannot fully explain to you the thrill I

got turning up at the Paramount or MGM studios to have the
gateman say, 'Welcome, Mr Myers, you are expected,' and being
directed to park on the lot.

David moved The New Seekers and The Springfield Revival
to LA and provided them with nice living accommodation
and weekly living allowances. He staffed up the office, taking
Glenn Wheatley, an old Australian associate he had brought to
London, over as vice-president. (I have to say that in corporate
America, every employee seems to be a vice-president. If a VP is
meeting with you, you are supposed to feel that you are important. You soon learn that the VP in charge of internal/external
transit is what we would call a doorman. GTO Inc. had a staff of
four, two of whom were VPs.)

Glenn was twenty-three and in Australia he had been a
member of a very successful band called The Masters Appren-
tices and, as is the way with pop stars, he was married to a
successful model. Glenn was ambitious and eager to learn
and I liked him immensely. He did not get on with David,
whom he claimed was unreasonably abusive and aggressive. If
so, I certainly never saw this side. At the end of 1974, Glenn
went back to Australia. He soon became hugely successful
there, managing some of the country's biggest music stars and
owning a major radio station. By 1987, he was included in
the Top 200 rich list in Australia's *Business Review Weekly*. In
1999, he published his autobiography that was almost embarrassingly fulsome in his praise for me as his guide and mentor.
He inscribed the book to me: 'Without you this would never
have happened'. In 2000 I received a call from *This Is Your Life*
in Australia. Glenn was to be the subject, and they wanted to

fly me over as the 'surprise guest'. Unfortunately, I was in the middle of my production of *The Seven Year Itch*, starring Daryl Hannah, and could not get away.

In the 2000s Glenn got into trouble with the Australian tax authorities for putting his money in a tax scheme on bad advice. He called me from time to time and I gave him what little advice I could. Unfortunately, as he was a public figure, the Australian revenue decided to make an example of him. He was given a jail sentence and went bankrupt. After he was released from jail he struggled to get back on his feet. He came to London and I loaned him ten thousand pounds, no paperwork, no payback date, no interest, which he said 'saved his life'. According to social media Glenn is now extremely successful again, but in spite of my several requests to do so, he has not seen fit to repay the loan. Disappointing.

Back to LA, where The New Seekers were signed to MGM Records, which was headed up by twenty-seven-year-old Mike Curb – a very right-wing Republican who was active in politics and would later become lieutenant governor of California. He was sometimes known as Mr Clean for his vehement anti-drug stance. Richard Nixon gave Mike Curb the job of coordinating the entertainment for the inauguration of his second term as president in 1973. Glenn was given the job of getting the talent to Washington. Glenn and The New Seekers flew in a jumbo jet of celebrities and retainers including Sammy Davis Jr and Pat Boone. Glenn made sure that everything went to plan on the night. The Nixon administration were famous for their appreciation of services rendered and Spiro Agnew, the vice-president, thanked Glenn and asked if there was anything he might be able to do as a thank-you. Glenn mentioned that he had been trying unsuccessfully for a year to get green cards – American work permits – for himself and his wife. Two weeks later, the cards arrived.

The other vice-president of GTO Inc. was Eileen Bradley, who had previously worked as a magazine journalist and had a good feel for the teenage market. Many years later I saw Eileen again when she was working as a well-connected agent for magic acts. I had an idea to make a musical based on the life of the famous escapologist Houdini. Magic was all the rage in Las Vegas entertainment and, ever the opportunist, I asked Eileen to fix me up with a meeting with the management of a large hotel and casino to see if they would put it on. The man I saw thought it was a great idea. He asked me what the running time would be and how much the show would cost to mount. As the show had not been written, I did the honest theatre producer thing and made up my answers. An average stage musical lasts around two and a quarter hours and, wishing to sound real, I said 'Two hours twenty.'

'No good,' he said. 'No show in our casino can last more than an hour, it keeps people away from the tables.'

'We can have a one-hour version,' I hastily replied.

'How much would it cost to put on?'

In those days, you would aim to budget a West End musical at no more than four million pounds, but knowing that Las Vegas loved things lavish, and not wanting to sound cheap, I said. 'Ten million dollars.'

He shook his head. 'You have to spend at least forty million dollars on a Vegas show,' and that was the end of that conversation.

Another ex-GTO Inc employee I met in later life was Billy Sammeth, a very talented man whom David had hired. Bill would later go on to manage Cher and Joan Rivers. Some time in the eighties, I popped in to see Billy at his office when he was managing Cher. He was sitting with his head in his hands. Cher was due to open that night in Vegas – a very big deal – but was two pounds over her desired weight and refusing to go on. Eventually she relented, but Billy probably lost more than two pounds in weight from aggravation. Billy ended up having lawsuits with both Ms Cher and Ms Rivers. The joys of management.

David and his team worked hard on improving the awareness of The New Seekers in America. They arranged tours including supporting Liza Minnelli in 1973. They appeared on the Johnny Carson show and also did a three-week stint in Las Vegas, but these activities contributed little to the coffers of GTO Inc. David signed some local acts including Angel, a handsome-looking rock band cast as the goody-goody antithesis of Kiss, just as The Beatles were perceived in relation to the Rolling Stones. They were signed to Mike Curb at MGM, who was keen on having wholesome artists on his label. He had signed The Osmonds to cash in on the success of The Jackson 5 and was generally into what you might call white-bread acts.

I introduced David to Alan Price, the brilliant keyboard player who was having a good career as a solo artist. I had been an admirer of Alan's talent from his days with The Animals. In fact, he totally changed my opinion on the musical ability he had, as well as that of many of his contemporaries, when I watched him playing around on the piano between recording at a Mickie Most session. Growing up, I had been a great jazz

fan. My idols were musicians like Oscar Peterson and Errol
Garner. I really liked the pop records that I heard in the sixties,
but I was somewhat patronising about the musicians behind
the voices. I always assumed that the players were experienced
studio professionals, which, of course, they often were. Alan,
who was truly a gifted musician, made me much more respect-
ful of the music-makers of his generation. Because these guys
often only needed three or four chords, it did not mean that
they were not masters of many more. My humble apologies to
all concerned for my unspoken thoughts at the time. When
Alan asked me to manage him in 1973 I jumped at the chance.
He wanted to break America and I booked him on a short
promotional tour. Alan was petrified of flying and he took a
strong cocktail of whisky and Valium to get himself on the
plane from the UK. The tour ended up at The Troubadour, LA's
most famous small venue. The tour was too short to have any
real impact on the American market and, sadly, Alan did not
like David's management style and asked me to release him
from his contract, which of course I did.

David also put together The Sarstedt Brothers. Peter Sarstedt
had had huge success in 1968 with 'Where Do You Go To (My
Lovely)?' It reached UK No. 1 and fourteen other countries, but
he had had little success since then. His elder brother Rick also
topped the UK singles chart under the name of Eden Kane,
with 'Well I Ask You'. The youngest brother, Clive, had made
records under the name of Robin Sarstedt but by 1972 none of
the siblings had much of a career. Their sister Lorraine worked
as David's personal assistant. David put them in an LA studio
and they made *Worlds Apart Together*. They toured a little in the

UK but the album was not a success, and they eventually went
their separate business ways.

Rick (Eden Kane) had married Charlene Groman, a nice
Jewish girl from LA. (In certain circles – my mother – the
phrase 'Jewish girls' is *always* proceeded by 'nice'.) After GTO
Inc. closed down I kept in touch with Rick and Charlene and
in an oblique way Rick was a catalyst that helped me persuade
Dick Leahy to sell GTO Records to CBS in 1978. It is quite
a nice story, which I will relate when I get on to writing about
GTO Records. In researching this book, I discovered that Char-
lene was a half-sister to the actress Stefanie Powers of *Hart To
Hart* TV fame – also a nice Jewish girl: who knew? Stefanie
Powers starred in my West End stage production of the musical
Matador in 1991 and I had no idea of the connection.

In May 1974, The New Seekers no longer wanted to teach the
world to sing in perfect harmony, and disharmoniously broke up.
It was front-page news in the UK, and a great disappointment
to their thousands of fans around the world. The most probable
reason was that, after years of success, they had no money. The
group formally declared that they no longer considered GTO
to be their managers. They were signed to us individually and
we sued them for breach of contract. Where there's a hit there's
a writ, and the writs were soon flying back and forth like kids
fighting with paper airplanes. They sued us for under-account-
ing. They employed a top firm of accountants to audit our books,
but nothing untoward was found. One of them told me that he
thought that I was just smarter than his accountants. A back-
handed compliment if ever there was one. The audit did show
that, strictly in accordance with the provisions of the manage-

ment contract, the group's earnings had been eaten up by their regular cash advances and expenses.

As a standard management agreement of the time, we took 20 per cent of the gross income, and all of the expenses incurred on their behalf were deducted from the balance. Please note that our own expenses of running our offices substantially reduced our commission. The New Seekers were on wages from the day that David put them together. Unlike so many of their contemporaries, they never had to starve before they had success.

When a band starts on the road, they are usually happy to travel economy, share rooms and generally live a modest lifestyle. As they become more successful, understandably, they want to travel in more comfortable style. Now here is the thing. Every manager of a reasonably successful band has the same problem. Having risked a great deal of money in the band's development, you sometimes get lucky, they have some success and you start to recoup. The band become stars and want to live like stars. If the manager is responsible, he warns them gently, and then not so gently, that they should be aware of their financial position. *But*, people – some sincere, some hangers-on – surround the bands and sow the seeds of discontent. Why, they ask, does the artist not have big cars/houses/drug supplies, whatever? Often a wannabe manager adds fuel to the flames.

I present you with the manager's classic dilemma. If you responsibly restrict your artists' spending, eventually they feel aggrieved and want to leave you. If you let them spend recklessly, they will end up broke. You may recall that Bowie fell out with Tony Defries because he had no idea that he alone was paying for the lifestyle that Tony encouraged him to adopt. Elton John eventually had a falling-out with his long-term manager, John Reid, as did Bob Dylan with Albert Grossman. It is easier to make a list of the artist/manager relationships that did not end in financial acrimony. Peter Grant and Led Zeppelin, Jim Beach and Queen, and Bill Curbishley and The Who quickly come to mind. The Beatles were loyal to Brian Epstein until the day he died, even though he had made terrible deals for them.

So, faced with the dilemma, what would you do? Would you do the 'right thing': protect the artist from himself and take the chance that he would leave you? I don't think so. Like me and most other managers I knew, after your due warnings had been ignored, you would pragmatically keep your artists happy and your own family secure, by letting the artists indulge in the lifestyle they wanted. Of course, if the artist is hugely successful for years they get rich in spite of themselves or their cynical management. Elton John is richer than his ex-manager. He's quite probably richer than you and he is certainly richer than me.

With The New Seekers there was another possible reason for their break-up. After five years together they had had enough of each other. In my own view, any discord was not helped by the fact that although Eve Graham had been the lead voice on every previous hit, Lyn Paul took the role on 'Beg Steal or Borrow', the Eurovision Song Contest entry, and 'You Won't Find Another Fool Like Me,' a No. 1 hit in 1973 written by Geoff Stephens and producer Tony Macaulay.

As a Christmas present to me, the girls in my office went into the studio with the track and recorded 'You Won't Find Another Boss Like Laurence'. The line 'Those Cuban heels for high-pow-

ered deals' sticks in my mind. I plead guilty to the Cuban heels
… well, it was the seventies.

The break-up became extremely acrimonious between the
group members themselves. Peter Doyle, one of the original
members, who sadly died young of throat cancer in 2001, had left
the group in 1973. Marty Kristian and Paul Layton bought the
rights to the name from Eve Graham and Lyn Paul. In subsequent
years, they reformed the group in various incarnations, including
some ex-members of The Springfield Revival. Eve Graham briefly
rejoined The New Seekers in 1976, in a line-up which included
musician Kevin Finn. Eve subsequently married Kevin and they
had a happy marriage until Kevin died in 2016. Lyn Paul went
on to have a career on stage, starring in *Blood Brothers*. Marty
and Paul took advantage of owning The New Seekers' name by
making soundalike re-recordings of all of The New Seekers' hits,
without using Eve or Lyn and licensing the recordings to Polydor,
who had the original recordings. This seriously devalued the original recordings that I owned, but it was a smart move and I do not
blame the boys for doing so. The dispute spluttered on for years
until Marty and I eventually ruined the day of several West End
lawyers by coming to an amicable settlement.

The London office had been financially supporting GTO
Inc. since the day it started and David had not managed to sign
anyone to contribute at all significantly to the running of the
LA operation. I had no animosity towards David, but after the
breakup of The New Seekers, I decided that it made no business
sense to carry on draining our resources indefinitely. I put it to
David that if GTO Inc. were not self-supporting by 31 December 1974 we should close the office down, even if there were a

promise to sign The Beatles on the next day. David was not happy. I bought Keith Potger's minority holding in the controlling company of the group so that I had a majority vote. I was never obliged to legally use my controlling vote to ride roughshod over David but – as with all divorces – it was a little messy. David did manage to walk away with the house in Beverly Hills and a nice sum of money and I kept the company. We were both a little unhappy with the deal that we made, which is always a good sign of fairness. Most importantly, we remained friends.

David decided to get back into radio and moved Robin and his four children to Hawaii. That did not work out as planned and he moved his family back to LA. He got involved in film production and in 1982 made *The Pirate Movie* based on Gilbert and Sullivan's *Pirates of Penzance* in Australia, and was co-producer of *Flight of the Navigator* for Disney. Neither of the films were box-office successes and he did not manage to get another film made. He went back to Australia and went into the restaurant business.

I had stayed in touch with David after GTO Inc. closed and tried to be helpful where possible. In 1993, whilst in LA, I met up with him again. He had moved back without his family, which did not surprise me as I figured that Robin had had enough of packing up the kids on yet another major move. I met with him for lunch at a restaurant in Beverly Hills, expecting him to tell me that he and Robin had split up. He said that he had something to tell me which he found difficult and I, rather smugly, said that I thought that I had worked out why he had moved to LA alone.

'Well,' he said, 'I have always been gay.' I was so shocked that my pasta went all over the restaurant's mirrored walls.

David's story was not unusual, but it was nonetheless heart-breaking. He had felt that he was gay since he was a teenager but thought that it would 'go away' when he married and had a family. It did not, and having had the painful life of keeping his secret for twenty years of marriage, circumstances in Australia obliged him to come out to his wife, kids and mother. I was extremely fond of David and Robin and felt great compassion for all of the family. To make matters worse, David soon found out that he was living with AIDS. This was in the nineties, when the illness was more debilitating and more life-threatening than medicine has made it today. David was unable to work but still endeavoured to support his family, all of whom stayed close to him. I helped him out as much as I could. At one point he planned to move to Spain with his boyfriend, a Mexican, and I offered our house in Majorca for him to live in as a first step but he didn't make the move. Eventually I became weary of supporting his schemes, all of which revolved around the gay community and in my view were highly unlikely to succeed. Unkindly, I just stopped calling him.

In 2011, I got a call from Marty Kristian. He and David had made up after some thirty-odd years, David was coming to London, and they were having a New Seekers reunion. Marty wanted me to appear as a surprise guest, which he thought would be 'the icing on the cake' for all concerned. I was not proud of the way I had treated David in the later years and would love to have gone along to try and make amends. Unfortunately, it was impossible for me to get there, but I asked Marty to give David my number so that we could arrange to meet. I got a very cold call from David saying that he was not keen to meet with me because

I had failed to keep in touch with him for the last few years. I did point out that phone calls work two ways, and that maybe it would be nice to meet up. I then received an email from David saying that he had no wish to meet with me. I had told a mutual friend in Australia that I had stopped calling David because I was fed up with his mainly gay-based business ideas. The friend, who was obviously not a good friend to David, had felt impelled to tell him so. I would have liked to have had a chance to explain to David that I had no homophobic prejudices; I just did not believe that his ideas were commercially viable.

If David had a business fault it was a blinkered persistence, which could sometimes work against him. He would go on and on browbeating Mr A to agree to something that Mr A really did not want to do. He would then do the same thing with Mr B and Mr C, until they also reluctantly agree to be part of the deal. Inevitably one of them would have second thoughts and pull out and the deal would collapse like a pack of cards.

David died in 2012 following a hip operation. He was surrounded by his still-loving family – none of whom, I am sure, will think kindly of me, which is a shame because, probably unknown to them, I did help David out financially quite a lot in the years following his illness.

I led into the GTO Inc. story by saying that it had eaten up the five hundred thousand pounds that I had received from the Bowie deal with Defries. In truth, I do not recall what the losses of GTO Inc. actually were but it was not, as they say, chopped liver. Looking back, I do not regret the cost to me of having supported an LA office that failed. Gertrude Stein once famously said of LA, 'I went there, and there was no there, there.' This was not true if you were involved in the entertainment business in the pre-Silicon Valley seventies and eighties. GTO Inc. was struggling but my other business ventures made me a perceived success, something vital to make it with the LA in-crowd.

I guess I have enough shallowness within me to have thoroughly embraced the bullshit of LA. For me it was exciting and vibrant. I had lots of friends there, many of them UK expats and we did not take ourselves or each other too seriously. The Chateau Marmont, now a five-star hotel, but then delightfully seedy, was the hangout for visiting Brits. Peter Brown, the ex-Apple publicist, an extremely urbane English gentleman, used to arrange a monthly dinner for the expat community at The Dome restaurant on Sunset Boulevard. One such occasion was to celebrate the Queen Mother's birthday. My 'date' for the evening was Hermione Gingold, a once extremely famous English actress who starred in *Gigi*, *The Music Man* and many other major films. Now in her eighties and living in LA, in her youth Hermione was a friend of the Queen Mother who, before she became Queen of England, was the Charleston-loving Betty Bowes-Lyons.

Hermione, in spite of her age, was as bright and feisty as a teenager. She clearly shared her old friend's alleged love of a gin and tonic, and during the dinner she regaled us with wonderful stories of the twenties when she and Betty were leading lights in young British society. Of course, the names she scurrilously bandied around were meaningless to us, but she several times confided in me in her cut-glass English accent, that 'Betty was a bit of a gel, dontcha know.' Just for the record, when I dropped Hermione home, I did not go in for a drink.

28. ARCADE RECORDS

For those of you who are too young to remember, there was a time when you could not buy compilations of various artists. In 1972, I was instrumental in the birth of the compilation business. In fact, I have been credited with actually creating it. A bold accolade that I would be foolish to deny.

There were a number of factors that serendipitously came together to cause me to get into the compilation business.

1. In 1972, I had reel-to-reel tapes in my offices that were capable of taking tracks that I chose from different vinyl recordings and putting them onto one cassette. More importantly, I had a kid in the office who knew how to do it. I used to make my own cassettes of music I liked by different artists and also made up compilations requested by friends.

2. The brothers-in-law. Every successful Jewish businessman has at least one brother-in-law. Sometimes one he has to support and sometimes one who contributes to his success. I got lucky with both of mine. Marsha had two half-brothers, Michael and Larry Levene. They had inherited their father William Levene's business, which supplied market grafters

with product lines to be sold via demonstrations. By 1972, they were in the business of selling TV-promoted kitchen gadgets and the like to the retail trade.

3. The Levene brothers' big competitor was a company called K-Tel, a Canadian company also owned by a family brought up in the market grafting business, selling similar products.

So how did it all come together? One day in early 1972 Michael Levene told me that one of his spies had reported to him that K-Tel had put out a TV-promoted record of polka music in the US that had sold phenomenally well. Could I come up with something similar in the UK for the Levenes? I explained that there was a huge descendant population of middle-European immigrants in America and the polka was the music of their heritage. The nearest thing to polka I could think of in the UK was clog-dancing, the knees-up, or Morris dancing, none of which was ever going to be a winner.

There was a company called Pickwick Records, which I had noted did very well making soundalike recordings of twelve recent chart hits and quickly getting them into Woolworths and other mass outlet stores. What if I could persuade record companies to license us the original hits that we could put on a single LP?

Michael was insistent that not only would the content have to be good, the record would have to be a genuine bargain. We came up with the idea of pricing the records at the same retail price as conventional albums, but putting twenty tracks onto one record rather than the usual twelve. Squeezing that many tracks onto a 12-inch vinyl album would slightly reduce the quality of the playback, but not, I thought, enough to spoil the listening of the average consumer. Anyway, the ethos of the TV marketing industry was 'It's for selling not for using.'

My first call was to EMI, the company with the biggest roster of artists at the time. I met with Ron Tudor, the MD, who was not enthusiastic but said that he would look into it. At our follow-up meeting, Ron told me that his legal affairs department had told him that there was no provision in their artists' contracts that allowed them to be put onto albums with other artists and there was a further doubt – twenty tracks on one LP, sold for the same price as a current album, would be a budget album and that meant a different royalty rate. Generally, EMI were living up to their reputation as being the Ministry of Pop, so I tried RCA – with a similar outcome.

All this took some time and I then got a panic call from Michael to say that his spy had told him that K-Tel's own spy had told the company's founder and boss, Ray Kives, that I was trying to put together a complication of hits, and they were now trying to do the same. The competition between K-Tel and the Levenes was intense and sometimes I got confused as to who was spying for whom.

I was close to John Fruin, the head of Polydor, who were The New Seekers' record company. He loved the idea, railroaded his legal department to make it happen, and it did. The Levenes were great believers in the approach now known as 'Does what it says on the tin' and we called the album *20 Fantastic Hits by the Original Artists* – to distinguish it from the Pickwick soundalike releases. I had three of my own recordings on the LP, The New Seekers' 'Beg, Steal or Borrow,' Johnny Johnson's 'Blame it on the

Pony Express,' and Edison Lighthouse's 'Love Grows ...', and an interest in the publishing of two other tracks, so I was also earning as a supplier. Happy days! K-Tel's *20 Dynamic Hits* hit the market a week or so before us but – slight puff of the chest here – our content was much better than theirs and we easily outsold them.

The Levenes and I became partners in a company called Arcade Records, named after Arcade House, GTO's building. Our first release was announced to the trade in a front-page article in *Music Week* in July 1972. In the same edition, there was a report that Pickwick had obtained an injunction against a company called Multiple Sound, who were also releasing soundalikes, for using the name 'Pick Of The Pops'. Multiple Sound was owned by Ian Miles, who later started the record arm of Ronco – a company in competition with Arcade and K-Tel – but they had little success with their releases. They did, however, do well with TV merchandising of weird gadgets like a device that made your old wine bottles into vases.

The Levenes did all of the marketing and distribution for Arcade Records, and my office made the repertoire selections and negotiated with the record companies. The Levenes' marketing was quite brilliant. On the basis that our TV campaign was driving customers into the shops, he offered the retailer a smaller margin. In addition, unlike conventional record companies, they offered the retailer full sale-or-return privileges. The pitch was that the retailer had nothing to lose by stocking our records. This was true, although some chains were initially resistant to the smaller margin before eventually realising that they were losing out on sales. All retailers, even Woolworths, the biggest mover of records at that time, gave in and stocked Arcade Records.

In no time Arcade had fully staffed offices in Germany and Holland. Larry opened an office in Paris but was frustrated by being unable to buy cost-effective TV time and soon closed the operation. We also became partners in PPL in Germany, a company making TV commercials. PPL was based in an abandoned swimming pool in Munich. It was a very creative atmosphere and I loved to spend time there.

Germany was by far the biggest market. K-Tel continued to be strong rivals but we usually won when it came to fighting for the most current hits. I really understood the record industry and used this knowledge to great advantage. I knew that one of the more difficult financial problems for a major record company was managing their pressing plants. They were obliged to have the capacity to deal with the demand created by a hit, but often were not aware of the extent until a record was released. This meant that most majors had idle capacity that they were obliged to keep in case. I would offer the record companies the contract for pressing a particular Arcade release, which could utilise their spare capacity. If they had an artist whose advance was unrecouped, I would offer to get that artist onto one of our records to help with the recoupment. I also had existing relationships with many of the writers, producers and managers of artists we wanted. If the record company was reluctant to give us a particular track, I could call one of the people behind the record and tell them that they were missing out on income because their record company would not license it to Arcade. Wherever possible, I chose a track in which a business friend had an interest, and that generally helped me within the industry. I was still seen as a hot source of talent so the record companies preferred to keep me happy.

K-Tel knew that Arcade was a family business, but at the 1975 Midem, Ray Kives, one of the owners, frustrated with usually coming second in the race for product, asked me what I would want to defect to them, which of course I would not even consider.

I did not want the record companies who were licensing us their product to realise how successful we were. In the UK I had managed to keep Arcade releases out of the charts, but in Germany both Arcade and K-Tel records were listed and the trade magazines also published their market share. In one quarter, Arcade and K-Tel had almost 25 per cent of the German market between them. When we made compilations, the majors sort of understood that it would be difficult for them to compete as they would have to agree with their rivals how many tracks each would have, who would do the pressing, etc. But when we started to make best-ofs for single artists, the majors began to wonder why they could not do this themselves. Over the years I persuaded major record companies to license us Elvis, the Rolling Stones, The Beatles, The Kinks, Hot Chocolate, The Beach Boys, The Everly Brothers, Johnny Cash, Diana Ross and some big local artists. We convinced them that there was some mystique about our operation. They believed that we had a secretive market-research department helping us to choose the less obvious compilations. In fact, with my trusted and brilliant lieutenant Sylvia Curd, I simply used to browse the record departments of the major department stores, Kaufhof in Germany and Vroom & Dreesmann in Holland, to see what was selling well in the budget record department.

We learned that the Germans, for instance, liked trumpet and saxophone records. There was a little-known American saxophone player called Billy Vaughn. I put together an album of familiar old songs like 'Sail Along Silv'ry Moon', 'Lili Marleen' and 'La Paloma' and it sold around half a million copies. An album of Nini Rosso, a trumpet player, featured a similarly unfashionable repertoire and almost was as great a success. One of our biggest-selling artists was the dolorously voiced Jim Reeves, an album that I could never listen to past the first track without falling asleep.

What kept the majors from entering the TV-selling market for a long time was their need for a business plan, especially in Germany, before they risked investment. What they did not know was that K-Tel and Arcade never had a business plan. We both operated with the market grafter's mentality that we all grew up with. Those of you who read my early history may remember that I worked in the market for about five years while I was a poorly paid accountancy articled clerk.

When an album was launched, Arcade had to commit to buying TV time and also make sure that we had reserved pressing capacity to meet the hoped-for demand. We would put an album out and if it was not working, Michael Levene would cancel the TV time and the pressing orders and worry later about the flack that inevitably came his way. There was a lot of schmoozing and many generous Christmas presents. We were very much a seat-of-the-pants operation, and the majors could not operate that way.

The biggest seller we ever had in the UK was *Elvis – 40 Greatest Hits*. The tracks that I licensed from RCA were pretty much already available on Camden, their low-volume budget line. Once again my inside knowledge of the business was the key.

I knew that RCA had recently bought out all of Elvis's future royalties for a huge sum of money and I convinced them that this was a way of quickly getting some back. I agreed an advance of just sixty thousand pounds, but eventually the record was so successful, Arcade paid them several hundred thousand pounds. We sold over two million copies, and at that time it was one of the highest-ever selling albums in the UK. As was normal, we had a three-year deal with RCA to exploit the rights. Elvis died in August 1977, two weeks after our deal ended. Had we still had the rights, we could have sold another million. In 1978, RCA put out a pink vinyl version of the same compilation, with a different cover but the same name.

There is a kicker to the *Elvis – 40 Greatest Hits* story. I had become close to RCA executive Mel Ilberman, who was then Colonel Parker's contact man at the company. Arcade Records had a gold disc made for Elvis that I took to Mel in New York, in the hope that he would pass it on to The King. He had a better idea. 'I'm flying to LA tomorrow to make a courtesy call on the Colonel. Why don't you come with me? You'll be doing me a favour, I really have nothing to talk to him about.' An offer I could not refuse.

I called my friend Freddy Bienstock, a partner in Elvis's publishing company, who promised to ask the Colonel if there was a chance of presenting the disc to Elvis in person. That evening Freddy told me that the Colonel's office was on the MGM Studios lot and Elvis would be there for costume fittings for his next (awful) movie. The Colonel was going to ask him to stop by. I was more excited than a sophisticated music executive should be – meeting Elvis was something that was as close to meeting a deity as this agnostic Jew was ever going to get. But the Colonel the next day gave the devastating news that Elvis's costume-fitting had been cancelled so he wasn't coming in. I was obviously disappointed, and as I recall so was Mel. I was about to leave them to their business but Mel asked me to stay. He was right – they really had nothing to talk about. Mel went through the release schedule for the next album, the Colonel whinged about RCA's slow accounting and that was it. Mel, no doubt eager to get away, excused himself but suggested that I stay for a few minutes and chat to the Colonel about the success of the Arcade release.

I had earned a living working as a market grafter. Colonel had at some point pre-Elvis also worked as a market grafter at county fairs where punters paid to watch his 'dancing chickens'. The chickens were placed on a heated plate and danced, as one would. The Colonel saw the two of us as kindred spirits and I was with him for a fascinating two hours. He ran the merchandising wherever Elvis appeared, and always stayed by the sales booth taking the cash. One wonders if he accounted for this to Elvis as part of their 50/50 agreement. One suspects not. He kept a stock of all of the merchandise in his office and gave me a range of samples as a going-home present. The gifts would not have been of interest to my young kids, so rather than carry them home, I gave them to the maid at my hotel. Who knew? I do know that Elvis got the gold disc. Very recently a friend of mine visited Graceland and sent me a photo of the Arcade gold disc on a wall, with hundreds of others that had been presented to Elvis over the years.

In 1982, a fourteen-page supplement in *Billboard*, the most important international music trade magazine, celebrated ten years of Arcade success. They reported that Arcade's turnover in 1981 was fifty million dollars. I cannot remember if that was true or something I made up to impress the industry. Probably the latter.

The major record companies, helped by ex-Arcade employees, eventually realised that there was no real mystery to our operation, and that they were mad to supply Arcade or K-Tel with product. They gradually went into TV marketing their own catalogues. Arcade got the dregs and began to lose money on some of our releases. It was obvious that our days in the record business were numbered. In 1983, Richard Branson – a smart man if ever there was one – made a deal with EMI to start releasing compilation albums for UK majors. *Now That's What I Call Music!* is, at the time of writing, up to *Now!* No. 96. Arcade, wisely, had already given up the UK market, by the time *Now!* arrived, and the series rang the death knell for K-Tel and Ronco.

We initiated the *Billboard* magazine supplement partly to promote the fact that I had taken Arcade Germany into the video business. In 1980, home VCR was exploding, and shops were opening all over the country to meet the public's demand for films to be played at home. The problem was that the major film companies were not yet making their product available. They had not worked out if the market was to be in rental or sales, if their rights even provided for home use, what the division of income between the various stakeholders in a film in this new media would be, etc. I realised that the shops had to fill their shelves with films. By now I was in the film world and I was able to source titles not owned by the majors, which the shops grabbed even though the content was generally awful. Inevitably, as with the record business, the majors soon worked out their problems, made their films available to the video market and that was the end of Arcade Video.

Arcade itself folded in 1983 and Herman Heinsbroek, the bright man I had poached from CBS Holland to run our Dutch company, took over the valueless company and re-launched the brand into the mainstream music business with great success.

In 1991, Michael Levene and I had another shot at working on a record together. Larry Levene had gone into the property business and Michael had a successful online sales company called Best Direct. As the name implies, products were not available in stores and customers bought directly in response to clever TV commercials and infomercials. You will remember them well. In fact, as a genre, they are still going. These ads had a key moment, the CTA – Call To Action – triggering the punter, sorry, the customer to, 'Order now and be sent absolutely free a …'

Michael was nostalgic for the happy days in the record business and both of us were nostalgic for the money that we earned from Arcade Records, so he asked me if I could think of a record package that he could sell. Not an easy task, as by then the majors had ceased to license any of their catalogues to outsiders. But the radio station Classic FM had started in 1992 and was proving a great success broadcasting best-known melodies from classical music. Clearly there was a market for popular classics, which we could combine with the public's desire for 'collectables'. I decided to put together a ten-CD set of the most well-known composers, knowing that there would be a wide choice of snatches of instantly recognisable melodies that could be used to make a great TV commercial. The package would have to be good value, which was not a problem. The actual cost of manufacturing each CD was less than fifty pence. The value to the consumer was what was on it, so the challenge was to pay as little as possible for the content.

Decca Records had by far the best roster of classical artists, but I realised that they would be expensive to deal with and, quite rightly, very fussy about the quality of the recordings. By now, I was completely indoctrinated by the Michael Levene mantra of 'They're for selling not for using', so I bought the content from Henry Hadaway, who owned a huge catalogue of schlock recordings by well-known names – or at least featuring artists whose names were to become well-known even if they weren't at the time of the recording. Henry's 'Frank Sinatra records' were by the Tommy Dorsey Orchestra in the forties when Sinatra was the unaccredited singer with the band. Their Beatles recordings were when they were the backing band for Tony Sheridan. If Henry could have found a recording where Chuck Berry had clapped along, it would have been sold as a Chuck Berry record. You get the picture. Most of his product was retailed through garage forecourts and other retailers who sold purely on price.

For very little money, I bought the best-known recordings of the ten most popular classical composers including Mozart, Beethoven, Chopin, etc. The recordings were by such 'quality' names as the Bratislava Radio Orchestra or the equivalent of the Huddersfield Philharmonic, if there had been one. They made up ten CDs which could be sold on TV for a very large margin of profit. I had to come up with the additional 'absolutely free', something as an incentive to order. *Now!*'s classical music had been given a boost when the legendary trio of Pavarotti, Carreras and Domingo appeared on worldwide television in a concert broadcast at the time of the 1990 World Cup. The Three Tenors' recording of the evening had sold in its millions. Obviously a CD of the three tenors would be an amazing incentive to 'Call and order NOW'. Back to Henry Hadaway.

Sure enough, Henry sourced recordings by each of the three famous tenors. They were not singing together as they did on the famous World Cup concert and the quality of the recordings was awful, but it was for selling, not for using. Some had been pirated from radio broadcasts, some recorded illegally from live concerts. You could actually hear an audience member coughing on one of the recordings. *But* I had a CD that could legally be called 'The Three Tenors'. Am I proud of creating this really inferior compilation? Absolutely *not*. But in 1992 my glory days in the music business were long behind me and my income from my old catalogue was diminishing. Luciano, Placido and Jose, or 'the boys', as I like to call them, saved my financial arse.

Michael made a great TV commercial, the collection was an enormous success and I did very well out of it indeed. There were very few complaints about the quality of the recordings. I believe that most consumers bought it with the coffee-table book mentality, that it was for displaying rather than for listening.

Michael Levene died in 2009 after a very long and debilitating illness. I had known him since he was ten years old and he was best man at my wedding to Marsha. He was not only my brother-in-law and a good business partner, he was also my friend and I still mourn his loss.

The power of TV is now even greater than it was during my days with Arcade. Radio play used to make instant record stars.

Now it is reality TV that spews out telegenic chart toppers. But the choreographed manipulation of audience reaction bothers me. Voting for the back-story as much as the talent. The boom-boom-boom-boom heartbeat before the tearful winner inevitably declares, 'It's like a dream come true,' and the losers glottal-stop, 'I'm guh-ed.' I have a horror that one day the election of a new Pope will not be announced by white smoke coming from the Sistine chapel. Instead the eligible cardinals will be lined up on that famous balcony overlooking St Peter's Square. There will be the boom-boom-boom-boom heartbeat before His Holiness, newly elected by viewers' telephone votes, is announced to the world by a deep, echoing voice from the sky.

Why am I so incensed by reality TV? To be honest, partly it is because starting a pop music talent show was an obvious opportunity, open for all. Like many of my contemporaries, I am consumed with envy/rage/bitterness that I did not think of doing it myself.

29. MIKE LEANDER –
ROCK AND ROLL PT. 2

Mike Leander's musical talent really bloomed in the sixties. He helped Keith Richards with the arrangement for the 1964 record of 'As Tears Go By', the song written for Marianne Faithfull by Keith and Mick Jagger. He also did the string arrangement for The Beatles' 'She's Leaving Home'.

Marianne made ten singles for Decca Records between 1964 and 1969. The producers included Andrew Loog Oldham, Tony Calder and Mike Leander. Mike worked on the tracks variously as studio engineer, arranger and orchestra director. Some records were released under the name Marianne Faithful with The Mike Leander Orchestra. RCA released 'Migration', a highly acclaimed orchestral record by The Mike Leander Orchestra. Decca released a single by The Mike Leander Orchestra of 'The Letter'/'Hey Jude', all now collectors' items. By the time Mike started working with me at Gem, Marianne was at the height of her dance with heroin. She was literally living on the streets, but Mike thought she might still have some of her early magic. He brought her to see me and I agreed to take her on as a Gem artist. She had no home, no possessions and no hope. We found her somewhere to live, paid the rent and gave her some money to buy food. From my point of view, this signing was as much an act of charity as a commercial decision.

Unsurprisingly, the Marianne Faithfull sessions did not work. Mike found it difficult to get a decent performance out of her. She often did not turn up to the studios, where we had expensive studio time, technicians and musicians booked and waiting. Mike brought her to see me in the office. Pasty-faced and sweating, she promised that, if I gave her another chance, she would turn up to the studio straight. She did not keep her promise and it was all very sad.

One night, Marsha and I were sitting at a table at Tramp, a fashionable disco of its time. Marianne made an entrance into the club, escorted by Richard Cole, Led Zeppelin manager Peter Grant's archetypal rock-soldier roadie. I knew him from my past involvement with Peter and the band. Marianne, who looked like an emaciated black-and-white sketch of herself, acknowledged me with a perfunctory nod and sat at a table across the room. A while later, Richard came over and requested that I send a bottle of champagne to 'my artist's table'. I knew that 'my artist' had a recording session scheduled with Mike the next day and I declined to buy the champagne. My counter-offer to arrange for a car to take Marianne home at a reasonable hour was rejected and, *quelle surprise*, she did not turn up at the studio the next day.

Drug addiction is of course a terrible disease, and I have real sympathy for those it afflicts, and even more sympathy for the family and friends who have to look on. But, on a business level, it is really difficult to deal with an addict whose behaviour wreaks havoc with other people's careers. Alcohol, of course, can be just as destructive. Mike did manage to finish an album with Marianne called *Masque*, but I did not think that it was good enough to deliver to Bell Records for release. Years later, I licensed the album to a budget label, who retitled it *Rich Kid Blues*. I will never recoup my costs, which does not concern me, but it would have been nice if my altruism had helped Marianne with her drug issues. Sadly, it did not. There was an attempted suicide in New York in the eighties, before Marianne got herself into rehab and bravely straightened herself out. Since then, to her great credit, she has managed to survive not only being Mick Jagger's ex, but also all the drugs and her scandals du jour in the sixties, including the alleged novel use of a Mars bar. In her teens, she was the pulchritudinous fantasy behind many a young man's locked bedroom door. If you want to know why, look up clips of *The Girl on a Motorcycle* on YouTube. Marianne is now taken seriously as a singer and has celebrated her fiftieth anniversary in showbiz with a world tour. According to an excellent BBC documentary about her, broadcast in February 2019, she is enjoying her current musical success and her family life with her son and grandchildren. Good for her. In the documentary she also acknowledged her debt to Mike Leander and Gem for getting her off the streets in 1970. So, I suppose, good for us.

At this time, Mike would book studio time to work with no particular purpose other than to experiment with sound, with the help of studio engineer John Hudson. It was to encourage creativity like this that I had started Gem/GTO. Very few record companies would allow their signings to just fool around in a studio without knowing why they wanted the time and without budgetary restrictions. I was content that neither Mike nor Tony Macaulay would waste my money to no purpose, and they were never obliged to seek my 'permission' to book a studio.

Mike was a multi-instrumentalist who could play drums, guitar, bass and piano. I once popped into Mayfair Sound where Mike, alone in the studio, was recording and found that he had placed wet towels on the drum skins in an attempt to get a sound that was in his head but that he was struggling to reproduce in the studio. He had looped his drum sound time and time again and he and John Hudson were experimenting with moving the mic around and using the technical effects that the studio's recording desk had to offer. Mike had also multi-tracked some guitar riffs using a technique that I had seen him practising in his office. When alone, Mike – a brilliant musician who was not a great guitarist – sat there for hours experimenting with retuning a guitar to enable him to play chords by using his cigarette lighter like a steel guitar slide. We had a running joke of me popping my head round his door almost daily, saying, 'Anything that you want me to hear?' and Mike replying, 'Not yet, old bean.' For that studio session, he had also had in musicians John Rossall and Harvey Ellison to lay the down the horn sound. I was yet to hear the melody to go over it, but the drum sound went through my body as if the bass drum were inside my head. It was an unbelievably exciting track.

Around April 1972, Mike booked in at Mayfair Sound to work with David Essex, who unavoidably cancelled at the last moment. Rather than waste the studio time, Mike went to the studio to continue to work on the track that he had been sweating over for the past few weeks. He took a singer called Paul

Raven that he occasionally used for demos to put a voice on the track. When he had completed his mix, Mike came into my office and said, '*Now* I have something that I want you to hear.' The track featured Paul's voice, which was not great, but the record was not about his voice. It was Mike mixing it onto the track that he had taken hours and hours to perfect.

Rather than waste time and money recording a B-side, Mike played me a remixed version of the same track with the drum sound brought up and instrumental apart from the chorus, bringing up the guitar for the basic melody. We decided that it would make an interesting – and cheap – B-side. Logically the A-side was called 'Rock And Roll Pt. 1', and the B-side was 'Rock And Roll Pt. 2'.

Singer Paul was not physically pop star material. He was nearly thirty, a little overweight and balding. We discussed the advisability of finding a younger singer with a more appealing natural look to re-voice the track for release. Mike told me that he would give Paul a writer's credit to soften the blow of not being on the released version. In the event, Mike – a kind man – decided that it would be too cruel to Paul to replace him. Paul had been working as a singer for fifteen years without success and it would have been a big blow. This is the story of the record that morphed Paul Raven – born Paul Gadd – into Gary Glitter.

Almost twenty years later, Glitter was charged with child pornography. He rightly became persona non grata to the rest of the world, as he is to me and this book. Glitter cruelly damaged the lives of his victims. He also damaged the financial position of many of his professional associates. With records produced by Mike, his backing musicians had carved out a good career of their own as The Glitter Band and that was halted overnight. Sadly, Mike Leander died in 1996 and Glitter's criminal conviction cut off the flow of royalties to the Leander estate.

The success of 'Rock And Roll Pt. 2' in America in a way lead to the creation of GTO Records. The record went to US No. 7 and Dick Leahy at Bell Records UK urged his boss Larry Uttal, head of the American Bell Records, to quickly take Gary over to the States to promote it. If he had done so, there was every chance that the record could have been an US No. 1 and paved the way for Glitter to have the string of hits there that he had in most other countries of the world. The problem was that Larry had sold Bell to Columbia Pictures three years earlier. He had taken Columbia shares for the sale and the quoted price of Columbia shares had now dropped by about 75 per cent. Larry had a three-year contract to run Bell and was insisting that Columbia made good his loss before signing a new contract. In the meantime, he was purposefully doing nothing to help the company

Larry Uttal was not a particularly likeable man and had over-played his hand with his bosses. Instead of giving him the deal that he demanded, they let him go and appointed Clive Davis, one of the best men in the record business, to take over as the new head of Bell. Clive Davis had been the uber-successful head of CBS Records in New York, having signed a string of major artists to that company, including Bruce Springsteen, Simon & Garfunkel, Billy Joel, Chicago and Aerosmith. Clive had been fired by CBS in July 1973, ostensibly for charging the cost of his son's bar mitzvah to the company. This is a ridiculous offence, and something that Clive denies to this day. Even if it were true, Clive was making millions for the company, signing big-selling, prestige artists, and sacking him for charging fifteen thousand dollars of personal expenses made no business sense. To his immediate bosses, this would have been like you or I using the company phone for personal calls.

The truth was that CBS Records was owned by the company that owned CBS News, a station that was constantly critical of President Richard Nixon. Tricky Dicky, as he was rightly known, was determined to have CBS reigned in. He seized on the fact that CBS Records' black music arm might be using drugs as payola, something that was common to most record companies. The CBS corporate board – concerned that they might lose their broadcasting licence – did what they considered to be the right thing by immediately firing the head of their record company. Using the excuse of his financial malfeasance, Clive Davis was actually marched out of his office by security guards. The whole record industry was aware that his vilification was a farce, and he was soon appointed as a consultant to Columbia Pictures, a company that at that time was not associated with CBS. Clive was the hottest record executive in the world and it was quite likely that Columbia manipulated the situation to get Larry out and Clive in.

The changes at the top of Bell made Dick Leahy reconsider his own position and I seized the opportunity to offer him a 50 per cent partnership in the new GTO Records. I had been most impressed with him. Apart from the product I supplied, and Bell's US acts, he had signed a number of good UK-based artists, most notably the hugely successful Bay City Rollers. He was passionate about records, understood the business inside out, had 'great ears' – industry shorthand for an ability to pick hits – and most importantly he had great rapport with artists. I had been flirting with him for a while about him someday joining me in starting a GTO Records division.

I told Dick that I would make a deal with a major record label to finance the company but he would have complete autonomy in the choice of artists and running of the business. This had obvious appeal to Dick, but by the same token if he chose to leave Bell, he could have walked into almost any job in the UK record business. He was a cautious man and he wanted time to consider his options. Clive Davis had asked him to fly to New York to discuss his staying on with Bell, and I wanted to see Clive to discuss the missed opportunity of bringing Gary Glitter to America.

We flew over to New York together to meet with Clive. He is a remarkable man, a couple of years older than me, and even today when most of our contemporaries are long retired from the music business or in the Rock'n'Roll Hall of Fame in the sky, he is still an active force to be reckoned with. I understood Dick well enough to not bring up his joining me, leaving him deep in thought as to what his next career move should be. Privately, I thought that he would stay with Bell. Clive Davis was a music executive legend. He loved his artists, and fought for them, as did Dick. There was no question that as soon as Clive got behind the desk, the calibre of artists that Dick would be looking after in the UK would be among the highest in the world.

The meeting that we all had was one that I particularly remember. Backed up by Dick, I complained about the fact that Bell had blown Gary Glitter's chance of making an impact in America by refusing to bring him over. Clive had signed major international artists to CBS and he was totally disinterested in what he considered to be a one-hit disco dance record performed by a strange-looking man dressed in tinfoil and a dodgy wig. He was dismissive to the point of rudeness, as he focused his attention on trying to persuade Dick to stay. Clive's ego was apparent as he explained that he was changing the company's name to Arista and would have unlimited backing to sign any artist that he wanted. He saw Dick as being a vital part of his plans to make sure that his artists were properly looked after in the UK, as well as relying on Dick to raise the standard of artists that were signed in the UK office. I felt sure that Dick would say yes to what was obviously a great opportunity. I said nothing during Clive's proposition, which was just as well because he talked to Dick as if I were not there. I was not offended. Indeed, if anything, I admired Clive's line of seduction, clearly perfected by his pitch to artists, and I took mental notes. The meeting lasted a long time. I was convinced that Dick would stay with Clive and – thinking of the pastrami sandwich I could get at the Stage Deli across 6th Avenue – I was near to excusing myself.

Clive finally sat back, a smug look on his face, and asked Dick, 'So what do you think?'

To my amazement, Dick pointed his thumb in my direction and said, 'Thanks for the offer, but I think I'll start a record company with him.' The look on Clive Davis's face was priceless. I said a cheery goodbye to the dumbstruck Clive and we left.

Clive, however, managed to do quite well without Dick, signing Aretha Franklin, Whitney Houston, Hall & Oates, Barry Manilow and many other big stars to the Arista label. Later when I asked Dick why he had turned Clive down, he said, 'He was dismissive of our artist, he was rude to you, and he fancies himself a bit too much.' So GTO Records was born. Under Dick's guidance it would be an important player in the UK business, and it deserves, and will later get, a chapter on its own.

Some time in 1977 Nicky Chinn came to see me about managing The Sweet. Nicky wrote the band's hit songs with Mike Chapman. They were also managing the band but finding it difficult to do so, possibly because of lead singer Brian Connolly's severe drink problem. Nicky was an interesting man. He came from a family that was successful in business and I felt that he did not have the pride that he should have in his own achievements. Although his songs sold millions of copies, he seemed somewhat embarrassed by their bubblegum nature. I assured him that he should not have been as he was responsible for some of the greatest glam-rock hits of the era, like 'Blockbuster'.

The Sweet were a great example of how a record can be a huge hit with a song that does not stand up on its own. There are very few, if any, cover versions of The Sweet's 'Blockbuster', which was a huge No. 1 record when it was released in 1973. The same anomaly applies to voices. Nobody would deny the value of Jagger's voice to Stones records, but neither would you hear a good song and say, 'I'd like to hear Mick Jagger singing that.'

It was not difficult to put together an extensive tour for The Sweet. I took James, my then seven-year-old son, to see them and naturally went backstage to meet the band. As we went into the dressing room, there was such a groupie fest going on, I had to spin him round and take him out.

I was also asked by Maurice Oberstein head of CBS Records, to manage Sailor. The band had had a couple of hits with 'Girls, Girls, Girls' and 'A Glass of Champagne'. 'Girls …' was particularly successful, knocking 'Bohemian Rhapsody' from No. 1 in 1976. I had met the group's leader Georg Kajanus and guitarist Phil Pickett some years earlier when I had signed them to Gem as Kajanus Pickett without getting them any success. Georg was a difficult man. CBS had brought over ex-Beach Boy Bruce Johnston to produce a new album, and early on in the recording process Bruce told me that he was giving up as he was 'too old and too rich to put up with Georg's shit.' Phil Pickett went on to write and work with Boy George, co-writing 'Karma Chameleon', one of the best-selling singles of all time worldwide. I still see Phil from time to time. Nice man.

30. GTO RECORDS – DICK LEAHY, DONNA SUMMER, BILLY OCEAN, HEATWAVE

Dick Leahy was born a year after me and was raised in Dagenham, east London – very much the town of the Ford motor company. Most of his family worked for Ford and it was expected that Dick would do the same. However, he had no wish to follow the family path. Passionate about pop music, he got a job in the A&R department of Philips Records. Dick soon established himself as having 'ears'. He was poached by Larry Uttall, who was setting up a UK office for Bell, and part of Dick's job was to look after my Gem output.

Dick was good at his job and extremely well respected within the industry. I soon had it in the back of my mind that, should I ever want to start a record company, I would want Dick to head it up. I casually planted this idea in Dick's mind when it was obvious to me that Larry Uttal was having trouble with Columbia, his parent company in New York. Dick did not react to my suggestion. He was a very contained man other than when he was talking about music, and I was content to let the thought of running a GTO record company stay with him.

I have already told you how Dick spontaneously accepted my job offer during a meeting with Clive Davis, when he turned down a very attractive job. I was aware that once it was known that Dick was leaving Bell, he would have many offers to join other companies and I had to move quickly to get him to come and join me before he changed his mind. I offered him a 50/50 deal with the promise of great autonomy. For the first time in his business life he would, to all intents and purposes, be his own boss. Dick was very happy with this proposal, but I knew I had to get the deal signed before he was seduced away by offers from the major record companies.

I used my frequent practice for getting deals concluded: get the principal and their lawyers in a room together with a secretary and have no one leave the room until the deal was agreed and signed. In this case – to make the process more seductive – I took Dick, his lawyer Tony Russell, my lawyer Martin Walford and my secretary Pat Grace to the south of France. I kept a twenty-two-foot motorboat in Cannes called *Ziggy Stardust*, courtesy of Mr Bowie. I anchored *Ziggy* in a very pleasant bay, and the five of us plus Pat's typewriter sat on the boat, enjoying the Mediterranean sunshine and some nice white wine from a chiller bag until we agreed the partnership deal and signed off the contracts. It was a happy negotiation and would prove to be a happy deal.

There was no problem in finding a major record company to finance the operation. Dick was highly rated and I had established myself as someone to do business with because of my success with Bowie, Glitter, The New Seekers and the other hits that had emanated from Gem/GTO productions. Although we

were yet to sign an artist, there was competition amongst the
major record companies to secure our product. Eventually we
settled on Polydor Records, who financed the company through
advances against royalties that we would earn from future
product. We gave Polydor the rights to distribute our product
throughout the world, excluding America, where their operation was not particularly successful. We decided that instead we
would licence our product on an artist-by-artist basis in the US.

Although Dick was happy to be in business with me, he was
very keen not to be seen as an employee running my record
label. With my support, he took offices in Mayfair and had a
distinctive logo designed for GTO Records. He put together
a great staff, many of whom went on to have brilliant careers
in the music industry after GTO was sold to CBS Records:
Di Graham, my ex-secretary, ran the international division.
She went on to become a top executive at CBS in Paris and
then head of BMG International and eventually head of Arista
Records. Paul Kinder – who was my office boy – asked if he
could also move over to work for Dick. I happily approved and
Paul became head of A&R. He went on to have a successful
career with Virgin Records. The head of regional promotion was
Edward Christie, who had started working for me as a chauf-
feur, then moved on to my film division to be in charge of print
movement. But music was Edward's first love and I persuaded
Dick to take him on.

GTO Records were in business before the EU and it was
not unusual to own rights only for the UK. We were offered
distribution for many artists owned by American record companies, most notably Donna Summer, the most successful artist

that we licensed. When 'Love To Love You Baby' was a hit, we bought Donna a mink coat as a thank-you gift. Donna's recordings were owned worldwide by Casablanca Records. Casablanca was owned by Neil Bogart and he and I got to know each other quite well. He once told me one of the great stories of the music business: when he started Casablanca, he had no success for a long time. He had put all of his money into the band Kiss and nobody was buying their first album. He was so low that he went to the beach and walked into the sea with stones in his pocket with the intention of ending his life. He told me that he stood in the sea for hours then said to himself 'Fuck it.' He went back to his office and rented a Rolls-Royce to cheer himself up. A few weeks later Kiss suddenly took off big time, and Neil was in business. Casablanca then went on to become one of the most successful disco record companies of the time, signing the Village People as well as Donna Summer.

I almost took Neil Bogart into the film business. I had acquired the rights to make Elton John and Bernie Taupins's 'Benny and The Jets' into a film and Neil was going to finance it. As with most film projects, it did not happen – but that didn't stop us having a great time talking about setting the story on LA's Venice Beach where roller disco was the craze of the month. I tried it myself but my portly five-feet seven-inches did not feel comfortable amongst the tall, slim, blonde Californians. Tragically Neil died of cancer at the age of thirty-nine and he was much mourned by all who had known him.

GTO's first hit in 1976 was 'Only You Can' by Fox. The band's lead vocalist – British-Australian Noosha Fox – went on to make a cameo appearance in *Side By Side*, a film I produced which was directed by Bruce Beresford. It was his first film outside of his native Australia. Bruce went on to be an A-list Hollywood film director and never mentions *Side By Side* in his credits. I can understand why … it was a rubbish film!

GTO Records' most successful homegrown artists were Billy Ocean and Heatwave, both major artists in the seventies. Billy Ocean, who is still going strong, was a great coup for the label. He is the biggest-selling UK black solo artist. A great singer, and a lovely man, Billy was managed by Laurie Jay. In the 1980s when I was not doing well, I almost went into the management business with Laurie. He had lost Billy as a client but he had a nose for talent and there were a couple of his acts that I thought showed great promise. Unfortunately, Laurie was far too cavalier in his business dealings, which is probably why Billy left him, and I did not pursue a relationship. Laurie died in 2017 and I have been told that in recent years when he was struggling financially, Billy helped him out.

Heatwave were an extremely important and influential band in the UK disco/funk scene. It was Paul Kinder who brought the band to GTO Records and they were a fantastic signing. Formed in Germany by ex-American serviceman Johnnie Wilder Jr, they moved to the UK where Johnnie teamed up with Cleethorpes-born Rod Temperton. Dick signed them in 1976 and put them into the studio to be produced by Barry Blue – real name Barry Green (not much of a change!). Barry had a hit as a singer in 1973 with 'Dancin' on a Saturday Night', but was more comfortable behind a sound desk than in a TV studio. Barry produced a string of hits for Heatwave but much of the band's success was due to Rod's writing and their dynamic stage act.

Johnnie Wilder was an incredible performer and always brought the audience to their dancing feet. His performance was almost acrobatic. His career took a different turn after a tragic car accident left him paralysed from the neck down. A true musician, although no longer a dancer, he carried on for many years and became a successful gospel artist. He died in his sleep in 2006.

The band had already suffered a dramatic loss when guitarist Jesse Whitten was killed in a stabbing incident in 1978 and the band's Swiss bass player Mario Mantese was also stabbed after a party at Elton John's house. He was left in a coma and became blind, paralysed and mute but miraculously recovered his health and has gone on to write about his near-death experiences. Even by the standards of rock'n'roll, Heatwave certainly had more than their fair share of tragedy, but they left a great legacy with their music. Rod Temperton, of course, went on to be a major songwriter – most famously writing 'Thriller' for Michael Jackson.

GTO Records had thirty-seven hit singles and fifteen hit albums in the four years before we sold the company to CBS (now Sony Records) in 1978. Dick Asher, the American head of CBS UK, had asked me a few times if GTO Records was for sale. Although we had an important roster of artists, Dick's main reason for wanting to buy GTO Records was a desire for Dick Leahy to run CBS in the UK. I really wanted to make the sale because in my opinion the price bandied around very much reflected the anticipation of Dick's services as head of CBS. For me it was an easy 'Yes' but as part of the deal Dick would be obliged to enter into a long-term service agreement to run GTO as part of the CBS group, in the hope that he would soon take over the running of CBS UK. Once again, I did not pressure

Dick into selling. He knew of CBS's interest and I just bided my time, whilst reminding Dick that a big cheque was only a phone call away.

One memorable day, when Dick and I were in LA, we were invited to a pool party at a large Norma Desmond-style mansion that was for sale on – where else? – Sunset Boulevard. I was shown around and it was really incredible. A hallway that looked as big as the Albert Hall, and countless rooms. The standout memory was the huge ballroom. At one end there was a wall, which at the touch of a secret switch opened to reveal a speakeasy-type room where, in the days of prohibition, there would have been a bar stocked with illicit booze. A door in this room opened to a blocked-off tunnel which led to the neighbouring estate. Apparently there was a network of these tunnels between all of the estates on Sunset which guests could use to escape from any police raid.

It was a typical LA party, scattered with tall, tanned California blonds both male and female. There was a bar next to the pool, dispensing chilled white wine and champagne. As we lounged – or frolicked may be a better word – in the pool, by anyone's standards, it was better than being in Dagenham, Dick's home town.

Dick, his face in the sun, said, 'I could get used to this, Laurence.'

'It's a phone call away,' I reminded him.

'Make the call.'

And so I did. A few weeks later, Dick, Tony Russell and I were ensconced in a large suite at a Park Lane hotel, along with Dick Asher, his business affairs team and a secretary. It was a

Laurence Myers-style meeting with everyone agreeing not to leave until the deal was done. Proceedings started at about 10 a.m. Negotiations went smoothly but by one o'clock there was still one huge sticking point, which was something to do with Heatwave. I cannot remember exactly what it was but Dick Asher said that it was a deal-breaker. Some two hours later, Dick Asher conceded and the deal was finally completed on our terms, and here is why …

It was a Friday, which is most important to my story. As with many of us, the person Dick was most fearful of upsetting was his wife. Dick's wife Sheila was quite a formidable character, and Dick had mentioned to me that he had to catch an early-evening flight to be back in New York so that he could attend Sheila's nephew's bar mitzvah the next day. When we reached the impasse, I declined to order lunch and said that I needed to speak with Dick Leahy and Tony about it privately. We retired to our room where I told Dick and Tony that we should talk about football or anything else to kill some time. After about an hour, the CBS lawyer put his head round the door and asked if we were making progress. 'Sadly not,' I replied. Half an hour later we went back in and I told Dick Asher that regretfully, we could not agree. Asher, desperate not to miss his plane, threw up his hands and conceded the point. The secretary deleted the contentious clause and we all signed off on the paperwork. Asher dashed off to get his plane and we all ordered room service on CBS's room charge.

Part of the deal obliged Dick Leahy to work for CBS as head of GTO, but there was no legal obligation for Dick to take over the running of CBS UK. And, in spite of Dick Asher's entreaties, Dick did not move over to CBS. He was not being difficult but, having had an inside taste of the politics in a big record company, he did not want to be part of it.

After Dick left CBS he went into the publishing business with Bryan Morrison, signing George Michael as a songwriter. This was in the eighties. I was not doing well and considering setting up a new company with my ex-employee David Mintz. Wham! did not have a manager and I asked Dick to arrange a meeting with them to pitch for the job. Dick sent Andrew Ridgeley to meet us. Without George Michael, I knew it was just an empty gesture, but nevertheless I appreciated the respect that he showed me in setting up the meeting. When Wham! stopped and George went on to have his brilliant solo career, Dick virtually managed him for some years. As I mentioned earlier when writing about Freddy Bienstock, he asked me to help with negotiations for a new administrator of George's catalogue, which was very flattering. Dick was a brilliant partner for me. He used to call me when I was on holiday to tell me that all was going well and there was nothing to worry about. He has retired to Spain and I wish him well.

A word about singers who are precious about their voice. Lots of singers will not record in the morning because their vocal chords have yet to wake up. Others insist on days off on tour to rest their voice. In 1987 the phenomenal Tom Jones made a record from me called 'A Boy From Nowhere'. It went to UK No. 2, his highest entry for seventeen years. Tom was doing a UK tour when the song started racing up the charts. The tour was so tight that there seemed to be no gap for Tom to record the desperately needed promotional video. Without any fuss, Tom walked off stage after his Manchester gig, went straight to the studio and recorded the song to camera in a couple of takes at about two o'clock in the morning. The next day he performed on stage at his next scheduled date. You can see Tom perform the song on YouTube, and you should. I believe that he is the greatest male singer the UK has ever produced and on 'A Boy From Nowhere' he is at his balladic best.

The song, produced by Mike Leander, was written by Mike and Eddie Seago for a stage musical called *Matador*, which I later produced on the West End stage, casting the young John Barrowman in the title role. John sang the song beautifully on stage, but he is the first to admit that Tom's version was hard to follow. Mike stuck with his old friend and writing partner, Eddie, to write the lyrics for *Matador*. Eddie had never written for theatre, his lyrics were poor and I begged Mike to drop him and let me bring in the highly acclaimed theatre lyricist Don Black, but, ever loyal, Mike would not. The reviews of the show were unkind, some particularly critical of Eddie's lyrics and I believe that the show might have had real success had Don been brought in.

Show business – everything about it is appealing.

31. GEM RECORDS – MY SWAN SONG IN THE RECORD BUSINESS

In 1979, after the sale of GTO Records to CBS, I was approached by Bob Summer – the worldwide head of RCA Records – to start a new record company to be distributed by RCA. He had once offered me the job of head of RCA UK but I had declined on the basis that it did not pay particularly well, so obviously he thought well of me. I decided to use the Gem name for the new company because it had been so lucky for me as a production company recording Bowie, Glitter and others.

I made a three-year deal under which RCA would – unusually – provide us with our overhead expenses budget as well as a generous budget for recording artists. Under my Gem deal with Bell Records I got paid a sum of money on delivery of each record. After recording costs there was little left over for overheads and the deal only worked for me because we started having hits from day one. I managed to negotiate the great deal based on my theory that record company executives were mainly concerned about the impact of a bad deal during their own tenure. With that in mind, I offered RCA an interest in the

Gem artists for ten years after the deal ended, thus enabling Bob to carry forward any loss by RCA to a time when it was reasonable to assume that he would be long gone. It was a risky deal for RCA because – with the overheads covered – there was no pressure to make profits to survive. They quite reasonably insisted that they approved any artist that we signed, and I was contractually bound to fly to New York on a regular basis to present artists to Bob for his approval. Such was the profligacy of the business at that time, I got him to agree that RCA would pay for me to fly over on Concorde, the new supersonic jet service run by BA. The fares were exorbitant, but it only took three and a half hours to New York and with the five-hour time difference, you actually arrived before you left.

At the time I had David Simone working for me as an in-house lawyer. He had been introduced to me by my brother-in-law Larry Levene. He was twenty-six years old, and was very much into the music business. He had been social secretary at his university, booking big bands. I appointed David as head of the new Gem Records. David put together a good team. He brought back ex-GTO Records employee Edward Christie as head of A&R; Clifford Gee was head of marketing; Golly Gallagher was head of promotions. Although Gem did not do well, all of these guys were talented and went on to have success within the industry. When I knew that Gem was coming to an end I encouraged David take a job as head of business affairs at Arista, where he was soon moved up to be MD. He was then head of Phonogram before moving to be chairman of MCA. He went to the USA to start UNI Records for MCA, then joined Geffen Records where he was head of A&R. He is currently a very successful manager living and working in New York and remains a close friend.

Edward Christie started Abstract Records, an independent record label dealing with the heaviest of heavy metal bands and Abstract Distribution in the States. Both companies did extremely well. He sold his interests in 2017. He lives in London with his wife Yvonne – also a clever person – who, through her glamour model agency, started the *Sun*'s Page 3 girls in 1970.

After leaving Gem, Golly did very well as an independent record plugger until he was exposed on TV for hyping records up the charts by buying multiple copies of singles. He bought from independent record retailers who reported their sales to the compilers of the singles charts. He would give the singles back to the shop owner or manager, who could then resell them and keep the cash.

Gem Records' biggest hit single was 'Born To Be Alive' by Spanish/French artist Patrick Hernandez, which made UK No. 10. We picked it up for the UK at Marsha's insistence after she and I heard it being played at Whisky À Gogo at Midem in Cannes. Claude Pellerin, a Frenchman who owned the record world, had cleverly arranged to have it played in the club, in the hope that it would help him sell it internationally – and it worked. David and Edward were not excited to put the record out as it was a Gary Glitter soundalike. Musical tastes were diversifying and moving away from the domination of wide-appeal artists that had given me success in the past. David and Edward were quite rightly looking to have Gem perceived as a record company for the future and when I insisted that we released 'Born To Be Alive', they considered it a step backwards.

When it started rapidly climbing up the charts, they forgave me. A Top 10 record is something to be proud of, but I had been so spoiled by the many No. 1s of so many previous records, that I, personally, could not get too excited.

I secured the right to release the soundtrack of *The Wanderers* – a GTO film crammed with great sixties hits. It made the album charts. After the Gem deal, I licensed it to third parties and it was a consistent seller for another twenty years or so, eventually recouping the loss I made on the film.

Looking to the future, David and Edward were impressed by Trevor Horn, a multi-instrumentalist/producer whom they signed with his band Garbo. Garbo was not a success for us, but they were right about Trevor. He called his next band The Buggles and had an instant No. 1 with 'Video Killed the Radio Star' through Island Records. Trevor also masterminded the promo video for the song, which was the first clip to be played on MTV. He went on to be one of the most important producers of the eighties.

Again, moving away from my comfort zone, we signed Samson, a stereotypically shock-rock heavy metal band put together by Paul Samson. The band's drummer, Thunderstick, wore an evil-looking leather mask over his face and played in a cage on stage. The lead singer was Bruce Dickinson, widely acclaimed as a great artist in heavy metal. We made an album called *Head On* with Samson. It briefly made the charts but was not a big seller. The band were fighting with their management, always a problem for the caught-in-the-middle record company. In all honesty our promotion department's DNA was more mainstream pop, so we did not really know how to help them.

We were contacted by Sanctuary Records, a successful company that had signed top heavy metal band Iron Maiden and desperately wanted Bruce Dickinson to take over in the band as lead singer. As a condition of releasing Bruce, David sold the Gem album to Sanctuary for more than its cost: a brilliant deal.

Gem had a couple of other minor hits but the most successful signing was the UK Subs, a punk band signed to Gem by Edward. I commissioned quirky director Julien Temple, young and up-and-coming – to make a short film about them to release as support to the main feature that my GTO Films then had on general release. The film *Punk Can Take It* was a very clever parody of wartime newsreel, portraying the punk movement as under attack from conventional society. John Snagg, a still recognisable voice of wartime news reporting, did the stylised commentary. Julien is now a respected maker of off-beat movies, and he directed *Habaneros*, a brilliant documentary on Cuba. It being a small world, the film was produced by Richard Conway, the son of great friends of ours.

UK Subs were important to Gem Records, giving us half a dozen Top 50 hits, but I had no sense of connection to them or to their music. As I have frequently mentioned before, I had a passion for songwriters. Whilst none of my writers could, or even tried to, compete with the lyrics of Cole Porter or Johnny Mercer, they wrote clever lyrics, contemporary to the day. The UK Subs' songs had lyrics like: 'Tomorrow's girl is pissing in your ear.' I rest my case. It was a UK Subs gig that decided me that it was time to go. Marsha had already opted out of the role of Manager's Dutiful Wife. In ten years of tirelessly supporting me in my work, she had developed her own career as a very successful antique dealer and was tired of schlepping to gigs. A couple of months earlier, we had gone to see Heatwave perform a sold-out concert at what was then the Hammersmith Odeon (currently the Eventim Apollo). The band's charismatic front-man Johnnie Wilder Jr – arms up, stabbing the air, was chanting 'Ooh, ooh,' to the driving beat of Rod Temperton's 'Boogie Nights'. I was up there 'Ooh-oohing' with the best of them. The packed audience leapt to their feet to join in – except one person. I looked down and there was Marsha, sitting unmoved.

I indicated with my head that she should jump up and join in the fun.

Nothing.

More 'ooh-ooing' and emphatic head-messaging from me for Marsha to jump up and have an 'ooh, ooh'. Still nothing.

On stage, Johnny worked up a sweat. The audience worked up a sweat too, particularly ripe when outstretched arms exposed sweaty armpits. As the song ended, Marsha used her head to indicate that I was to sit down next to her, which I did. She leaned over and whispered in my ear. 'Enough with the ooh-oohing. Next time take me to see Streisand.'

Then it was my time to opt out. The Subs were playing a sold-out gig at a regular punk venue and, having never seen them perform, I decided to go and enjoy their success. Picture, if you can, a seedy venue in a seedy part of north London. An audience of punks are there, many with spiky mohican hair, their pierced faces, ears (and no doubt other parts unseen) decorated with metal skulls, chains and other ornamentation that is mysterious to me. Charlie Harper, the UK Subs' charismatic leader, is on stage sneering 'Stranglehold' – one of their hits – to his adoring fans.

At Charlie's feet, in the mosh pit, more punks are body-slam-
ming each other as they pogo up and down. They show their
further appreciation by spraying family-size globules of spit over
the band, making pretty rainbow effects in the stage lighting. I, a
rictus smile on my face, am trying to pretend that I am enjoying
the show. Next to me is an unsmiling punk, his punk lady-friend
next to him, his doppelganger apart from her metal-studded
leather-clad boobs. Some of the audience are 'weekend punks',
their mohicans artfully slicked back for their day job in a bank,
but these two are the real thing.

Mr Punk, his eyes fixed on Charlie Harper, is slurping a pint
of beer, his head nodding viciously in time to the ear-bashing
mono-melody coming from the stage. Without warning, he
pukes voluminously down his punk, black leather jacket. The
vomit glides from the jacket, explodes over his punk standard
issue Doc Martens, splattering vomit on to my Gucci loafers. But
here's the killer. Mr Punk does not move. He does not acknowledge any dilemma. He does not apologise. He just carries on
drinking his beer and nodding in time to the music. My own
instinct to move away is hampered by the carpet, so filthy that
my sick-patterned Gucci shoes are sticking to it.

I should not mock punk. Charlie Harper, with an ever-changing line-up of musicians, still works. His fans, some still in
uniform, are loyal. He still sells some records and makes a
modest contribution to my catalogue.

Pioneered by my old house guest Iggy Pop, punk was part
of a social movement arising out of the anger of the disenfran-
chised youth around the world. It was a genuine influence on the
music of the day. It also influenced fashion, and the 'punk look'

frequently reappears on catwalks even to this day. Unlike the sometimes physical warfare between mods and rockers in the sixties, punks did not go out on a Saturday night looking for a fight. The fact that I have chosen to mock punk behaviour that particular Saturday night at the Camden Palace I think reflects badly on me, but reinforces that I just didn't 'get it' as I didn't 'get' heavy metal. The music did not drive mainstream rock and pop out of the market but I took my antipathy to these genres as a warning sign. Music-business executives who made their judgements based on public trends, irrespective of their personal taste, could thrive in the music business as they got older. My success in the music business came because my musical taste coincided with much of the record-buying public. Clearly the times, they were a-changin'. Rap did not start to evolve until the nineties but – had I carried on – I would have felt completely redundant.

My deal with RCA was coming to an end. I was forty-two, had lost my enthusiasm for the business and I decided there and then, in my vomit-splattered Gucci shoes, that I had reached my sell-by date. It was time for me to say 'Thank you and goodbye' to the music business.

My journey had not been without its highlights. Some artists would not have had the careers that they did without my influence. My thumbprint was on records that had sold more millions than I can count. My reputation was still such that I could call anybody in the business to get an immediate 'No' which, if you think about it, is almost as good as a 'Yes'. The reluctance of people at the top to muck you about is, I believe, a mark of your stature in any business and I felt that I was quitting when I was just about ahead.

I can't believe that it was fifty years – a *half a century* – ago that I worked with the Rolling Stones, David Bowie, The Beatles and record-makers Mickie Most, Mike Leander and Tony Macaulay. There were many other talented people who I worked with on both sides of the microphone who also put my kids through private school.

I earned a lot of money in the music business and lost a lot in the film business, with no regrets. I would possibly have done as well or even better had I stayed in my previous career, as an accountant, but I was never in music for the money. I loved what I did. I mixed with talented, exciting, vibrant people at a time in the development of popular music when London was the place to be. To some extent, we were all riding on the crest of the British Invasion that was taking over the American music charts. Part of this was because some of the most successful British bands were in fact playing music 'borrowed' from black American artists. Middle America's moms, who did not like the idea of a poster of Chuck Berry, Muddy Waters – or even the overtly sexy Elvis – on their daughters' bedroom wall, happily drove their kids to see those cute English boys with their cute haircuts and cute English accents. Those moms even liked the Rolling Stones I think because, in the privacy of their own bedrooms, they fancied Mick.

Over the past fifty years, other than mankind's determination to continue to kill each other over religious differences, the world has changed. Technology has changed the music-buying habits of the young. Fifty years ago, young people listened to their music in the privacy of their bedrooms on inferior record players. Homes had one telephone line, and mum and dad rationed teenage use. There were very few hours of TV with youth appeal and, as often as they could, teenagers disappeared from their homes to meet their friends, passing their younger siblings playing happily in the street. Kids did not get routinely mugged, stabbed or abused, and, generally speaking, their parents were rightly not concerned for their offspring's safety, even without the invisible umbilical cord of the yet-to-be-invented mobile phone.

Music is now bought – or more often pirated – and downloaded onto mobile phones and many devices called 'I' something that I would just as soon never have to learn about. You can ask your little box called Alexa to play any song that has ever been recorded, without even saying 'Please', and she will oblige. There are no record stores where kids can gather on a Saturday morning to listen to the latest hits before they buy. Kids now 'gather' on social media sites and establish firm friendships with other kids that they have never met.

In previous generations, popular music was recorded using big bands or orchestras. Many homes in the sixties still had a piano in the parlour, but it was a difficult instrument to learn, and money had to be found for lessons. You only needed a cheap guitar to play rock'n'roll and three easy-to-learn chords gave kids an extensive repertoire. I even learned them myself, taught by Mickie Most.

All over the UK, groups were formed, collars were turned up à la Presley, and the sales of Brylcreem rocketed. Thousands of kids dreamed of making their living playing music, and although most didn't, some did. Two kids called John and Paul did rather well and changed the way that the world viewed youth.

The 2i's basement cellar, where so many UK artists started their careers, has long gone, but if it were still there, like many of the pubs that used to book bands, it would now be hosting stand-up comedy, the new rock'n'roll.

The legendary Woodstock festival put on at a farm in the Catskill Mountains in 1969 was pretty much a one-off at the time. Following the example of Mr Eavis, who started the Glastonbury festival on his farm in Somerset the following year, half the farms in the UK seem now to be putting on festivals. Music fans are very well entertained at these mega-concerts by great shows, which the majority of the tens of thousands attending watch on giant screens. I am not at all critical of this. The fans have a great time and there are very few stars who do not play these events. Interestingly, most of the top attractions at these events are well-established names who have been performing live for some years.

Pop stars are now fast-tracked to fame by reality shows. Some contestants will last but most will fail, not having learned their trade schlepping around the country to badly paid gigs, crammed into a Ford Transit van. Apart from jealousy that I have no financial interest in these programmes (something that I have touched on before), the reason I particularly dislike them is that the audiences allow themselves to be manipulated to scream with delight when a contestant reaches a high note or, in some cases, any note at all. The people who vote from home are often influenced by the contestant's 'back story' – the more emotionally upsetting the better when it comes to getting votes. The owners of the shows sign every artist who might prove to be popular – as would I in their position – but I believe that these shows are bad for the business. They are unfair competition for artists who are striving for success the hard way, working for years to try to capture a following.

The major record companies, Universal, Sony and Warner Music, control about 80 per cent of the music sold in the world. Also, in my view, a bad thing. Artists can, and do, bypass the establishment and find success, but it is rare. Do I sound like an out-of-touch grumpy old man? I hope so, I worked hard for the right to be one.

I loved my time in the music business. Many years ago, Andrew Oldham adopted the slogan 'Happy to be part of the industry of human happiness' for Immediate Records. On reflection, it was a very corny sentiment but – for me – it was true. Music does bring happiness, especially when it makes you want to get up and dance. It is an integral part of our memories and, like me, I am sure that you identify certain times and events in your life with certain songs. I still get a kick out of hearing a song on the radio that might never have been exposed to the public without my involvement and, although I no longer get up and dance as well as I used to, there is definitely still a twitch in my legs.

ACKNOWLEDGEMENTS

Thank you to my family and friends, who have encouraged me to write this book for many years (probably to stop me telling them a story that I have told them many times before…)

For help with turning my sometimes hazy recollections into something tangible, I'd like to thank Clare Lockhart for her research, editing and general encouragement.

For giving their time and generously allowing me to plunder their own material, I'd like to thank and acknowledge Kevin Cann (*Any Day Now: David Bowie The London Years 1947–1974*); Peter and Leni Gillman (*Alias David Bowie*); Fred Goodman (*Allen Klein: The Man Who Bailed Out the Beatles, Made the Stones, and Transformed Rock & Roll*); and Tony Zanetta (*Stardust: The David Bowie Story*, written with Henry Edwards).

For sharing their memories with me and reminding me what a blast we had, I'd like to thank Angie Bowie, Eileen Bradley (former V.P. GTO Inc); Jon Brewer (film-maker and former Gem employee); Dana Gillespie (former Gem artist and close friend of David Bowie); Don Hunter (former Gem employee who brought in Stevie Wonder); Penny Leander (my dear departed friend Mike Leander's wife); and Anya Wilson (former Gem record plugger).

For their help with getting this book published, I'd like to thank my copyeditor Lucian Randall, John Bond and George Edgeller at whitefox Publishing, and Simon Levy who designed the cover.

I am indebted to you all...

INDEX

A&M Records 239
Abba 52, 105; 'Waterloo' 52
ABKCO (Allen And Betty
    Klein COmpany) 67–8,
    129–30, 142
Academy Awards (1973) 240
Ad Lib club, London 42
ADP Ltd 169
Albion Records 238, 239–40
Alexander, J. W. 124–5
Anderson, Stig 52
Angel 245
Animals, The 35, 37, 41, 46, 47,
    48, 57, 58–9, 60–1, 64, 66,
    67, 68, 89, 118, 121, 245–6;
    'Baby Let Me Take You
    Home' 37; 'The House of
    the Rising Sun' 35, 37, 41,
    118
Anka, Paul 180–1
Apple Corp 152–6, 208

Apple Records 145, 154
Arcade Records 209, 255–68
Arcade Video 264–5
Archies, The (animated TV
    series) 55
Arden, Don 46–9, 87, 88, 101,
    146
Arista Records 147–8, 277–8,
    282, 291
Arnold, Martin and Morrow
    119
Asher, Dick 285–8
Astoria Candy Stores, Finsbury
    Park 17–18, 21–2, 24–6, 61,
    205
Astoria cinema, Seven Sisters
    Road 17–18, 24–5, 61,
    205
Atlantic Records 143, 163
Attenborough, Richard 20
Average White Band, The 146

Bacharach, Bert 104

Bag O' Nails, London 42

Bart, Lionel 43–5, 105

Bassey, Shirley 103, 163

Beatles, The 37, 40, 56, 58, 59,
     68, 88–9, 103, 111, 115,
     116, 123, 124, 130, 132,
     133, 134, 140, 145, 151–6,
     160, 163, 179, 189, 196,
     208, 232, 245, 249, 251,
     266, 269, 298, 299; 'Hey
     Jude' 145; 'She's Leaving
     Home 163, 269; 'Yesterday'
     116

Beautiful (musical) 55

Beck, Jeff 69, 147, 148–50; 'Hi
     Ho Silver Lining' 147

Bee Gees, The 46

Bell Records 164, 165, 195,
     271, 274, 275, 276–7, 280,
     281, 290

Bell, Kenny 185

Belushi, John 95–6

Benjamin, Louis 107

Beresford, Bruce 284

Bergman, Jo 135

Berlin, Irving 50, 103, 115, 116;
     'I'm Dreaming of a White
     Christmas' 115

Berry, Chuck 46, 146, 266, 298

Berry, Dave: 'The Crying
     Game' 99

Best Direct 265

Beuselinck, Oscar 110

Bev's Blenheim Club, London
     32

Beverley Hills Hotel 83–4, 216;
     Polo Lounge 157, 159

Beverley Sisters 18

Bienstock, Freddy 116–20, 143,
     262, 288

Bienstock, Miriam 143

Bingenheimer, Rodney 188,
     224

Bisset, Jacqueline 74, 79, 80, 82,
     83, 86

Black, Don 45, 104, 161, 173,
     289; 'In One of My Weaker
     Moments' 162

Blackburn, Nick 184, 185

Blackburn, Stan 134

Blake, David 83

Bloom, Jack (father-in-law)
     31–2, 62, 63

Bluestone, Stephanie 126

Boccelli, Andrea 160–1

Bogart, Neil 283

Bolan, Marc 144, 163, 172, 186

Bonham, John 101

Bowie, Angie 75–6, 176–8, 181,
     191, 192, 193, 198, 203–4,
     212, 215, 217, 218, 219–20,
     222–4

Bowie, David 7–8, 76, 144, 170,
     171–98, 203–34, 235, 236,
     237, 241, 248, 253, 281,

Bowie, David *cont.*
290, 298; 'All The Young
Dudes' 211; 'Andy Warhol'
192; *BOWPROMO* 194–5,
196; 'Changes' 206–7; 'Holy
Holy' 186; 'Life On Mars'
192, 206, 207, 210; 'The
Man who Sold the World'
181, 184; *The Man Who Sold
the World* 183, 188, 189, 195;
'Memory of a Free Festival'
186; 'Oh! You Pretty Things'
186; 'Space Oddity' 173, 178,
181, 195, 196; 'Suffragette
City' 208; *The Rise and
Fall of Ziggy Stardust and
the Spiders from Mars* 197,
206, 207, 208, 209–10, 211;
Young Americans 217
Bowie, Zowie (Duncan Jones)
223–4
Boyd, Pattie 136
Bradley, Eileen 244
Brandt, Jerry 57
Branson, Richard 264
Breaking Glass (film) 238
Brewer, Jon 187, 193, 210, 222
Brewer, Liz 187
Brill Building, The, New York
54, 55, 118, 170, 187
Brolly, Brian 162–3, 164
Brooks, Elkie: 'Pearl's A Singer'
53

Brown, Peter 254
Buddy Holly Story, The (film)
148
Budgie (musical) 161–2
Burdon, Eric 121–2
Burrows, Tony 166, 167

Caine, Michael and Shakira 42
Calder, Tony 124, 269
Callander, Peter 51, 104
Cameron, Ray 131
Cann, Kevin: *Any Day Now*
212–13
Cannes Film Festival 71,
73–83, 228–31
Canvey Island 29
Capitol Records 234
Carlin Music 117, 119
Carter, Alan 31
Carter, John 99–100
Casablanca Records 283
Cats (musical) 162–3
Cavern Club, Liverpool 152
CBS Records 67, 195, 247,
265, 274–5, 277, 279, 282,
285–8, 290
Chandler, Chas 121
Chappell Music 118
Cher 51, 52, 245; 'Little Man' 52
Chinn, Nicky 278
Christie 102; 'Yellow River' 102
Christie, Edward 282, 291, 292,
293, 294

Chrysalis Group 184, 185, 187, 194

Cinema Shares 83, 84

Clark, Petula 32

Collins, Joan 157, 158, 159, 174

Conn, Les 172–3, 176

Cook, Roger: 'Blame It on the Pony Express' 167, 257–8

Cooke, Sam 56, 124, 125

Cooper, Alice 205

Cornish, Mel 166–7

Cosby, Bill 92, 94

Cramer, Billy J 59

Crawdaddy Club, The, London 124

Crewe, Bob 51

Cromwellian, The, London 42

Crosby, Bing: 'White Christmas' 50–1, 116

Curb, Mike 243, 245

Curd, Sylvia 260

Curtis, Tony 94–5

Czar 187

d'Abo, Mike 112

Daily Mail 68

Dave Clark Five, The 57, 59, 124

David, Hal 104

Davidson, Dennis 78, 82

Davies, Ray 69

Davis, Clive 148, 274–5, 276–8, 281

Deane, Marvin 92

Decca Records 18, 40, 126, 127, 128, 129–30, 133, 142, 160, 163, 266, 269

Deep Purple 93

Defries, Tony 171, 174–5, 176, 178–9, 181, 183, 184, 185, 186, 187, 189, 190, 193, 194, 195, 196, 200, 201, 202, 203, 204, 205, 206, 208, 209, 211, 212, 213–22, 223, 224, 225–7, 228, 231, 233–4, 235, 236, 241, 248, 253

D'Imperio, Joe 56

Dobson, Anita 161, 162; 'In One of My Weaker Moments' 162

Donegan, Lonnie 155

Donovan 69, 98–9; 'Catch The Wind' 98; *Sunshine Superman* 99

Drai, Victor 86

Dubin, Al 53

Duff, Mickey 176

Dunn, Bill 96–7

Dylan, Bob 92, 98, 210, 249

Eastman, John 151–2

Eastman, Linda 151–2

Easton, Eric 124, 125, 126, 127, 128, 133, 138, 142

Eden, Peter 98–9

Edison Lighthouse 166, 167, 170, 258; 'Love Grows (Where My Rosemary Goes)' 113, 166, 167, 258

Edwards, Henry: *Stardust – The David Bowie Story* 218

Ellis, Terry 184, 185, 194

Elton John 104, 111, 147, 189, 248–9, 283, 285; 'Bennie and The Jets' 147, 283

Elvis – 40 Greatest Hits 261–2

EMI records 39, 40, 56, 58, 59, 60–1, 64–6, 68, 96, 128, 196, 257, 264

End of the Rainbow (play) 238

English, Scott 147–8; 'Hi Ho Silver Lining' 147, 148; 'Mandy' 147–8; 'Rhinestone Cowboy' 147

Epirotiki cruise line 73, 77–9, 80, 81–2

Epstein, Brian 56–7, 151–2, 179, 249

Epstein, Clive 152

Ertegun, Ahmet 143

Essex Music 180, 181

Essex, David 207, 272

Eurovision Song Contest 52, 145, 249

Factory, The 197, 198, 204

Faith, Adam 103, 161, 162

Faithfull, Marianne 136, 140–1, 207, 269–71; As Tears Go By' 269

Feldman, Marty 16

Fenton & Co 54

Fine, Mort 85

Finer, QC Morris 109–10, 111

Finsbury Park Empire, London 18–19

Finsbury Park, London 16, 17–26, 82, 172, 241

Fish, Michael 183

Foundations, The 107

Fox: Only You Can' 283–4

François, Claude 180

Freddie & The Midnighters 89

Frischauer, Willi 72

Fruin, John 25

Fury, Billy 38, 163, 179

Gallagher, Golly 291, 292

Garbo 293

Garland, Judy 155, 238

Gavin, Bill 76, 77, 78, 79

Gavin, Jane 77

Gee, Clifford 291

Gem Productions 65, 113, 164–8, 169–234, 269–79, 280, 281; merger with Toby Organisation and birth of GTO 235–54

Gem Records 274–8, 280–301

Gem Toby Organisation Ltd
    235–54
Gerber, Peter 171, 213, 217
Gerry and The Pacemakers 59
Get Yourself a Girl (film) 57
Gibbs, Chris 140
Gillespie, Dana 181, 192, 194,
    198, 215, 220, 224
Gilliam, Terry 96
Gillman, Peter: *Alias David
    Bowie* 171, 177, 213, 227
Gingold, Hermione 254
Glancy, Ken 206
Glastonbury Festival 192, 193,
    300
Glitter, Gary 206, 208, 237,
    272–4, 276–8, 281, 290,
    292; 'Rock And Roll Pt. 1'
    273; 'Rock And Roll Pt. 2'
    273, 274
Goldstone, John 96
Good Earth 144, 146, 191
Goodman Myers and Co.,
    Chartered Accountants
    31–4, 35, 67, 91, 92, 121,
    126, 130–2, 134, 143–4,
    149–50, 164–5, 169
Goodman, Ellis 31, 33–4, 35,
    36, 135–6, 143, 149–50,
    165, 169
Goodman, Gillian 34
Goodman, Manny 32
Gordy, Berry 199, 200–1

Grace, Bob 184, 185–6, 193,
    194
Graham, Di 282
Grant, Peter 36, 40, 46–7, 48,
    81, 100, 101, 111, 249, 270
Greek Tycoon, The (film) 71–86,
    96
Greenaway, Roger 167; 'Blame
    It on the Pony Express' 167,
    257–8
Greenfield Hammer 167
GTO Films 71–86, 96–7, 146,
    293, 294
GTO Inc 258, 271; birth of
    235–54
GTO Records 112, 113, 122,
    164, 173, 237, 239, 247,
    274–89, 290, 291

Hadaway, Henry 266, 267
Hair (musical) 51
Haley, Bill: 'Rock Around The
    Clock' 38
Hampton, Christopher 104
'Happy Birthday' 116
Harrison, George 96, 136, 151,
    154, 155
Hawkes, Chip 102
Heath, Geoff 180
Heatwave 206, 284–5, 287, 295
Heinsbroek, Herman 265
Hemmings, David 228, 229–31
Hendrix, Jimi 41, 42

Henroid, Henry 87–90
Herman's Hermits 40, 58,
    60–1, 64, 66, 67, 68, 89, 99,
    124, 186; 'There's a Kind of
    Hush' 99
Hernandez, Patrick 292–3;
    'Born To Be Alive' 292–3
Hickey, Jane 170
Hill & Range 118
Holder, Noddy 115
Hollies, The 103
Hopkin, Mary 144–5, 146;
    'Knock, Knock, Who's
    There?' 145; 'Those Were
    The Days' 144–5
Horn, Trevor 293
Horton, Ralph 176
Hot Chocolate 99; 'I'll Put You
    Together Again' 99
Houdini 244
Howard, Alan 102
Hudson, John 271–2
Hunter, Don 199–200, 201, 202
Hunter, Ian 211
Hype, The 172, 210

Idle, Eric 96
Iggy Pop 188, 204–5, 209, 211,
    212, 296–7
Ilberman, Mel 196, 224–5, 226,
    262, 263
Immediate Records 124, 125,
    301

Impact Sound 127, 128

Jagger, Mick 7, 124, 126, 129,
    131, 134–6, 137, 138, 139,
    140–1, 142, 143, 179, 223,
    228, 269, 271, 278, 298
Jay, Laurie 284
Jeff Beck Group, The 148–9
Jeffery, Mike 41, 46, 57
Jesus Christ Superstar (musical)
    163–4, 181
Johnny Johnson and His
    Bandwagon 167, 170, 207,
    257–8; 'Blame It on the
    Pony Express' 167, 257–8
Jones, Brian 124, 126, 130, 131,
    137–9, 140
Jones, John Paul 101
Jones, Tom 75, 103, 183, 288–9;
    'A Boy From Nowhere'
    288–9
Joseph, David 118, 235–7, 240–1,
    242, 245, 246–7, 248, 250–3
Joseph, Robin 236, 251, 252
Judy (film)155, 238
Just A Gigolo (film) 228–31

Kags Music 124, 125
Kanaar, Nick 109, 110
Kane, Eden (Rick Sarstedt)
    173, 246–7; 'Well I Ask
    You' 246
Kass, Ron 154, 157–8

Katz, Dennis 196
Kelly, Clive 64–5
Kemp, Lindsay 192
Kennedy, Teddy 72–3
Kinder, Paul 282, 284
King, Carole 55
Kingsway Recording Studios,
    Holborn 41
Kinks, The 69, 260; 'Sunny
    Afternoon' 69
Kirshner, Don 54–5
Kiss 245, 283
Kives, Ray 257, 260
Klein, Allen 54–68, 71, 75, 79,
    82, 83, 84, 96, 107, 111,
    125, 126, 127, 128–9, 132,
    133, 134, 133, 136, 138,
    140, 141, 142, 143, 151–2,
    154, 155, 156, 157, 165–6
Klein, Beth 67, 165
Klein, Betty 57, 58, 61, 62–3,
    67, 154
Klein, Jody 142
K-Tel 256, 257, 258, 259, 260,
    261, 264
Kurtz, Normand 109, 195, 203

Laginestra, Rocco 196, 203–4
La Trattoria Terrazza, London
    41–2, 104,175
Leahy, Dick 112, 122, 164,
    239–40, 247, 274, 275–6,
    277–8, 280, 281–2, 285–8

Leander, Mike 91, 104, 145,
    160, 163–5, 166, 167,
    168, 170, 187, 190, 195,
    207, 208–9, 228–30, 230,
    231, 269–70, 271, 272–4,
    289, 298; 'A Boy From
    Nowhere' 288–9; 'Early in
    the Morning,' 163; 'Lady
    Godiva' 163; Migration'
    269; ; 'Rock And Roll Pt. 1'
    273; 'Rock And Roll Pt. 2'
    273, 274; 'The Letter'/'Hey
    Jude' 269
Leander, Penny 145, 187,
    228–9, 231
Led Zeppelin 36, 40, 42, 81,
    101, 111, 249, 270
Lee, Alvin 187
Lee, Calvin Mark 177
Lee, Peggy: 'Is that All There
    Is' 53
Le Gavroche restaurant,
    Mayfair 154–5
Leiber, Jerry 53, 103
Lennon, John 68, 151, 152,
    153, 154–6, 223, 232, 299
Leopold Joseph & Sons 140
Les Ambassadeurs, London
    62–4, 68
Levenberg, Annie
    (grandmother) 14
Levenberg, Peter (grandfather)
    14, 15

Levene, Billy 29

Levene, Larry 48–9, 255–6, 258, 259, 265, 291

Levene, Michael 255–7, 258, 261, 265, 266, 267

Levine, Colin 23

Levinson, Bob 240

Lewis, Sir Edward 127

Lindsay-Hogg, Michael 153

Lippman, Michael 223, 225, 226, 227

Little Richard 87–8

Locke, Josef 19

Lockwood, Joseph 39–40

Loewenstein, Prince Rupert 140–4

London Records 130, 132

Long John Baldry 112

Lubin, Alan 146

Lulu 69

Macaulay, Tony 104, 107–13, 164, 166, 167, 168, 170, 173, 190, 195, 207, 208–9, 249, 272, 298; 'Baby, Now That I've Found You' 107; 'Blame It on the Pony Express' 167, 257–8; 'Love Grows (Where My Rosemary Goes)' 113, 166, 167, 258; 'You Won't Find Another Fool Like Me' 112, 249

Mackintosh, Cameron 44–5

Macleod, John 107, 108, 109, 112

MainMan 213–14, 215–27, 233

Manfred Mann 99, 176; 'Semi-Detached Suburban Mr James' 99

Manilow, Barry 119, 147–8, 277; 'Can't Smile Without You' 119; 'Mandy' 147–8

Mardas, Alex 153

Marquee Club, London 42

Martin, Bill 104

Martin, George 37, 40

Martino, Al: 'Here In My Heart' 38

Mason, Barry 104, 166

Mastorakis, Nico 71–3, 74, 76, 78–9, 80, 81, 82

Matador (stage musical) 239, 247, 289

Mataxa spirits 73

Max Wall Funny Man (film) 20

Max Wall Society 20

May, Brian 105, 161, 162; 'In One of My Weaker Moments' 162

MCA Records 163, 164, 291

McCartney, Paul 144–5, 146, 151–2, 154–5, 228, 299

McCrindle, Robert 109

mechanicals 114–15

Mellencamp, John 233

Mercury Records 183, 184, 188, 189, 197

'Merry Christmas Everybody' 115

Meyers, Bobby 73

MGM Films 60–1

MGM Records 60–1, 67, 243, 245

Michael, George 112, 239, 288

Mickie Most and the Playboys 36

Midem (Marché International du Disques et de l'Edition Musicale) 50–3, 68, 122–3, 180, 260, 292

Mike Leander Orchestra, The 269; 'Migration' 269; 'The Letter'/'Hey Jude' 269

Miles, Ian 258

Milkwood 199

Mills, Gordon 163, 183

Minnelli, Liza 44, 245

Mintz, David 288

Mitra (Indian clerk) 32–3

Mixtures, The: 'The Pushbike Song' 118, 120

Monkees, The (TV series) 55

Monty Pythons' Life of Brian (film) 96–7

Moon, Keith 146, 228

Moore, Dudley 192

Moore, Roger and Luisa 42

Morrison Leahy Music 239–40

Morrison, Bryan 239, 288

Morrissey, Paul 204

Morrow, Geoff 119

Most Brothers, The 36

Most, Chris 41–2, 43, 51, 151

Most, Dave 40–1, 69

Most, Mickie 35–7, 40–3, 46–8, 51, 56, 57–9, 60–1, 64–6, 67, 68–9, 87, 88, 90, 91, 99, 125, 128, 131–2, 145, 147, 148, 167–8, 172, 174, 186, 190, 191, 245, 298, 299

Motown 37, 199–203

Mott the Hoople 211; 'All The Young Dudes' 211

Multiple Sound 258

Murray, Alex 36

Murray, Mitch 51, 104, 105

Music Week 201

Myers (née Bloom), Marsha (wife) 24, 28, 29, 31–2, 34, 41, 43, 44, 50, 51, 53, 59, 61, 62, 63, 67, 101, 105, 119, 144, 145, 154, 159, 165, 191, 208, 228, 229, 255, 267, 270, 294–5

Myers, Alan (cousin) 15, 16

Myers, Alice (mother) 13, 14, 15, 17, 20–1, 25, 26, 247

Myers, Beth (daughter) 165

Myers, Cyril (cousin) 29–30

Myers, Gerry (father) 13–14, 16, 17, 25, 26

Myers, James (son) 101, 195, 278

Myers, Laurence: articled clerk to firm of chartered accountants, Holborn 21, 31; Astoria Candy Stores and 17–18, 21–2, 24–6, 61, 205; bingo operation 29–30; birth 11; bongo playing 20–1, 27–8; childhood 11–16, 17–21; children 67, 101, 165, 195, 278; FCA (Fellow of the Institute of Chartered Accountants) 27–8; film promotion *see individual artist, company and film name*; first home 32; Goodman Myers and Co., Chartered Accountants *see* Goodman Myers and Co., Chartered Accountants; Jewish Ancestry 12–13, 14, 21, 23, 30, 61, 94, 152, 172, 247, 255, 263; market grafter 21–4, 168, 255–6, 261, 263; marriage *see* Myers, Marsha; music, career in *see individual artist, company and event name*; newspaper reporter

Myers, Laurence *cont.*
for *The Daily Express* 21; parents *see* Myers, Alice *and* Myers, Gerry; pirate radio and 87–91; Second World War (1939–45) and 11–15, 17, 24; *Ziggy Stardust* motorboat 211, 281

Myers, Marlene (cousin) 16

Myers, Peter (son) 67, 101

Myers, Roger (brother) 24, 61, 67–8, 144, 146, 191

Napier-Bell, Simon 100

Nashville Teens, The 40

Nate'n Al's, Beverley Hills 53

NEMS 152

New Seekers, The 112, 206, 235, 236, 237, 241, 242, 243–4, 245, 247–8, 249–50, 252–3, 257, 281; 'Beg Steal or Borrow' 249, 257; 'I'd Like to Teach the World to Sing' 235; 'You Won't Find Another Fool Like Me' 249

New Vaudeville Band, The 99–101; 'The Bonnie and Clyde'. 101; 'Uncle Gabriel' 101; 'Winchester Cathedral' 99–101

Newley, Anthony 173–4

Nixon, Richard 243–4, 275

Novello Awards 173, 174

Oberstein, Maurice 279

Ocean, Billy 284

O'Connor, Hazel 238–40

Oldham, Andrew 42–3, 68,
    123–4, 125, 126, 127, 130,
    132, 134, 138, 142, 196,
    269, 301

Oliver: 'Good Morning
    Starshine' 51

Oliver! 44, 45

Olympic Airlines 74, 79

Onassis, Aristotle 71–3, 85

Ono, Yoko 68, 154, 156

Osbourne, Sharon 46

Osmonds, The 245

Page, Jimmy 101

Pallenberg, Anita 138

Papas, Irene 74, 80, 82

Paramor, Norrie 39, 40

Park Theatre, Finsbury Park 18

Parker, Colonel 118, 196, 214,
    262, 263

Patterson, Robert 187

Peppermint Park, Covent
    Garden 146

performance royalties 115–16

Performing Rights Society
    (PRS) 115–16

Perrin, Les 132

Philips Records 164, 178, 183,
    190, 280

Pickett, Phil 279

Picket, Wilson: 'In The
    Midnight Hour' 134

Pickwick Records 256, 257, 258

pirate radio 87–91

Pitt, Ken 176–7, 178, 179, 183

Plant, Robert 101

Platz, David 180

Polydor Records 52, 235–6,
    241, 250, 257, 282

Poole, Brian 102

Pork (play) 197–8, 215

Post Campbell, Bruce 92

Potger, Keith 120, 236, 237,
    251

Powers, Stefanie 247

PPL 259

Presley, Elvis 38, 53, 94, 103,
    109, 118, 119, 179, 195, 196,
    203, 215, 231, 260, 261–3,
    298; 'Heartbreak Hotel' 38;
    'Let's Be Friends' 119

Price, Alan 118, 245–6

Pryor, Richard 92

Punk Can Take It (film) 294

Pye Records 69–70, 98–9, 107

Quarrymen, The 155

Queen 105, 161, 249

Quinn, Anthony 72, 73, 74, 76,
    79, 80, 81–2, 83

Radio Caroline 87, 89

Radio Luxembourg 90

Rafferty, Gerry 187; 'Baker
    Street' 187
Rainbow Theatre, London 18,
    205
Rak Management 40, 100, 101,
    168
Rak Music Publishing 40–1,
    69, 168
Rak Records 40, 41, 68–9,
    167–8
Raskin, Gene and Francesca
    145
RCA Records 52, 56, 189,
    195–7, 203–4, 206, 213,
    224–7, 257, 261, 262, 263,
    269, 290–1, 297
Red-Faced Sam 23
Redlands, West Sussex 136
Reed, Les 104
Reed, Lou 204–5, 211, 228
Reg, aka Chicken 22
Reizner, Lou 177
Rice, Tim 105, 163, 164
Richard, Cliff 38, 39, 44, 103,
    179
Richards, Keith 124, 126, 129,
    136, 137, 138, 139, 146,
    269; 'Living Doll' 44
Richmond Theatre, London
    20
Ridgeley, Andrew 288
Rivers, Joan 92, 245
Rolling Stone 188–9, 198

Rolling Stones, The 7, 9, 42, 68,
    121–44, 155, 163, 167, 171,
    179, 196, 200, 232, 245,
    260, 278, 298s
Ronco 258, 264
Ronson, Mick 172, 187, 193, 203,
    204, 210, 220, 222, 227, 228
Ross, Diana 199
Rowe, Dick 160
Russell, Tony 281, 286–7

Sailor 279
Sammeth, Billy 245
Samson 293–4
Sanctuary Records 294
Sarstedt Brothers 173, 246–7
Sarstedt, Peter: 'Where Do You
    Go To (My Lovely)?' 173,
    246
Saturday Night Live 95–6
Schroeder Music Publishing
    107–11
Schroeder, Aaron 109
Schwab, Corinne 223, 224
Scott, Ken 189, 190, 191, 194,
    196, 209
Second World War (1939–45)
    11–16
Seekers, The 120, 236
Shapiro, Helen 59
Sheffield, Norman 161
Shuman, Mort: 'In One of My
    Weaker Moments' 162

Side By Side (film) 283–4
Silver, Roy 92, 93, 94
Simone, David 291–2, 293
Simone, Nina 51, 52
Sinatra, Frank 75, 109, 180–1,
    182, 266; 'My Way' 180–1;
    'Strangers In The Night'
    181
Sinatra, Nancy 57
Slade: 'Merry Christmas
    Everybody' 115
Slim Miller Entertainments
    236
Smith, Greg 92
Society of Distinguished
    Songwriters, The (The
    SODS) 103–6
Sonny and Cher 51, 52
Spago, Los Angeles 157
Spector, Phil 36
Spencer Morris, Lee 68
Springfield Revival, The 237,
    240, 242, 250
Springfield, Dusty 103, 237
St John, Sue 157
Star-Club, Hamburg 88–9
Starr, Freddie 89
Starr, Ringo 151, 156
Stephens, Geoff 98–101, 104,
    112; 'You Won't Find
    Another Fool Like Me'
    112, 249
Stewart, Rod 148–50

Stigwood, Robert 46
Stoller, Corky 53
Stoller, Mike 53, 103
Stooges, The 188
Sugar, Alan 24
Summer, Bob 52, 290–1
Summer, Donna 206, 282–3;
    'Love To Love You Baby'
    283
Sunset Boulevard (film) 104
Survivor, The (film) 229
Sweet, The 278; 'Blockbuster'
    278
synchronisation fees 116–20

Taupin, Bernie 104, 147, 283
Telefunken 88, 90, 91
Temperton, Rod 284–5, 295
Temple, Julien 294
Tetragrammaton Records
    92–4
Thompson, J. Lee 85
Tiny Tim 93–4; 'Tiptoe
    Through the Tulips' 93
Titanic Music 184–5
Tittenhurst Park 155–6
Toby Organisation 235–7
Townsley, Sir Edward 127, 128
Tramp nightclub, London 42,
    157, 229–30, 270
Tremeloes, The 102
Trident Studios 161, 190, 191
Tudor, Ron 64, 257

20 Fantastic Hits by the Original Artists 257–8
2i's coffee bar, Soho 36, 40, 300
Tzuke, Judie 146

UK Subs 294–6
Underwood, George 211
Universal Studios 85
Uttal, Larry 164, 274, 275, 280

Vigoda, Joe 202–3
Vincent, Gene 46, 87
Visconti, Tony 144, 145, 146, 172, 183, 190, 191, 230, 239

Wakeman, Rick 191–2
Walker Brothers, The 122–3; 'No Regrets' 122
Wall, Max 19–20
Wanderers, The (film) 293
Ward, Brian 209
Warhol, Andy 189, 192, 197, 198, 204–5
Warner Music 112, 301
Warren, Harry 53
Warrior Records 35–6, 174
Watts, Charlie 130, 131
Watts, Michael 207
Webber, Andrew Lloyd 104, 105, 162–3, 164, 229

Weiss, Larry 147; 'Hi Ho Silver Lining' 147, 148; 'Rhinestone Cowboy' 147
Weissleder, Manfred 88–9, 90, 91
Wexler, Jerry 163
Wham! 288
Wheatley, Glenn 242–4
Whittingham, Sylvan 166
Who, The 146, 249
Wilde, Marty 38
Wilder Jr, Johnnie 284–5, 295
Williamson, James 209
Wilson, Anya 166–7, 186, 187
Wonder, Stevie 193, 199–203
Wood, Ronnie 148
Wright, Chris 184
Wyman, Bill 121, 131
Wyper, Olav 178

Yardbirds, The 42, 100, 101
Yellow Pages 102

Zanetta, Tony 171, 197, 204, 215, 216, 217–22, 223, 224, 227, 228
Zellweger, Renée 155, 238

ROGERSTONE

8·11·19

Y021376